ASO EBI

T0324332

AFRICAN PERSPECTIVES
Kelly Askew and Anne Pitcher
Series Editors

Aso Ebi: *Dress, Fashion, Visual Culture, and*
Urban Cosmopolitanism in West Africa,
by Okechukwu Nwafor

Unsettled History: Making South African Public Pasts,
by Leslie Witz, Gary Minkley, and Ciraj Rassool

Seven Plays of Koffi Kwahulé: In and Out of Africa,
translated by Chantal Bilodeau and Judith G. Miller
edited with Introductions by Judith G. Miller

The Rise of the African Novel:
Politics of Language, Identity, and Ownership,
by Mukoma Wa Ngugi

Black Cultural Life in South Africa:
Reception, Apartheid, and Ethics,
by Lily Saint

Nimrod: Selected Writings,
edited by Frieda Ekotto

Developing States, Shaping Citizenship:
Service Delivery and Political Participation in Zambia
Erin Accampo Hern

The Postcolonial Animal: African Literature and Posthuman Ethics
Evan Maina Mwangi

Gender, Separatist Politics, and Embodied Nationalism in Cameroon
Jacqueline-Bethel Tchouta Mougoué

Textile Ascendancies: Aesthetics, Production, and Trade in Northern Nigeria
edited by Elisha P. Renne and Salihu Maiwada

The Black and White Rainbow: Reconciliation, Opposition,
and Nation-Building in Democratic South Africa
Carolyn E. Holmes

Aso Ebi

*Dress, Fashion, Visual Culture,
and Urban Cosmopolitanism
in West Africa*

Okechukwu Nwafor

University of Michigan Press
Ann Arbor

Copyright © 2021 by Okechukwu Nwafor
All rights reserved

For questions or permissions, please contact um.press.perms@umich.edu

Published in the United States of America by the
University of Michigan Press
Manufactured in the United States of America
Printed on acid-free paper
First published May 2021

A CIP catalog record for this book is available from the British Library.

Library of Congress Cataloging-in-Publication data has been applied for.

ISBN: 978-0-472-07480-8 (hardcover : alk. paper)
ISBN: 978-0-472-05480-0 (paper)
ISBN: 978-0-472-12866-2 (e-book)

Library of Congress Control Number: 2021935578

ACKNOWLEDGMENTS

In writing this book I am indebted to several individuals. I wish to say that the first major funding I received to complete this book came from the African Humanities Programme (AHP). I thank Andrzej W. Tymowski and the AHP team for their generous support that enabled me to conclude this manuscript.

I wish to acknowledge my enormous debt to Patricia Hayes, an exceptionally benevolent scholar, who was committed to my scholarship and took an enormous amount of time to read my works over the years and offer helpful advice. Her wonderful insights assisted in giving form to my void thoughts during the early period of this project. I also owe my special gratitude to Gary Minkley, Elisha P. Renne, Corrine Kratz, late Ivan Karp, Sandra Barnes and Nina Sylvanus for their painstaking efforts in reading through this manuscript.

I thank Ciraj Rassool, Leslie Witz, and Premesh Lalu for making me stay back at the Center for Humanities Research (CHR) of the University of the Western Cape (UWC), South Africa, after my studies in the African Programme in Museum and Heritage Studies. Directly or indirectly they reshaped my ideas, which enabled me to prepare for the daunting task of future intellectual battle.

Colleagues and scholars at the history department and CHR at UWC were like a knowledge pool from where I drank. Some of the scholars I benefited from at UWC include Surren Pillay; Heidi Grunebaun; Maurits van Bever Donker; Paolo Israel and his wife, Jung Ran Annachiara Forte; Charles Kabwete; Steve Ouma Akoth; Mduduzi Xakaza; Vilho Babangida Shigweda; Napandulwe Shiweda; Stanley Baluku; Toni Ngonaldo Ngodinashe; Jeremiah Arowosegbe; Jade Gibson; Olusegun Morakinyo; Abdul Jawondo; Melanie Boehi; Phindi Mnyaka; Zuleiga Adams; Jane Taylor; Lameez Lalkhen; Michelle Smith; Thozama April; Van Laun; Bianca Paigè; Tinashe Maware; late Emile Maurice and Noëleen Murray, who is now the director of the Wits City Institute at the University of the Witwatersrand. I will not forget the invaluable assistance of Helena Pohlandt-McCormick, Andrew Lampretch, George Emeka Agbo, and Ruth Simbao.

Eric Shepherd, former director of the Interdisciplinary Center for the Study of Global Change (ICGC), University of Minnesota; Karen Brown, deputy director of ICGC, who eventually became the director when Eric left; Sara Braun, administrator at ICGC; and the late Kate Kulkahen, financial secretary at ICGC, were there for me during the fall of 2011 when I arrived in Minnesota. I thank you all. Eric and Karen introduced me to the erudite scholar Joanne Eicher, who read through my manuscript and made meaningful contributions. Joanne's in-depth understanding of Nigerian fashion became an inestimable resource from where I drew heavy inspiration.

Over the years, my book was strengthened through generous funding that took me to different academic centers. One of these academic centers is the African Studies Centre (ASC) of the University of Michigan (U of M) Ann Arbor, where I spent six months as the University of Michigan African Presidential Scholar (UMAPS) in 2018. I wish to thank especially the former director Kelly Askew, who first expressed faith in my work and advised me to submit my prospectus to the University of Michigan Press. I also thank the director of ASC, Andries Coetzee; the associate director, Laura Beny; Henrike Florusbosch; Cindy Nguyen; and Sandra Schulze. They made difficult things look simple in my eyes, and no amount of accolades can describe their contributions to the successful completion of this book. In addition, I am grateful to Derek Peterson of the University of Michigan Department of History; Omolade Adunbi of Afroamerican and African Studies of U of M; and Christine Feak of ASC, U of M, who read the early drafts of this book and offered me useful comments that helped me resolve some of the questions I raised.

I owe a debt to Pamila Gupta of the Wits Institute for Social and Economic Research (WISER), University of the Witwatersrand. Pamila was my host during my last months as a Mellon Fellow on Photography and Visual Culture at WISER. I also thank the director of WISER, Sarah Nuttall, and Achille Mbembe.

I thank Raymond Silverman, a professor in the office of History of Art, at the University of Michigan. Ray's kindness and hope in my work were inexplicable, and he was instrumental to my return to Ann Arbor after my UMAPS fellowship. Staff and colleagues at the History of Art of the University of Michigan listened to my presentations and made meaningful contributions. I thank especially the chair, Christiane Gruber; my colleague, Ashley

Miller, David Doris; Kevin Carr and Megan Holmes. Staff such as Jeff Craft and others facilitated my arrival in Ann Arbor in 2019.

I am grateful to Chu Krydz Ikwuemesi of the University of Nigeria, Nsukka; Sylvester Ogbechie of the University of California, Santa Barbara; Chika Okeke-Agulu of Princeton University; Smooth Ugochukwu Nzewi of the Museum of Modern Art (MOMA); Laura de Becker of the University of Michigan Museum of Art; Iheanyi Onwuegbucha of CCA Lagos, Kerstin Pinther of Ludwig-Maximilian University Munich, Ozioma Onuzulike, Sarah Adams, Bright Eke, Ndidi Onyemaechi Dike, Ola Oloidi; Obiora Udechukwu; Chike Aniakor and Chijioke Onuora for the different occasions we shared together and their invaluable advice.

I want to thank Pita Ejiofor, Ilochi Okafor, Boniface Egboka and Joseph Eberendu Ahaneku, former vice chancellors of Nnamdi Azikiwe University (NAU), Awka, Anambra State, Nigeria, and the current vice chancellor of NAU, Charles Okechukwu Esimone. These vice chancellors generously granted me the leave that made my numerous academic travels possible.

I thank Emeka Ezeonu for his brotherly love and encouragement. Thanks as well to my colleagues at NAU: Clifford Ezekwe Nwanna, Valerie Nnodu, Charles Egolum, Ike Odimegwu, Tracie Ezeajugh, Alex Asigbo, Joel Igbokwe, Emman Okunna, Ifeanyi Enete, Kevin Okolie, Chinedu Chukueggu, Ebele Emengini, John Nwadike Amifor, Azuka Nzoiwu, JohnBosco Ojiakor, Ivan Okonkwo, Chidiebere Onwuekwe, Late Pius Ekekwe Nwankwo, B. O. Njelita, and the late Ifedioramma Dike. Special thanks also go to Frank Ugiomoh, Best Ochigbo and Osa D. Egonwa.

In its eventual wrap-up in 2018, several important contributions made this book a reality. Most especially, I am grateful to the University of Michigan Press and the African Perspectives series editors, Ellen Bauerle, Kelly Askew, and Anne Pitcher, for giving this book their full support, for believing in it, and for their responsiveness to the nitty-gritty that shaped it. I thank editorial assistant Flannery Wise and my production editor Mary Hashman.

My parents, Chief Michael Ifeatu Nwafor (Omechalunia) and Mrs. Maria Nneka Nwafor, bore the pains that came with my entire life as an academic. Their immeasurable sacrifices during the course of my career cannot be forgotten. I will not forget Chukwudi Ezeodili who took the initial task to nurture my precocious talent at Nsukka quite early in life. I express my profound gratitude to my in-laws G. C. Uju and Reke Uju who have been very supportive throughout my career as an itinerant academic.

Finally, a special thanks to my wife, Nkiru, and my children, Ijeoma, Chinua, Chioma, and Chisom, who have made this work possible through their love and encouragement. For many years, all of you endured the painful gap I created in your lives by my incessant travels. The message you sent to me was clear, strong, and sharp: that neither distance nor time could "kill" your love for me. I appreciate and love you all.

CONTENTS

INTRODUCTION
Aso Ebi: Dress, Fashion, Visual Culture,
and Urban Cosmopolitanism in West Africa   1

CHAPTER 1
Aso Ebi and the Fashioning of Bodies in Colonial Lagos,
1860s–1960s   24

CHAPTER 2
Cheaper Clothes in a Fluctuating Economy, 1960–2008   51

CHAPTER 3
Coloring Wealth, the Crowd, and Class   78

CHAPTER 4
Fractured Materiality and the Political Economy of Intimacy   96

CHAPTER 5
Framing the Mutual Life of *Aso Ebi* in Lagos:
Copies, Copying, and Fashion Magazines   121

CHAPTER 6
Surfacist Aesthetics and the Digital Turn   158

CONCLUSION   181

Notes   189

Bibliography   211

Index   235

Digital materials related to this title can be found on the Fulcrum platform
via the following citable URL: https://doi.org/10.3998/mpub.11649792

Introduction

Aso Ebi: Dress, Fashion, Visual Culture, and Urban Cosmopolitanism in West Africa

Kelechi Obiesie, a housewife who lives in Lagos, was preparing for her younger brother's wedding coming up on November 11, 2019, in Onitsha, Anambra State, Eastern Nigeria. Her major concern was the dress she was supposed to wear on the wedding day. Her dress would constitute part of a uniformed group that would appear in photographs with the couple on the wedding day. Her brother lives in Onitsha, while Kelechi lives in Lagos, about ten hours away.

Her younger brother's wife-to-be, Rita, had bought two different sets of large quantities of textile materials intended for these uniformed groups to wear. One of these was a pink lace material with some flowered designs. It cost her ten thousand naira (about 28 USD) per five yards. The other material she bought was a greenish material known as *ankara*, which cost her five thousand naira (about 14 USD) per five yards.

Rita sold the lace material to Kelechi and twenty of her friends at the cost of fifteen thousand naira (about 42 USD), making a profit of five thousand. These twenty friends would dress in this pink lace material, sewn in their different styles, during the wedding, where they would forge solidarity with Rita and her husband.

Rita also sold the green *ankara* material to about thirty other individuals, including friends and relatives, at ten thousand naira per five yards. Two months before her wedding, I kept track of Rita's wedding transactions. On the wedding day, all of those who bought the materials from her, including Kelechi, appeared at the venue and flanked Rita and her husband. A photographer known as Hector, commissioned for the event, took different shots of these uniformed groups (figs. 1a and 1b).

This complex transaction of uniformed individuals is called *aso ebi*. Kelechi and her friends who dressed in the pink lace uniforms are referred to as *aso ebi* women, and their uniformed fabrics themselves are described as *aso ebi* materials. What is striking in these dress designs is that the women are all dressed in the same pink uniforms but different dress designs.

Kelechi's tailor in Lagos, who, for this book, prefers to use the name Tkbridals, her business name, owns a shop in a corner of Sabo market in Yaba, Lagos, where many tailors occupy a section of the market (fig. 2). Tkbridals not only sews *aso ebi* for retailers like Kelechi, but she also sews for the big names who have established large fashion business networks with *aso ebi*. These big names accept contracts from their clients and sublet to Tkbridals, who sews for them. While most of the owners of the big fashion names are neither tailors nor seamstresses, they have established a huge social media outlet that enables them to reach clients from all over the world. According to Tkbridals, "Most of my clients reside in the United States and the West. Usually a dealer on *aso ebi* gets the measurement of those living in the United States planning *aso ebi* and then sends them to my WhatsApp." She opened her phone and showed me WhatsApp photos of different dress materials and styles, each with measurements sent to her by some of the big names: "The dealers send the styles and the measurements to my WhatsApp, and I sew them and package and send them back to the United States. I don't know most of the clients because they come through the dealers, who have popular websites where my clothes are advertised." For the sake of protecting her business, she refused to mention the big names. Kelechi's transaction with Tkbridals was different. Instead of allowing Tkbridals to select from her archives of designs, Kelechi brought her own design concept from a fashion magazine she got from her friend in Lagos. She could not bring the entire magazine, so she took a photo of the dress with her cell phone.

Tkbridals works with different textile materials from a variety of companies for her *aso ebi* designs, such as Da Viva, Vlisco Dutch wax, *atiku*, *george*, Woodin *ankara*, and Chiganvi *ankara*.[1] She opened her phone again and showed me her web page named Tkbridals, which is suffused with a selection of different sewn materials and styles of *aso ebi*. She said people also contact her through her blog and that keeps her business going.

During Rita's wedding many photographers, including Hector, their commissioned photographer, and uninvited ones such as Topklass, were seen

Figure 1a. Kelechi Obiesie and her friends during Rita's wedding. Photo: Hector.

Figure 1b. Kelechi Obiesie and her friends during Rita's wedding. Photo: Topklass Events.

Figure 2. Tkbridals. Lagos, 2019. Photo: Okechukwu Nwafor.

photographing most of the women dressed in *aso ebi*. A few of those who did not dress in *aso ebi* uniforms seemed awkwardly detached from the midst of the colorful uniformity. After Rita's wedding reception, some women were seen with gifts of an umbrella, given only to those dressed in *aso ebi* uniforms. Kelechi and her friends were seen with different colors of umbrella gifts. Those who did not dress in *aso ebi* were left without any gift.

The unique circumstance of Kelechi's *aso ebi* experience is the fact that she traveled from Lagos in Western Nigeria to Onitsha in Eastern Nigeria, a distance of about 250 miles, to attend her brother's wedding and participate in the *aso ebi*. The juxtaposition of these two locations is important in order to underline the complex cultural and geographic scope of *aso ebi* in Nigeria and beyond. It simply and immediately shows how a practice that originated among the Yoruba in the western part of Nigeria has permeated other ethnic groups and regions of Nigeria and beyond. Lagos and Onitsha thus illustrate this underlying component of origins and expansion that is central to fashion discourses, especially from cosmopolitan centers to the hinterlands.

Most Nigerians have always placed emphasis on clothes. In Yoruba language aṣọ means "cloth" while ẹbi means "family." Literally, *aso ebi* means "family cloth." As the name implies, families, friends, and groups usually wear *aso ebi* as uniforms to signify unity during most social events such as weddings, birthday parties, housewarming ceremonies, and others. In wedding preparations, such as Rita's, for example, *aso ebi* is always on the priority list.

I employ *aso ebi* to show how a fusion of clothing, fashion, and photography have provoked and heightened a unique kind of urban visibility in Lagos. The desire and pursuit of this unique visibility signifies and shapes identities, social relations, and class while also giving rise to radical transnational economic connections and the postcolonial urban experience in the city of Lagos. Numerous transformations and transactions are caused by *aso ebi*: First is the transnational capitalist network in the textile economy instigated by *aso ebi* in Lagos: many individuals like Rita, preparing for one event or the other, flood the Lagos textile markets every day to purchase large quantities of fabric that will be used for *aso ebi* uniforms. Second is the large number of individuals who dress in *aso ebi* uniforms and converge in public places in Lagos to celebrate one event or the other, thus constituting what I call the "*aso ebi* crowd." In the case of Rita's wedding, more than fifty people dressed in *aso ebi*. Third is the huge tailoring business that *aso ebi* has provoked in the city of Lagos as numerous individuals search the city for adept tailors and designers who will sew suitable styles, such as Tkbridals, who sews for the big fashion names as well as for those with other, personal needs. Fourth is the fashion design innovation and the struggle for competitive design ideas instigated by *aso ebi* styles as seen in the case of Kelechi, whose friends wore different designs of the same pink lace material. Fifth is *aso ebi*'s recent ascent into the high-fashion genre in the city of Lagos. Sixth is the presence of insinuations of wealth, class, and politics of inclusion and exclusion that are now emerging among *aso ebi* groups. Seventh is the ubiquitous visual kaleidoscope *aso ebi* has prompted in popular photography, fashion magazines, online fashion sites, and other media. With these activities it is clear that *aso ebi* lies at the heart of a crucial urban imaginary posing a huge scholarly research promise in popular and visual culture scholarship. This book, therefore, may serve as the first, and most timely, comprehensive attempt to articulate the yearnings of many individuals who have ultimately anticipated this moment when such a ubiquitous social ritual in West Africa would receive the desired scholarly attention that will equally satisfy popular readership.

Aso ebi, most recently a pervasive clothing practice in Nigeria and West Africa, offers a fascinating way to examine the rise of fashion practices in Lagos and, in the difficult conditions of Nigeria from the 1960s on—with the country's political instability, economic turmoil, and growing inequality—how changes in moral, visual, and political economies have produced changing modes of social relations and different forms of cultural interrelationships.

What I have done here is to look at, for example, Kelechi's *aso ebi* as a textile fabric, as a visual culture and social practice: the history, social meanings, aesthetics, and economics surrounding *aso ebi*. In this way I foreground the power of *aso ebi* as a form of political language capable of unifying, differentiating, challenging, contesting, and exerting influence. I consider how *aso ebi* is represented in other popular forms—photography, the fashion industry, and digital media—to show how this cultural practice has gained ubiquitous impetus, use, and popularity in urban Lagos and the Western diaspora. In other words, it is my strong argument that *aso ebi* is not just "uniformed dress" as such but rather a practice that uses uniformed dress as a tool for much broader engagement in the quest for individual and collective visibility in the city of Lagos.

JUSTIFICATION OF LAGOS AS THE CENTER OF *ASO EBI* FASHION

The stories that build this ethnography were gathered between 2009 and 2019. I traversed the multiple sites of Lagos in search of multilayered transactions involving *aso ebi*. Relying on hundreds of interviews, participant observation, oral history, archival research, and scholarly texts, I examined processes through which *aso ebi* stories are woven into the fabric of the city. Some of the many instances where one encounters *aso ebi* are typically in informal, everyday conversations among Nigerians or other groups, public online forums on the internet, online fashion websites, in newspapers and fashion magazines, and especially among friends preparing for one form of social event or the other. My close association with these and other forums reinforced the ubiquitous impetus that *aso ebi* practice has garnered in recent times and that no doubt makes it an important research area begging for attention. In addition, *aso ebi* has generated a significant amount of controversy in everyday debate among Nigerians at home and in the diaspora such that there is a common association of *aso ebi* with Nigerian culture and tradition.

It is necessary to establish why this study is set in Lagos, a historically Yoruba city. *Aso ebi* is a Yoruba affair but has recently spread from the Yoruba region of Nigeria to other parts of the country where women from other ethnic groups participate in it. This was seen in the case of Kelechi, who, although an Igbo woman, traveled from Lagos to Onitsha in Eastern Nigeria to participate in *aso ebi*. It has also spread to other parts of the West African subregion. Its unbounded creative expansion has recorded an unprecedented promise in Lagos. The role of Lagos as the center of commerce in Nigeria and West Africa has attracted a peculiarly fashion-conscious populace from the hinterlands of Nigeria and other parts of the West African subregion at least since the fifteenth century. Located in a large lagoon that circuited into West Africa's Bight of Benin, Lagos forms part of the southern border of a region that stretches from the Volta River in the west to the River Nun in the east. With an estimated number of about 20 million people, Lagos was recently adjudged the most populated city in Africa and the fastest-growing city in the world, exploding from 288,000 in 1950, to 14 million in 2010, and to 23 million in 2015 (Anheier and Raj Isar 2012, 118). As one of the greatest hubs of urban culture in the African continent, Lagos poses a critical case study in urban fashionability. In the event where its visual cultures, especially through Nollywood (the Nigerian film industry) and the music industry, have constituted a pervasive form of consumer culture across the world, a study of *aso ebi*, a constituent part of this consumer culture, becomes very expedient.

Again, as a leading commercial circuit in colonial and postcolonial Africa, Lagos became a central site of imported textile and other goods, in exchange for slaves, during the sixteenth century. The expansion of import trade in textiles, manilas, cowries, and beads reached its zenith in the seventeenth century. By this period Lagos had constituted an important center of expanding local and regional trade, a feat made possible by its central location on the water route linking Benin, Ijebu, Allada, and Oyo's southern commercial termini (Mann 2007, 18). After 1760, European traders made continuous back-and-forth trips to Lagos, occasioning rapid transformation in its geographical stratification and a high influx of economic immigrants. Indeed, by the eighteenth century the transatlantic commercial circuit had provoked more politically conscious inhabitants who realized the potentialities of Lagos's positioning not just in the economic and political organization of their life but also in fashioning a city with a unique social life. Textile production and trading would play a major role in this fashioning. While trade in textiles with Africa's Gold Coast declined in the eighteenth century because of the decline in the value of Gold Coast gold, trade in textiles with Lagos boomed in this period. Merchants' records from the seventeenth century showed that a type of Yoruba cloth known as "Allada cloth" was transported from Oyo through the Lagos coast for sale on the Gold Coast by Dutch, English, German, and Swedish merchants. Such merchants' records have occasionally offered a brief description of Allada cloth as "plain or loom-patterned with either strips of brocading," with a lack of appropriate vernacular names for the process (Kriger 2005).[2] Again, cloth trading along the Ijebu-Ode axis, through Lagos to the Gold Coast, Senegambia, and Gabon, also points to the traffic in "Jebu cloth." Jebu cloth, apparently a derived lexicon from "Ijebu," a deep blue–striped cotton dyed cloth made through local dye pit by Ijebu-Ode women, was exchanged for Portuguese tobacco along the West African coast during the eighteenth century. Captain Hugh Clapperton and Richard Lander noted large-scale indigo production at Old Oyo in the 1820s. They also observed the presence of plain-dyed indigo fabrics and fabrics woven with indigo stripes (Lander 1967). In the same period, an Ijebu slave identified indigo-and-white-striped cloth as an important trade item produced by his people. What this means is that local fashion was already an entrenched way of life by the 1700s in that its export possibilities by even European slave dealers could puncture the colonial ethnographic visual economy where locals were positioned as nude, unclothed savages.[3]

No doubt, Lagosians and visitors to Lagos, in their endless to-and-fro travels, have engaged in the dissemination of popular dress styles from Lagos and across the other hinterlands in the subregion. This has defined an area of study for dress history and urban cultural forms. The need to understand the meanings of commodity culture in relation to *aso ebi* might suggest that

Lagos, as an important commercial center in Nigeria, has produced demographic entities that engage in the active production of everyday cultures through consumption or appropriation of commodities such as textiles (Moore 1993, 129).

The city has a significant role to play in the way we envision self, the way we act, and the way we fashion our lives such that fashion intensifies a multiplicity of social relations, increases the rate of social mobility, and allows styles to be appropriated across class boundaries (Ashley and Orenstein 1990, 314). The choice of Lagos derives from a need to recognize that city's role in fashioning postcolonial modernity in Nigeria and other West African subregions. As an important city in Nigeria, with its large population and its role in the nineteenth-century European missionary and colonization exploits in Nigeria, Lagos requires a historical study with regard to certain aspects of its life.

Fashion or dress style obviously reflects the changing phases of cultural and social development in any city. The fashion business of Lagos is strongly tied to the city's active social life, which enables endless design possibilities through *aso ebi*. Focusing this book on these design possibilities, therefore, entails a study of the African city as a modernity that emerged from a peculiar historical process. This requires a recognition of Lagos as a modernity where notions of wealth, subjectivity, and the city are fundamentally shaped through histories of colonial, postcolonial, and global encounters that are often hypothesized in discourses of modernity and globalization. Therefore, an attempt to comprehend and narrate an African metropolis is an attempt to see the city through its layers of *aso ebi* histories (Enwezor 2002, 20; Koolhas 2002, 175). If humans are metaphors for cloth in the Yoruba psychosocial world, then drawing a distinction between a Western model of the city and that of Lagos becomes easy, especially as a Western paradigm of the rise of the city poses a conceptual challenge for seeing through Lagos (Ash and Wright 1988, 11).[4]

SEEING AND BEING SEEN IN *ASO EBI* DRESS

Aso ebi, as I argue, is merely an act of seeing and visualizing everyday fashion. That most authors of fashion and clothing unanimously assent to the pervasiveness of "seeing and being seen" (Silverman 1986, 147) as the ultimate aspiration of the dressed body fits my descriptive model in approaching *aso ebi* as visual culture.[5] Again, a view of the visual culture of the city gestures a shift from art history to "the ethics and politics, aesthetics and epistemology of seeing and being seen," a paradigm in cultural studies that condenses the monumentality of culture from elite practices to a mundane means of existence (Mitchell 2002). It is this quality of visual and material culture to summarize simultaneously the everyday, the epic, and the remarkable that makes it such a powerful tool for analyzing *aso ebi* relations that structure the city of Lagos.

Through *aso ebi* I attend to social and visual culture practices that are implicated in concepts of wealth, solidarity, friendship networks, and an artisanal textile economy, among others. In a sense, I use *aso ebi* as a shorthand for a voyage into Lagos's low-end fashion networks. In doing this, I expand the meaning of "fashion" beyond its high-modernist application into local contexts in order to identify changing designs, individual imaginations, and ideas around body presentation.[6] There is no descriptive model that will be appropriate in defining fashion from a specific context. I therefore liken fashion to a repertoire of shifting ideas and imagination within the whirlpool of change.

One way to understand the transformation that has attended Lagos since the late nineteenth century is to examine how the multiple layers of the city's visual and social relations are imagined through fashion and dress. For example, in mid-nineteenth-century Lagos dress became a compelling factor in the realization of a new experience in social and cultural relations. This experience engendered a new ideology among the native Yoruba such that the Yoruba Ijebus, who were one of the first settler groups in Lagos, initiated a policy of ostracism that deployed dress as instrument of anticolonial resistance. This policy saw to the enactment of a law that banned European dress and lifestyles and banished missionaries from entering Ijebu land in 1852. By 1861, when the British forcefully took over Lagos through bombardment and the deposition of the *oba* (king), there ensued a new kind of identity formation and skirmishes that revolved around dress. The British; the returning slaves from Brazil, Cuba, and Sierra Leonne; the native inhabitants; and the missionaries were all entangled in a contentious debate about the meaning of appropriate dress style. Contrary to the history presented in mainstream colonial literature of the late eighteenth and early nineteenth centuries, these debates were instrumental in shaping the broader sociocultural life of Lagos even up to the postcolonial period. They also suggested how the image of colonial Lagos was not exclusively about domination and subjugation but also that of resistance and expressions of subjectivity. There is also evidence of how textiles aided the entrenchment of the slave trade in Lagos. Yet, studies of African textiles suffer this increased silence in literature about the slave trade and colonial literature about Africa's (under)development. I reveal these dynamics through the reading of *aso ebi* dress across a range of historical, social, and economic perspectives of textiles and cotton.

Before the early twentieth century, no linguistic historical evidence had established the coinage of "*aso ebi*" within the lexicon of Yoruba sartorial practice. The years between 1893 and 1929 have been described as a period of economic prosperity in Lagos. An increase in textile imports made clothes affordable to the growing urban population. This occasioned creative innovation from local textile producers and tailors. With the influx of these affordable textiles, the quest for *aso ebi* increased, especially among Christian societies who used them as uniforms. These uses spread to the social arena, where individuals had started using *aso ebi* as uniforms for different events. Women competed for fashion among themselves and made unbearable requests from their husbands in order to meet the increasing demands for *aso ebi*.[7] These demands came with family crises, as many husbands were unable to meet their wives' undue demands. From the first quarter of the twentieth century, around 1915, *aso ebi* thus sparked a major debate in Lagos. In many letters to the editors of such newspapers as the *Lagos Standard* and the *Lagos Daily Record*, among others, dress and *aso ebi* were beginning to reveal a provocative panorama of Lagos life in terms of aesthetic heterogeneity, pursuit of religious agendas, and expressions of an emerging cultural agency. Concerns about economic waste were ascribed to *aso ebi* while in certain quarters it was dismissed entirely as a creeping vile of Lagos sociality. This dimension of *aso ebi* suggests how the poetics of materiality that emerge from the practices of everyday life can offer a means of theorizing the mundane. Therefore, I take a panoramic viewpoint by approaching *aso ebi* not from a narrow thematic focus of just "uniformed dress worn as a form of solidarity" but from the interrelationship it has with different contexts: aspects of dress as fashion, designs, articles of social mobilization, textile economy, and urban cosmopolitanism, among others. In fact, I highlight a shifting perspective, beyond the linear framework, that configures how we might understand dress practices as merely banal, insignificant others. It enables us to understand how and why, for example, by the 1980s *aso ebi* became a yardstick for measuring wealth through one's network of friends dressed in *aso ebi* (Ugwu-Oju 1997).[8] It also enables an understanding of how, since the 1990s, there has been increasing redefinition of *aso ebi* practice that was occasioned by contemporary realities of economic changes, new understandings of solidarity, and the politics of fashioning cosmopolitan modernity. In certain instances, those who did not dress in *aso ebi* were treated as persona non grata and denied food and other forms of recognition during important ceremonies.

Again, in studying *aso ebi* I recognize another unique attribute of the Nigerian society where social gatherings have been restructured by the double binds of repulsion and attraction of *aso ebi* culture and where the logic of *aso ebi* is strongly embedded in the rhetorical professions of love and friendship. I significantly reveal the politics of exclusion and inclusion that are often expressed subtly or awkwardly in *aso ebi* through photography and fashion magazines. Thus, fundamentally, the union of *aso ebi*, popular photography, and fashion magazines has revolutionized the local visual cultural landscape in West Africa. This union also presents the creeping sense of egotism and/ or commercialization bedeviling *aso ebi* practice. Shifts in ceremonial hospitality are one way that *aso ebi* is caught up in changing moral and political economies in Lagos and other parts of the West African subregion. They also indicate how *aso ebi* shapes social relations and forms of interdependence.

Much of the literature on *aso ebi* has emphasized the solidarity indexed by the practice, a contemporary visible sign of "wealth in people" (Guyer and Eno Belinga 1995). But scholarly work on wealth in people shows that it had both harsh and supportive aspects, yet those harsher undercurrents have not received much attention in research on *aso ebi* as dress. That side of *aso ebi* emerged more clearly in Nigeria's decades of military and political maladministration—from the independence period of 1960 to the 1990s, when the middle class eroded. Beginning in the 1980s and through the late 1990s, the distraught middle class struggled to regain their lost statuses by reinventing themselves through *aso ebi*. In the process, *aso ebi* fed into the lawlessness of the military era in Nigeria (1970–1990s), through what the Yoruba call *Owambe*, meaning an unbridled quest to attend parties.

Indeed, *Owambe* became popular during the heyday of the military junta in Nigeria when contemporary sociality ate into the putrefaction of degenerate politicians, a period when *aso ebi* nurtured the lost glory of the dwindling middle class and glided through the emptiness of the social systems. Of particular note is how *aso ebi* constructs an idea of a sumptuous paraphernalia employed for the objectification of rank and the elaboration of class. Under this foundation the concepts of power, status, and visual culture clearly manifest as viable theoretical premises to launch my analysis of *aso ebi*.

The prescription and limitations of the moral economy in which *aso ebi* is produced and consumed are striking. *Aso ebi* serves as a specific social currency that mediates two contradictory logics of gift giving and commodification. I challenge the often-assumed moral economy of intimacy by interrogating ways in which *aso ebi* is "offered" by celebrants "for sale" as a gesture of friendship and imminent commensalism, yet it seems that the costs of refusal to buy the *aso ebi* removes the guests altogether from the cycle of counter-gifts/payments. I unveil the underlying difference in modes of celebrations; concepts of friendship, family, and the logic of economic necessity inherent in *aso ebi* in Lagos; and how these specific moral and political economies come together.

Considering the umbrella gifts that Rita bought with the proceeds of her *aso ebi* sales, for example, I contend that the nature of "gifts" and "counter-gifts" that attend *aso ebi* practice demands a proper historicizing and theorizing. A proper historicizing of "gift giving" and "norm of reciprocity" in *aso ebi* immediately brings Annette Weiner's (1992) *Inalienable Possessions* to mind. However, prior to Weiner's seminal work, the "give and take of reciprocity" seems to have assumed a magical power with the rise of capitalism in Western economies. Weiner argues that the idea of a return gift does not generate the thrust of exchange; instead what initiates exchanges is the radiating power of keeping inalienable possessions out of exchange. Weiner has emphasized the inevitability of enthroning difference during the course of keeping relationships and possessions. During this process, "nodes of power" are created by these differences. This, in turn, "delimits constraints against hierarchy." It is against these opposing forces that difference is established. However, there is a simultaneous craving and rejection for the power that difference generates. Weiner argues that this power is at once "simultaneously sought after, yet submerged; proclaimed, yet disguised; nurtured, yet defeated" (177).

I unveil similar inherent differences in *aso ebi*, especially in ways that shed more light on classic anthropological studies of gift giving.[9] I question varying romantic idealization of the world of gift exchange by showing how far from being politically innocent gift exchanges such as aso ebi often are.[10] There has been little attention to the nature of gift giving and conviviality that attend *aso ebi*, nor to its political and visual economic roles. While gifts have also been widely explored by scholars, their intersections with *aso ebi* still remain largely unattended to by scholars.[11]

I reveal how *aso ebi* is implicated in Nigerians' efforts to negotiate industrial and cultural exchanges through textile merchandising. How does fashion consumption inflect people's understanding of the power of cooperation and its resultant mass-consumerism? Through economic interdependence, *aso ebi* economy has defied the meanings of culture (in Lagosians' perception) and branched into the signifying logic of an industrialized economy. In this sense, *aso ebi*'s historical and material conditions also illuminate and enact the crisis of the postcolonial city. Within the lived experiences of such crises, *aso ebi* uniforms are deployed to resolve the crisis of identity by transforming mere cloths into tangible but malleable archives of social reality that enable their wearers to imagine, if not create, new identities and realities.

ASO EBI AS HIGH FASHION

Aso ebi has been creatively woven into urban fashion, and now it seems to dictate the trajectory of radical design ideas across Nigeria and beyond through social media. Looking at how Kelechi took a snapshot of an *aso ebi* dress design from her friend's fashion magazine, one can argue that no aspect of Lagos life is resistant to the domineering power of *aso ebi* as a promoter of urban style and as one of the revolutionary seductions of modern sartorial life in Africa. To add to many scholarly works on changing dress styles in Africa and the concept of fashion, including the role of tailors in Africa's dress practices, I argue that *aso ebi* is one of the major agents of dissemination of urban styles in Africa.[12] My routes across Lagos's urban metropolis suggest that thousands of street fashion styles in Nigerian and African women's wardrobe have found ideas in the web pages of fashion sites that promote *aso ebi* fashion, such as Tkbridals and BellaNaija. This has exposed the unprecedented research promise that *aso ebi* can generate.

Through the ubiquitous revelries I attended across Lagos, I saw how *aso ebi* has profoundly reorganized everyday lives in Nigeria and has almost imposed a totalitarian uniformity of socialization through events such as weddings, funerals, and birthday parties. That a majority of families in Nigeria and the West African subregion have engaged, or anticipated future engagement, in *aso ebi* makes it a social revolution and an infatuation of modern urban life. It is my strong argument that *aso ebi* offers a way to bridge the gap between "popular" readership and disciplinary academic boundaries.

Given the prevailing cosmopolitan influence facilitated by globalization and media technologies--one that is very evident in Tkbridals' WhatsApp transactions with her clients--*aso ebi* has become a mirror through which Lagos urban styles are viewed. Many soft-sell magazines are used to disseminate *aso ebi* styles. The social media sites of AsoEbiBella.com, *BellaNaija*, and others have created special web pages for advertising *aso ebi* dress styles. Many of the sites have become windows of exhibition and advertisement for numerous *aso ebi* designers in Lagos and beyond. Many fashion websites have attached "*aso ebi*" to their names and pushed for designs that merge local elements with cosmopolitan ideas. While Lagos's unending weekend events have become competitive stages where countless *aso ebi* designers test their creative wits, AsoEbiBella.com, *BellaNaija*, and other *aso ebi* websites serve as intermediate spaces where the conflicting interests of fashion designers, wearers, textile marketers, and photographers are harmonized. I weave together these discourses under the thematic thrust of *aso ebi* as the ultimate mobilizer of these hybridized identities and performed practices created within the contingent spaces of the city of Lagos.

Aso ebi is a form of social change, a means of individual and collective mannerism, offering an opportunity to endless design evaluation, observation, and socialization. Here *aso ebi* is deployed as a social uniformed dressing in Nigeria and as the embodiment of the multiple aspects of modern social imaginary, economic instabilities, moral economies, as well as political and visual cultural features of the city of Lagos. That all of these classifications are enshrined in the singular uniform of *aso ebi* suggests how *aso ebi* can transform an entire city's culture and stand as a formidable playground for adventurous lived fashion experiments and experiences.

ASO EBI: FASHIONING FRACTIOUS UNIFORMITY

By the late twentieth century *aso ebi* had become popular as a "family uniform" in Lagos. Since then its meaning continues to transmogrify with the passing years. It has extended to a broader social arena to include remote relations. In these relations, friends and strangers wear uniformed fabric to chart solidarity in weddings, birthday parties, christenings, funerals, political rallies, and other occasions. One salient point that resonates across *aso ebi*'s genealogies is the strong insignia of uniformity. As a uniform, *aso ebi* has survived the vagaries of economic, cultural, and social upheavals that came with what Hudita Nura Mustafa (1998) has described as "postcolonial crises." The potent force enshrined in this uniformed fabric of *aso ebi* draws attention to the fact that "uniforms shape who we are and how we perform our identities" (Craik 2005, 4). Indeed, one could understand from this book how uniforms specify a variety of responses in terms of changing values, identities, moods, and attitudes (4). *Aso ebi* is tactically deployed to play the games of social life by letting people adapt to groups they are part of. This radically invokes the question: "Do people wear uniforms or do uniforms wear people?" (5). The answer rests in the internal mechanisms and techniques of the human body in the "actualization of persona and habitus" (7) through *aso ebi*.

The "actualization of persona and habitus" is found in how, during weddings or other social events, most individuals wear *aso ebi* fabric of similar color but sewn in different, individual styles. Here the emblem of uniformity is found in the common color code of all of those who are dressed in *aso ebi* fabric, while the pursuit of individualism resides in multiple, distinctive, individual designs. While color serves as the unifying thread, it also obliquely insinuates the humanistic collectivity that the fabrics weave together. However, different individual designs signify the distinguishing indications of design professionalism or amateurism. Popular photographers swarm social events and photograph almost every woman dressed in unique *aso ebi*. Their interest more often has to do with the designs of the dresses than the beauty associated with the wearers; photographers sell most of the photographs to fashion designers and publishers of soft-sell fashion magazines in Lagos. Most of the fashion designers launch the photos on their websites, and through these sites the designs enter into the global visual economy of fashion consumption. The interesting thing is that women who attract the attention of most photographers are those whose designs are the most outstanding. In effect, photographing seems to identify and endorse the fashionably savvy within the sea of uniformity. Thus there is an awkward sense of ambivalence within the group solidarity of oneness. What also emerges is a distinguishing arena of socialization and demarcation. Again, quality of textile materials is seen as something that should demarcate the "elite" from the poor, yet I suggest that a democracy of sartorial performativity is resolved by *ankara*, a signifying text within the debate of "originality" and "copy." Here the body, as I argue, is a pervasive object dictating the debate around individual motives and collective identities, both of which are implicated in the "changing political, social and cultural world" (Hendrickson 1996). Indeed, clothing the body involves a bodily practice that mediates a personal realization of group values (Lock 1993). Clothing is thus subjective as well as socioculturally determined and often involves a projection of a befitting persona (Berreman 1962). In many African contexts, the projection of a befitting persona might be tied to group membership such that, according to Judith Perani and Norma H.

Wolff, "pride of family, political affiliation, social club association and even friendship can be demonstrated through wearing identical dress to show group affiliation (*aso ebi*)" (1999, 29). Most literature on dress in Nigeria does not mention *aso ebi*. The few that do so include it in the manner of Perani and Wolff, either in passing or as part of a minor remark in the course of their major writings.

From the above, it is not surprising that women scavenge the spaces of the city and the internet searching for an adept who could invent a unique design that will crown them champions of urban trend in Lagos. They rely not only on designers in the streets to construct their images of *aso ebi* but also on the ubiquitous designs found in fashion magazines and social media. Hudita Nura Mustafa has advanced the theory of *sartorial ecumene* in her study of the fashion industry in Senegal. By "sartorial ecumene" she means the "incorporation of objects and images of global origins into practices and circulations involving dress and bodily adornment" (1998, 22). She observes that "new media such as television and photography intensify the circulation of fashion" (22).[13] Mustafa's study in Senegal offers a clue as to how women in Lagos have depended on global images of *aso ebi* fashion styles to invent new styles in the city of Lagos. We see, for example, how Tkbridals appropriates and disseminates images of her fashion designs through online sources and how Kelechi took shots of *aso ebi* dress designs with her phone from her friend's fashion magazine.

These women become conscious of how they present themselves and attempt to control the impressions that others receive about them. Other peoples' reactions toward a person's presentation of self are important for a person's sense of worth (Essah 2008). Metaphorically, *aso ebi*'s communal solidarity is represented by the colors of dress, which are usually matching, while the internecine discord and disagreements within the practice are symbolized by individual designs, which usually differ. These disagreements are found in the protestation of some friends who refuse to adorn themselves in *aso ebi* because their friends are selling it at an expensive price, a discord that sometimes produces an inverse reading of *aso ebi*: friends have been denied both food and wedding gifts because they refused to wear *aso ebi*, and enemies who dressed in *aso ebi* may have received food and wedding gifts. In other words, this discord shows that subversion is embodied in *aso ebi* uniformity itself. It also suggests that uniforms sometimes transform foes into friends and friends into foes. It has become evident that *aso ebi* is a mechanism used to transform potentially distant relations into relations of illusory amicability. It shows that *aso ebi* solidarity is based on thin, ephemeral robes rather than thick, resilient bonds. Fashion is therefore fueled by the competition provoked within the perceived spaces of *aso ebi*'s convivial commensalism and fractious uniformity.

LOCATING *ASO EBI* WITHIN FASHION DISCOURSES

Some scholars of fashion have unveiled a number of the dominant influences that Western ideas of fashion have had on people's notions of clothing.[14] For example, in Gilles Lipovetsky's work *The Empire of Fashion* (1994), fashion is seen as a vital means of cultural expression that is fraught with political valence. Fashion for Lipovetsky is a "rising power" in contemporary society circumscribing not just clothing but all aspects of sociocultural life, from television shows to sexual practices to scholarly interests (4). He defines "fashion" more broadly as "a sociohistorical reality characteristic of the West and of modernity itself" that opposes the power of tradition and endorses the obsession for novelty and change (4). However, it is noteworthy that while invoking the notion of fashion, Lipovetsky talks mostly about dress. He connects the identification of fashion with dress to the historical fact that until recently the fashion process was most obviously embodied in the clothing people wore. I demonstrate the logic of inconstancy in fashion and how fashion has shifted from an embellishment of modern collective life to a force reshaping society itself in its own image. Framing his words in a rather fashionable way, Lipovetsky notes, "Fashion is in the driver's seat" (6). In line with Lipovetsky's argument that fashion fuels the aesthetics "of being seen, and of exhibiting oneself to the gaze of others" (29), *aso ebi* is not just the clothes people wear; it is also an embodied sartorial modernity shaping the quest for visibility in the postcolonial city.

It seems that from Lipovetsky's work one can infer that fashion has indeed been an empire in itself, certainly because it upholds Western notions of the individual. My work on *aso ebi* perhaps charts a more divergent perspective regarding fashion, this time not from the notion of the individual but in terms of group commonality. Lipovetsky's work attempts a sociopolitical and/ or historical analysis of cloth. However, it seems that even in its task to resolve the structural/agency problems that inhere in a more expansive, geo-cultural fashion discourse, the work adopts an ethnocentric approach to social process. I think his history of fashion ultimately treats clothing as a subject that may never be entirely comprehended through a narrow conceptual tool. While Western fashion, as argued by Lipovetsky, is structured by evanescence and aesthetic fantasy, I view *aso ebi* fashion, in the Nigerian context, as being informed by a sense of enduring aspiration and aesthetic permanence and as a form of clothing that is intimately linked to the production and reproduction of culture—not as a "superficial" phenomenon but rather something that weaves material culture into a deeper human engagement.

Many other authors have suggested how dress functions as a "social skin" by inviting us to explore the individual and social identities that the dressed body creates (T. Turner 1993, 15–39).[15] The contingent dynamic that inheres in these individual and collective identities of dress—in the case of *aso ebi*—may sometimes manifest as "considerable ambiguity, ambivalence, and, therefore, uncertainty and debate over dress" (372). *Aso ebi* as dress readily becomes a turning point of contradictory morals, driving contests in historical encounters, in interfaces across class, between genders and generations, and in recent global textile economic exchanges. Given these dimensions, I track the internecine wrangling *aso ebi* constituted in Lagos, over definitions of identities, especially as discussed from accounts of daily altercations among friends and families. These exchanges showed that failure to buy *aso ebi* from each other generated antagonism in colonial and postcolonial Lagos. They also revealed the deployment of aso ebi in the quest for political identities through anticolonial struggle in Nigeria by women in the 1940s. Most importantly, daily transactions in aso ebi are shaped by the dilemmas in the fluctuating textile economy as well as the evolving local rhetorics of social identities and solidarity.

Some studies have explored the place of exchange and appropriation in specific colonial contexts and the impact of such transcultural practices on postcolonial subjectivities.[16] Through such studies it is possible to understand, first of all, the varying ways in which fractious morality was encapsulated in the sartorial practices of colonial subjects; second, how dress is caught up in colonial power relations; and, third, the imagery of clothing in postcolonial social movements.[17] What most literature on African dress has treated sketchily is the local and social categories of uniformed dressing outside the domineering discourses of officialdom.[18] Through *aso ebi* I identify the juncture at which local agency manifested as a form of opposition or denunciation of the colonial sartorial style. I investigate this dialogue between the subject and the master in colonial Lagos. Through newspaper archives of late nineteenth- and early twentieth-century Lagos, I offer a departure from the prevailing literature on clothing practices during the colonial period in Africa, which so far does not give much voice to the locals.

Some authors have drawn accounts from diverse disciplinary boundaries to shape a history of fashion in Africa.[19] Some of these authors saw how dress becomes a way of constituting the "social position of a person in society" and is thus used as a mechanism whereby inclusion and exclusion can be advanced (Essah 2008, 16).[20] In order to adequately explore the instability, the social constructedness, and the internal heterogeneity of identity categories, I insert *aso ebi*—for the sake of an avoidance of epistemological ambiguity— into the city of Lagos not as a form of identity but as a phenomenon that defies any attempt to naturalize any group's practice as normative. Jean Allman's *Fashioning Africa: Power and the Politics of Dress* (2004) gathers together chapters touching on power and politics of dress in a fast-changing sociopolitical African environment to make compelling arguments concerning the mechanism of cultural assimilation through Western dress during the colonial and postcolonial periods. This provides avenues for further analysis into the historical as well as contemporary manifestations of such assimilations. In adding to this interesting argument, I deploy *aso ebi* to account for the processes through which Africans engaged the preponderant and rather global hegemonic trade around textile production and distribution. My account of textile economy traces the role of the West and other economic superpowers in the economic life of African textiles in Africa and how capitalist production has impacted the practice of *aso ebi*. Many Nigerians who practice *aso ebi* rely on massive influx of African prints from China and elsewhere to fulfill the burden of mundane ritual. Central to certain aspects of my investigation is the political and economic role of Africa's agency in negotiating industrial and cultural exchanges. The changes in the textile economy between China and Nigeria is traced from the economic life of *aso ebi* fabric in the Balogun textile market in Lagos, which is one of the biggest markets in West Africa. Through this I question the meaning of "culture" and "tradition."

In questioning "culture" and "tradition" in the context of Lagos, a very interesting idea to consider is Simidele Dosekun's argument that a "spectacularly feminine Lagos woman" cannot be denied the agency of mainstream fashion trademarks because of her preference for 'traditional' dress. What Dosekun's text illustrates is that as a spectacularly gendered style of Lagos women's cosmopolitanism, traditional dress counters Western capitalist modernity. As an imagined otherness, 'traditional' dress cannot be a victim of "cultural imperialism." It cannot undermine cosmopolitan femininity, neither can it deny Lagos women their deserving position as equal actors in the global sartorial debate, especially as they struggle to fashion a postfeminist self (2020: 87–112). Dosekun's idea on 'traditional' dress is an interesting perspective that I am inclined to pursue in this book: a reflective analysis of fashion from a low-end level.

Many fashion discourses in postcolonial scholarship prefer to go beyond what Thorstein Veblen (1899) describes as "the leisure class." Veblen's "leisure class" (a phrase for the elite class) and its amplified articulation in his concept of "conspicuous consumption" and wastefulness were taken from a Marxist and materialist paradigm of fashion. This paradigm thus enables an alternative theoretical reflection of fashion systems from postcolonial and decolonial contexts in *aso ebi*. The concepts of "conspicuous consumption" and wastefulness are seen in aso ebi's excessive and spectacular deployment of textile materials and other accompanying paraphernalia. It suggests how Nigerian women's wardrobes are deeply invested in, and superfluously bedecked with, hundreds of *aso ebi* dresses that accumulate from their weekly participation in social events. Yet, as a different kind of uniforms, these *aso ebi* dresses tend to outlive their usefulness immediately after each event.

Interestingly, *aso ebi* seems to endorse another important theoretical characterization of fashion developed by Brenninkmeyer (1973) in which individuals prefer fashion styles they already own rather than adopting a completely new style (see Welters and Lillethun 2018). This explains why "traditional" dress has endured in Nigeria and largely West Africa since the 1960s. In terms of the materiality of fashion, capitalist modernity did not alter this ubiquitous fashion choice, rather it contributed to its proliferation.

It would be appropriate to consider another theoretical framework existing between the discursive aspects of dress and relations of power surrounding the dressed body. A reflection on the analytical schemes between the embodied experience of dress and socializing experience of the dressed body is necessary in the context of this book, especially in approaching issues of fashion stylistics and individual differences within a space of collectivity. This approach is attractive as it reconciles the socially discursive world, which regulates the dressed body, with the lived embodied experience of the dressed body, which selects, feels, and wears clothing (Essah 2008).

CHAPTER SUMMARIES

Chapter 1 aptly articulates the struggle that existed between members of Lagos society in terms of dress and the meanings it embodied during the colonial era. In approaching the critical intellectual debates around colonialism in this chapter, dress is used to invoke the psychology of resistance that eludes some literature on colonialism. If the role of dress in shaping the decolonization process in Lagos is made clear here, what is more pronounced is the role of *aso ebi* dresses in this decolonization process. The core of this chapter is its recognition, highlighting, and historicizing of *aso ebi* dress practices, which up till now are still very much under-researched.

Chapter 2 narrates the story of the textile economy as a means for understanding how new forms of mercantile networks reinvented a web of histories around aṣọ òkè and *ankara* textiles in Lagos. I also investigate Lagos as a city where the discourse of "fake" and "original" is entangled in the transactions of Chinese and Nigerian textile economies. The devastating or gainful effects of late global capitalism, I argue, have probably enabled a greater number of individuals to participate in *aso ebi* culture.

In chapter 3 the relationship between colors of *aso ebi* textiles, class, and the crowd is explored. Here the presence of large numbers of people in *aso ebi* at a particular gathering demonstrates the wealth of the celebrant, who is expected to clothe and feed such numbers. However, the provision of free *aso ebi* to such numbers was a propensity that reigned among the wealthy and few middle classes in the early twentieth century and declined around the 1980s when the economic predicaments of the Structural Adjustment Programme (SAP) occasioned a decrease in people's sense of generosity. In other words, in an effort to excel in the politics of the crowd, individuals aspire to multiply the number of people who wear *aso ebi* during their social events.

Under the thematic thrust of fractured materiality and the political economy of intimacy, chapter 4 surveys *aso ebi*'s claims in the consolidation of relationships and how this claim has been dismissed with indifference by those who cherish their individualism and who view the claims as ephemeral rather than enduring. The spirit of *aso ebi* solidarity has been substituted by shallow, bodily attire. In Lagos, therefore, the social and cultural valences of *aso ebi* as a gesture of group conviviality have sometimes been overlaid by references to the politics of exclusion/inclusion therein. Many individuals buy *aso ebi* fabric to sell to their friends and use the proceeds to offset the wedding expenses. In the process, politics of exclusion and inclusion ensue.

While opening up issues around *aso ebi* and notions of popular photography, print media, fashion magazines, and group performativity in certain social events in Nigeria, chapter 5 shows that *aso ebi* has occasioned an explosion in the Lagos fashion business. Almost approximating a social convention, *aso ebi* employs its material accoutrements to construct the visible persona in the city. There is a healthy competition instituted by *aso ebi* in the Lagos fashion business whereby creativity in designs is driven by photographs of *aso ebi* groups in fashion magazines, Instagram, Facebook, WhatsApp, and other social media. Fashion magazines constitute a major vehicle for visual mobilization and intensification among the tailors and groups who wear *aso ebi*.

Chapter 6 reveals how *aso ebi* largely informed the revolution seen in digital Photoshop editing among Lagos photographers. The urge to appear in fashionable *aso ebi* dresses has influenced the surface reconstruction of most wedding photographs. I show that the proliferation of photographers in social events in Nigeria is a trend that came with *aso ebi* culture and has been made possible by the new technological capital of digital cameras and the digital photo lab. This is similar to Martin Lister's (1995) exploration of the technological transformation of the image and its implications for city life.

I attempt to address the aesthetics and politics of dress through *aso ebi*. I identify the discourse of dress as that which bears on one quintessential object sign: the human body. Finally, I conclude that *aso ebi* is being fed by the underlying visual and consumerist hype that underpin the late capitalist system as it unfolds in Nigeria. The tenor of the argument in the chapters as a whole connects *aso ebi* visuality, everyday experiences, and the economics of mundane living under late capitalism. In the process, individuals who practice *aso ebi* seem to have lost the sense of a "precolonial humanism" with which *aso ebi* was originally identified: there are no longer free gifts. Instead what obtains is a fetishization of various forms of commodity culture ranging from the textile economy, personality cults through mass-produced images in fashion magazines, exchange value in human relationships through gifts, and a form of exclusion achieved through the surface effects of digital photo editing. Indeed, I suggest that both fashion and photography emerge as two inseparable aspects of modernity that Nigerians sought before and after colonialism in the 1960s, during the economic crisis of the 1980s, and during the rise of digital photography and radical printing technology in the twenty-first century.

CHAPTER 1

Aso Ebi *and the Fashioning of Bodies in Colonial Lagos, 1860s–1960s*

During the fifteenth century, people of the Awori branch of the Yoruba from the west, Egba Yoruba from the northwest, Ijebu Yoruba from the north, and Bini (Edo) from the Benin empire to the east moved into the area now known as Lagos. These groups competed for supremacy in the region. As the earliest settlers, the Awori claimed chieftaincy and primordial rights to the land. The Awori also became influential in the political transition of Lagos from the colonial to the postcolonial period (Aderibigbe 1975, 3–5; Barnes 1986, 38). Their political structures instituted the *oba* (king) of Lagos during the fifteenth century through the authorities of the *oba* of Benin. With increasing wealth from slave trade deals, chieftaincy categories were constituted, and these chiefs ruled the town until the nineteenth century (Baker 1974, 7–18).

Ruy de Sequeira led the first Portuguese that arrived on Lagos Island in 1472. These Portuguese merchants eventually called the city "Lagos," the Portuguese word for "lakes." By the 1760s the Portuguese had established a flourishing slave trade. Enabled by the city's advantageous seaport, the Lagos slave trade enriched foreign merchants and local chiefs. The *oba* was remunerated with many articles of trade brought by the slave traders. Some of these articles were clothing materials that would eventually shape the *oba*'s wardrobe. As subsequent discussions will reveal, this clothing also constituted an object of political and cultural tension in colonial Lagos. Superior access to "money" and consumer goods further enriched and empowered the *oba*, whose influence would ultimately form the power politics of Lagos up to today.

By the nineteenth century liberated slaves from Sierra Leone known as the "Saros" returned to Lagos. Other slaves (of Yoruba descent), popularly known as the "Brazilians," were repatriated to Lagos from Brazil after the 1826–1835 slave revolts in Brazil. Still other slaves, liberated from Cuba and Brazil and commonly referred to as the "Agudas," also joined. Agudas were slaves from different ethnic groups who returned on their own accord from the new world to Lagos, as equals, to reintegrate with their origins. The Agudas were highly skilled technicians and introduced Brazilian architecture to their new settlements in Lagos and beyond. Brazilian architecture would eventually become preferred to the reigning European architecture because of the craftsmanship introduced by the returned Agudas. Ironically, some of the Agudas became wealthy slave dealers (Crowder 1962, 77).

British attempts to suppress the slave trade in Lagos culminated in a naval attack in 1851 and the deposition of the then Oba Kosoko.[1] The slave trade continued until in 1861, when Lagos was made a British colony. Being under the British colony, which had outlawed slave trade and dethroned local chiefs who traded slaves, Lagos was seen as a safe place. By this time, more slaves began to return from different parts of the West African subregion, and Lagos became more cosmopolitan. The year 1861 marked a turning point in the social, political, and cultural history of Lagos.

The significance of the post-1861 setting is crucial for an examination of the sartorial politics of colonial Lagos. For example, the slaves who came back from Brazil, Sierra Leone, and Cuba brought their own styles of dress, while Christian missionaries who came to Lagos after the British annexation in 1861 attempted to enforce certain uniformed dress for converts. Some local Lagosians were not amenable to sartorial changes and instead retained their so-called traditional attire. The colonial administrators and missionaries also brought sewing machines. This, then, raises the question of how these changes affected dress and *aso ebi* practice in colonial Lagos.

Against the backdrop of these developments, this chapter addresses two important issues: first, the politics of dress in colonial Lagos and, second, the origins of *aso ebi* in the city. In examining the politics of dress, I discuss how dress became a core argument among various groups in colonial Lagos, including the returned slaves from Brazil and Sierra Leone, the colonial administrators, the missionaries, Christianized Lagosians, and those opposed to Christian conversion. Located within these contests are issues of conversion, "proper" sartorial styles, and expressions of identity by different groups. Here, I argue that in approaching colonial literature, one needs to recognize certain forms of resistance that came with dress.

To interrogate the origins of *aso ebi*, I undertake a nuanced investigation of how Christian missionaries and colonial authorities may have aided its intensification. The impact of colonial uniforms and Christian churches' uniforms, I suggest, may have facilitated the spread of *aso ebi* uniforms. A caveat here is that the sheer difficulty of synthesizing specific histories of *aso ebi* is a topic I can merely raise rather than resolve in this chapter.

THE POLITICS OF FASHIONING THE BODY IN COLONIAL LAGOS: 1860S–1920S

The Yoruba constitute the dominant population in Lagos, which explains their control over the political and cultural life of cosmopolitan Lagos. Although the present Lagos is cosmopolitan, with people from other parts of Nigeria, the West African subregion, and elsewhere, politically the Yoruba still dominate present-day Lagos. It is also generally believed that they dominate the *aso ebi* practice in the city.

Accounts from the nineteenth century affirm that being well dressed played a significant role in Yoruba social hierarchies, with much importance being attached to the size, color, quality, and quantity of fabric (Euba 2002). Indeed the Baptist missionary William H. Clarke, during his sojourn in Abeokuta near Lagos between 1854 and 1858, observed that the Yorubas attached much importance to dress and that their love of fine clothes was unmatched. Clarke, however, recognized the ubiquity and variety of stylish and colorful dress in Yorubaland and felt it could equal any part of "civilized" society (1972, 237). In terms of sartorial dressing, the Yoruba may have exceeded Clarke's expectations; however, we cannot ascertain what his expectations were, nor do we know precisely what might have occasioned his surprise at the Yorubas' "stylish and colorful collection." Similarly, when the traveler and British consul Richard Burton visited Abeokuta in 1861, he noted that "people are tolerably well clothed. Dressy men wore shogoto, or loose cotton drawers fastened above the hips . . . and extending to the knee. The body was covered with a cloth gracefully thrown like a plaid over the shoulder" (1863, 102). It must be noted that this same style of clothing was a bone of contention between the Christianized Lagosians and the non-Christian locals in the 1880s: the Christians rejected it outright. As will be shown subsequently, the contention was championed by some key newspapers of this period in Lagos.

Yoruba popular thought often expressed, and continues to express, the relationship between dress, social hierarchy, and prestige. For example, the saying "*Irinisi ni isoni lojo*" translates as "One's physical looks combined with one's demeanor explains who one is." Another example, *"Bi a ba rinrin iya, ti a woso ise wo lu, igbakigba ni won fi i boni fun ni mu,"* means "If we walk disorderly and dress raggedly into the town, an unwholesome calabash will be used to serve us drinking water." Similarly, the saying goes that *"Eni to kan akanpo ewu ti kuro ni ile san tabi ko san,"* which translates as "The nobility of someone who is dressed in gorgeous garments is not in doubt" (Lawal 1996). Some of these sayings can be seen as a reflection of the wardrobes of most Yoruba rulers, who maintain status and seniority through conspicuous display of aesthetic forms, including clothing.[2] For example, Titilola Euba observes the importance of sumptuous and expensive dress materials acknowledged by the *oba*:

> Respect for seniority, and for the prestige of kingship symbolized by dress, is demonstrated by the action of Oba Akinsemoyin[,] who was on the throne at the arrival of the first Portuguese slave traders. When offered a dazzling piece of satin velvet, the astonished king promptly sent the material to the Oba of Benin as being worthy only of His Majesty. The king of Benin on his part encouraged the Oba of Lagos to continue his friendship with the slave traders. (2002, 140)

A. B. Aderibigbe notes that Losi, "the traditional historian," describes this costly piece of velvet as "one which when placed in the king's room made the room dark in the day and bright at night" (1975, 12). Losi's metaphorical allusion illustrates the importance attached to foreign clothes then. Alongside the encouragement by the king of Benin is the suggestion that the entrenchment of the slave trade in Lagos could have been facilitated by a mere piece of cloth. Support for this entrenchment is evidenced by other trade relations between the natives and the slave dealers in which textiles acted as a major article of barter.

Before the British takeover of Lagos in 1861, the traditional dress of the *oba* and his chiefs was a white wrapper worn toga-like in the Yoruba style and in the manner of Bini chiefs. The *oba* and his chiefs were also distinguished by the white cap that continues to be the official symbol of the Lagos chiefs whose origin is Bini as opposed to Yoruba. With the return of the slaves from Brazil to Lagos, the *oba* supplemented his status by appropriating the imported cloths brought by the foreigners—rich satins, velvets, damasks, and silks—while the simple white cap of former times was substituted with a top hat and with the admiral's cocked hat. By this period more foreign attire had clearly found its way into the *oba*'s wardrobe. Euba describes a photograph of Oba Akitoye thus:

> The earliest photograph of Oba Akitoye shows him wearing a top hat covered with patterned damask with the design of a crown conspicuously in front. He wears a long-sleeved white shirt of obvious European inspiration, but the shirt is full length, and underneath it, though not visible, is a white wrapper, the Gbariye, which is worn as a compulsory token of the Oba of Lagos, traditional costume. The long shirt is covered with a damask wrapper the ends which are thrown over the left shoulder in the traditional style. A pair of socks adds a touch of class. Most important for historical purpose is his staff, very new at the time, for it was given to him by the British to mark the treaty that enabled him to regain his throne from his nephew Kosoko, the slave trader par excellence. Engraved on this staff, termed *opa adehun*, is a promise to abolish human sacrifices, to end the slave trade, to promote legitimate commerce, and to protect Christian missionaries. It was signed on January 1, 1852. (2002, 142)

This style of dress has implications for subsequent dress style in contemporary Lagos. To illustrate, the present *oba* of Lagos still retains most of the paraphernalia mentioned above. The import of these Western dress materials into the *oba*'s dress must be observed in the context of their meanings during the late eighteenth and nineteenth centuries. By this period, fashion had become part of a more popular consciousness, and the mass manufacture of clothing emerged at the same time that individual status and uniqueness were being increasingly accentuated. Although damask, seen in the subsequent *oba*'s wardrobe, was already in vogue during the fourteenth century in Europe, it flourished at the height of the Industrial Revolution, between 1760 and 1815 (Wilson and de la Haye 1999; Jenkins 2003). It can be argued that at the end of the eighteenth century, benefiting from the growing trade in slaves and textiles that was occasioned by the Industrial Revolution, the Lagos native wardrobe radically transformed. Captain John Adams, who arrived in Lagos in 1789, described the articles of trade acquired by the *oba* of Lagos as consisting of "pieces of cloth, of Indian and European manufacture, iron bars, earthenware, a beautiful hand organ, the bellows of which were burst; two elegant chairs of state, having rich crimson damask covers, all in tatters; a handsome sedan chair without a bottom and two expensive sofas without legs."[3]

From the enlisted Indian and European textiles, it is therefore not surprising that the *oba*'s fashion, in the spirit of the new industrial and commercial age, was exercised most ostentatiously and conspicuously. And his mode of dress inadvertently signified, at the same time, the winding, disconnected historic and geographic route by which it arrived in Lagos. The new wardrobe of the *oba* was evident in a local's eyewitness account of Oba Akitoye in exile near Badagry in 1846: "The apparel of the king was certainly very costly and his splendour cast such a shade on the other chiefs that they looked like other common people."[4] From the *oba*'s wardrobe, one could easily conclude that the creative combination of Western and local attire provided a new sartorial vocabulary with which to communicate in the modernizing, social environment of Lagos. By this time vast imaginative and experimental promises, needed to forge new social and sartorial identities, were revealed to Africans through Western dress. Victoria Rovine sees this as "a language with which to speak back to the whites" (2001, 103).When the British took over Lagos in 1861, the local hierarchies that placed the British officials, missionaries, and traders on the aristocratic ladder were restructured. The indigenous Lagosians were consigned to the lower rungs, while the Brazil returnees and other black immigrants were among the middle class. The *oba* located himself among the esteemed bourgeoisie who made claims to a British connection. This new social grouping, obviously, was deeply resented by Indigenous Lagosians who believed that the Sierra Leaonean immigrants dressed so flamboyantly that they posed a sartorial affront to their *oba*.

Importantly, before this period, the *oba*'s influence was close to that of an autocracy and, as such, no ordinary citizen would dare outdress the *oba*. The British, however, diminished the *oba*'s influence, weakening his powers such that "ordinary" Sierra Leonean immigrants could now allegedly compete with him in stylish dressing. Essentially, what was understood as the *oba*'s attire then was the English top hat, which had become the standard fashion in England from the early decades of the nineteenth century and was the very hat favored by the *oba* as his crown. This symbolic usurpation of the *oba*'s status no doubt contributed to the antipathy existing between the Sierra Leoneans and the *oba*'s subjects. And this same antipathy was transferred to other groups of Yoruba returnees perceived as Creoles.[5]

The Yoruba Creoles, for example, loved fine clothes, a tendency that was manifested in the ladies who wore crinolines and high-heeled boots. Their love of high heeled boots was described as an evidence of their urge to be "civilized." 'Civilization' was used in most nineteenth century Lagos Newspapers as an idiosyncrasy that was tied to Western tastes and attitudes.[6] For this reason most of the immigrants saw it as a duty to use their foreign dress as a means of differentiating themselves from pagans, and this very attitude became the target of their critics. On the one hand, the Europeans deeply resented the competition posed by this class of nouveau riche, and on the other, indigenous residents equally hated the rivalry of those who placed themselves outside the jurisdiction of the established order.

Most Christian Yorubas and Saros (Sierra Leoneans) imitated middle-class Europeans in their mode of dress. The slaves returning from Brazil did the same, especially with regard to letting their hair grow and parting it in imitation of the whites, whose long hair was a symbol of their social standing. In Yoruba social practices, long hair and shoes were prerogatives of the kings, the former symbolizing his sacred power, the latter his control of wealth and prestige. Shoes were among the items seen as the "inspiration of civilization" that, according to Samuel Johnson, came with northern trade (2001, 14). In nineteenth-century Lagos, a fit dressing for a typical Yoruba Lagosian consisted of a "loin" cloth reaching to the ground, a large wrapper ending on the shoulders, and one or another of a large variety of hats. Subsequently, under Muslim influence, a pair of short trousers and "a kind of vest" became part of the wardrobe. The women wore the usual wrapper known as *iro* in Yoruba and head-tie known as *gele*. I shall return to *iro* and *gele* in subsequent discussions.

Suffice it to say that although dress was a bone of contention in nineteenth-century Lagos, it was also a symbol of identity among all the diverse groups that made up Lagos. Among all of these groups it was the Saros who carved a niche for themselves as those immediately following the whites in the ladder of ascending to the bourgeoisie. Most of the nineteenth-century newspapers gave many insightful revelations into the lifestyle of the members of the elite group. This group included the Saros who imitated the Europeans in their dressing and make up. Titilola Euba remarks that "the Saros were more or less unanimous in their passion to be civilized," and their social and economic access to the Europeans placed them on a surrogate standing with the white ruling class (2002, 147). Other groups were becoming accustomed with the Saros's penchant for European articles and lifestyle disclosed in their dress, food, and social activities. In the competitive bid to achieve elevated status and high social standing, and thus free themselves from the detestable lowliness associated with "the natives," the former slaves from Brazil held onto their Catholicism, which gave them a sense of equality with their former masters.

By the time Christianity started making a strong incursion into most groups during the colonial period, the idea of a dress code became a contentious one in the administrative and local settings of colonial spaces, including in Nigeria.[7] Intertwined here is a desire, on the one hand, by Christian converts to emulate a Western style of dress, and, on the other, by the so-called pagans to retain their traditional style of dressing. However, it seems that the Bible and the nectie emerged contemporaneously, and missionaries claimed that the dress of the Christians would be a "badge of distinction" that would set converts off from the rest of African society. In fact, "African" attire was seen as an impediment to the project of evangelization (R. Ross 2008, 125). During the mid-nineteenth century, many missionaries believed that converts who did not drink tea or wear European clothes lacked the genuine attributes of a Christian (Ayandele 1981, 36).

The *Lagos Observer*, in an editorial comment of May 7, 1887, spoke against "the Eastern fashion as worn by the Mohammedian around us; or the broad cloth thrown over the left shoulder and passed under the right arm as worn by the *gens togata*, now symbolized by the people of the Gold Coast." The editorial argues:

> Probably the only reason that can be urged at present for the use of the English dress on this coast is that the influence of the British nation is the most preponderating; and here we find history repeating itself, for when Britons were Gaulic slaves their improvised paintings and barbarous languages were replaced by the grace of their conquerors.[8]

There is a sarcastic tone in the writer's use of "the broad cloth thrown over the left shoulder and passed under the right arm as worn by the *gens togata*" of the Gold Coast and of "the Eastern fashion as worn by the Mohammedans around us." This repudiation by the *Observer* came as a result of the tensions arising between educated and Christianized Lagosians (who had embraced European dressing habits) in the late nineteenth century and their non-Christian and illiterate countrymen (who would not accept the European model of dress) (Echeruo 1977, 38).[9] In a letter to the editor of the *Times of Nigeria* of November 1, 1920, one Bello Babatunde Salami, while not dismissing the idea of Yoruba Muslims wearing their native *buba* and *agbada*, claims that native dress "is most degrading and unsuitable to the educational and social states of the educated Muslim."[10] He strongly argues that "the educated Muslim acting on and having firm faith in the belief previously stated will undoubtedly wear the European dress completely" and that "native dresses are a sort of disturbance to the anticipated professional works of the educated Muslim."[11] In this statement Salami canvasses a dress distinction between educated Muslims and the natives. His argument clearly indicates that education and religion became two distinct elements that must define aspects of dressing.

While Salami and the above commentators relied on religious paradigms for dress styles, the *Times of Nigeria* of May 3, 1920, chose to condemn the identification of "a particular dressing with a religion." The writer opposes the perspective that "dressing like Agbada and Buba are the Muslims and European suit and trousers the Christians" and suggests that "if one knows his duty towards his God, surely, the mere dressing up in any kind does not corrupt his religious morality and faith."[12]

If the *Times of Nigeria* of May 3, 1920, was equivocal in its dress advocacy, the *Lagos Observer* of April 2 and 16, 1887, was more definite in its support of "native dress": "It remains also to be seen in the near future what effect the European dress will produce on the constitution of West Africa." It went ahead to state how "the European dress is unsuitable in tropical heat, with a lurid sun overhead, dressed on a Sunday, in Winter suit, or with clothing of the finest wool importing an inflammable warmth to the system."[13] The *Observer* even went as far as advocating for "legislative measures against the indecent appareling in foreign dress, of our native female population."[14]

From the above, it is clear that a manifestation of a sartorial contest was at the heart of colonial/missionary expansionism with the corresponding antithetical responses that attended their modernizing mission. In allowing these contestations to constitute the editorial focus, most newspapers understood the emerging conflict that dress was beginning to generate in the imperial posts. In most of the newspaper columns, some writers took up the pedagogical task of educating Lagos residents of "how to dress well."[15] In the *Nigerian Pioneer* of July 28, 1922, the commentator's conclusions of "dressing well" were premised on moderation rather than on the controversy surrounding European and native dress: "If nothing else, it is the overdressing that destroys the charm and natural attraction."[16]

When the historic phenomenon of European domination is taken as the single most defining moment in history, colonialism takes credit for structures, events, and processes. Colonial discourse becomes even more pronounced when the story of expatriates in the social and political economy of most colonized states occupies a larger-than-life space in the cultural imagination of the "Other." In this context, the result could be the trivialization of the non-Christians and illiterate Lagosians' role in forging a sartorial agency during the colonial period in West Africa. By highlighting this sartorial agency, I identify a peculiar social and political structures at play in Lagos during the colonial period. More importantly, I want to suggest, the wearing of aṣọ òkè cloth "uniforms" by families in Lagos and in the wider Yoruba-speaking area of Nigeria may have occurred earlier than the colonial period at funerals and other major family events, thus contributing to the emergence of a dress culture like *aso ebi*. In view of the above, I suggest that passive submission under colonialism might not be taken as the singular historical logic for the genesis of "culture." In approaching the politics of fashioning the body in colonial Lagos, it would also be reasonable to recognize the significant roles played by these dress debates in shaping cultural understandings, especially between various groups in Lagos.

Also one needs to examine how these dress debates became most pronounced in the editorial columns of the *Lagos Weekly Record* and the *Lagos Observer* in the late nineteenth century. It was clear that contributors in both of these newspapers were manifesting this disagreeable idiosyncrasy by either supporting the cause of native dress or rejecting it. Apart from the *Lagos Weekly Record*, the *Lagos Standard* also vigorously championed these debates, in some cases, in support of native fashion (Byfield 2004, 34). In certain instances the *Weekly Record* and the *Standard* instituted a staunch campaign both against the rejection of Western fashion and in favor of cultural consciousness, through which they attempted to stimulate greater interest in African history, language, and culture (Omu 1978, 107). Unlike the large newspapers, O. E. Macaulay, Bishop Samuel Crowther's grandson and editor of the pro-government *Eagle* and *Lagos Critic* newspapers, argued for the abandonment of "the easy and free native cloth toga and sandals" and the adoption of the "costly and inconvenient dress, boots, shoes and hats" of the superiors. (Euba 2002, 155). This was viewed as a politically charged argument that was meant to bolster the English fashion business of Mrs. Crowther (the editor's aunt-in-law).

To some Lagosians, the "inconvenient dress" was a visible indicator of a creeping identity crisis that worked to undermine the mental power and psychological dignity of the Black African.[17] However, influenced by the dress reform movement against European dress that began in Sierra Leone in the late 1870s, some Christians discarded their dress and European names (Euba 2002, 155). One of these was Reverend Mojola Agbebi, the acclaimed demagogue of the Baptist Church in Lagos. In fact, in 1896, in a commentary in the *Lagos Standard*, he argued that European names and dresses were concrete reminders of Africans' ambivalent cultural and social positions: "Every African bearing a foreign name is like a ship sailing under false colours, and every African wearing a foreign dress in his country is like the jackdaw in peacock's feathers."[18] Another author in the *Lagos Standard* a year later dismissed European dress as unsuitable for the African climate and a symbol of mental bondage.[19] Other factions who championed the cause of African dress were led by Otunba Payne, the hardworking and influential registrar of the Supreme Court of Lagos, who declared that "the unanimous opinion of intelligent Africans is that health in West Africa is impaired, and lives shortened by the adoption of European tastes, customs and forms of dress" (Kopytoff 1965, 86).

By 1880 Richard B. Blaize, the wealthy Egba Saro merchant and the publisher of the anti-government newspapers the *Lagos Times* and *Gold Coast Colony Advertiser*, had already, through his local attire, influenced his daughters, Charlotte Blaize, who later got married to become Mrs. Obasa (the fashionable Sisi Obasa), and her younger sister, Mrs. Gibson (Euba 2002, 155). In 1890 Mrs. Gibson's wardrobe was already adorned with various combinations of traditional attire such as *adire* (tie-dye) wrapper and differently patterned prints such as the *buba*-like overblouse, head-tie, and shawl. Her sister, even more stylish, combined handwoven cloths, aṣọ òkè, and European prints, but this was only later in her life and apparently to distinguish herself from "rascals." The importance of aṣọ òkè at this moment cannot be overemphasized, and its influence on—and historical connection to—the sartorial development of *aso ebi* in twentieth-century Lagos will be discussed in subsequent chapters.

But what the foregoing discussion suggests is a kind of sociopolitical resistance in the emerging Lagosian culture under colonialism. The resistance has largely been ignored in the scholarly literature, with the result that analyses remain enmeshed within a narrow explanatory framework of relevant links with the sociopolitical climate surrounding, for example, Mrs. Gibson's 1890s. In fact, a review of the roots of Nigeria's colonial encounter with dress coupled with the social and political history of Lagos from the 1890s unveils a number of interesting convergences indicating that choice of dress was not materially dependent on colonialism but flourished in spite of it.

In further investigating the visceral resistance to the colonial system between 1800 and 1891, the Ijebus, one of the first settler groups in Lagos, pursued a policy of "splendid isolation" in which they treated British agents, missionaries, and non-Ijebu Yoruba as strangers. Their abhorrence for Europeans and their lifestyles resulted in the enactment of a native immigration law by the Awujale (the Ijebu king) banning missionaries from entering Ijebuland in 1852. The Ijebus were unwavering in their resentment of the seemingly domineering influence of European culture, such that Ijebu Saro (Sierra Leonean Ijebu) were rejected as members of their own community. In their eyes the latter "had betrayed their fatherland by adopting European religion, manners and clothing" (Ayandele 1981, 90–95). Thus it could be observed that the psychology of resistance was something that extended to anything deemed to have the slightest contact with European culture, including dress. And within these forms of resistance there was also a struggle for distinction, which gave rise to a deference toward existing sartorial attitudes of which *aso ebi* was a part. This attitude was initiated by the Saros. Records show that during weddings, Saro family members would wear the same uniforms as a symbol of their solidarity and to differentiate themselves from other members of the public (Bascom 1951, 492).

While some authors of colonial history and fashion alike have argued that dress practices were central to colonial rule and to postcolonial anxiety, it is necessary to note that toward the last decade of the nineteenth century, dress was deployed as a weapon of imperial denunciation in Nigeria.[20] This became more intense after 1895, to the extent that dress was one of many tools deployed in the struggle against incipient signs of racism instituted by British imperial rule in Nigeria. After 1896, segregation became so pronounced in Lagos that even in hospitals Black and White wards were separated (Byfield 2004, 9). The Church Missionary Society, which was then the leading missionary group in Lagos, abandoned its initial primary objective of establishing an African-led church, increased the number of white missionaries in Nigeria, and placed lesser-trained Europeans in supervisory positions over Africans who were more qualified. Furthermore, White missionaries' disapproval of Samuel Ajayi Crowther's appointment as bishop in 1891 had clear racist overtones. These developments contributed significantly to the creation and expansion of independent African churches. By this period, Nigerians in the civil service began to face color discrimination. In a number of instances, less-qualified Europeans were promoted over Nigerians, and there were disparities in salaries and benefits. Attempts were also made to create racially segregated residential communities and churches (Ayandele 1981).

Educated Nigerians were especially outraged by these developments, because they had agitated for more vigorous colonial expansion during the

1880s and 1890s, expecting to be Britain's partners in progress. They had not anticipated the heightened racism that accompanied colonial expansion. As a result, educated Nigerians began to reevaluate their enthusiasm for European culture. Doing so led to a renewed enchantment for African institutions and practices that hitherto had been denigrated by the Europeans. Such reevaluation was not unique to Nigeria; this ideological shift in Britain instigated similar rethinking in other colonies. For example, in Sierra Leone, the Creoles, descendants of African American and Jamaican immigrants, launched a dress reform movement in the late 1880s. Dress reformers saw the eradication of European dress as the first important step in bringing about a gradual independence from all European customs. They did not, however, adopt the dress styles of the indigenous communities in Sierra Leone. Instead they invented a new wardrobe that served to distinguish them from Europeans and from the communities in the hinterland, people they also considered "barbarian aborigines" (Spitzer 1974, 117; Mann 1985). The importance of this dress movement cannot be overemphasized. As is evident from the above, dress was a critical response and a dimension never envisaged by the colonialists. Again, this condition was not exceptional to Nigeria but also played out in other African nations.[21] This topic is further explored in subsequent discussions that attempt nuanced explorations of certain historical circumstances that suggest the rise and intensified use of uniformed dressing such as *aso ebi*.

THE RISE OF UNIFORMED DRESS AND THE IMPACT OF EUROPEAN MERCHANTS AND CHRISTIAN MISSIONARIES

The institutional power and social legitimacy embodied in the notion of uniform cannot be underestimated, especially during colonialism in Africa and other parts of the world. The values and ideals that the colonial authorities assigned to official clothing and decorations need to be studied more carefully in order to ascertain whether these have any influence on the rise of such attitudes as *aso eb* uniformed culture in Nigeria. Under British rule uniforms became a highly disputed aspect of clothing, especially as Africans became subjected to the colonial instrumentality of formal and semiformal uniforms in colonial offices and schools.[22] With the rapidly expanding imperial incursion, "colonial dress practice became increasingly rigid and formal."[23] While Africanist scholars have closely examined the broad debates surrounding clothing in the past decades, uniforms in colonial African society still require deeper contextualization within the ambits of imperial officialdom and socio-cultural significance.[24]

Although it is possible that *aso ebi* was already practiced before the nine-teenth century in Yorubaland, quite possibly the arrival of colonial adminis-trators and the missionaries intensified the practice. Lack of visual evidence to prove the existence of *aso ebi* before their arrival has become a challenge in tracing the point at which *aso ebi* was put to ubiquitous use in urban Lagos. This is especially so where the camera was part of the instrument of colonial rule and missionary evangelism. Photography was invented only in 1839, and by the mid-nineteenth century photographs of Africans expressing agency may not have been possible. Most photographs that circulated around the imperial outposts were mainly stereotypical photographs that advanced colo-nial missions.

By the 1840s and 1850s Christianity was introduced in Lagos through the efforts of liberated Africans returning home from Sierra Leone as well as through the endeavors of missionaries of various denominations. Notable among these denominations were the Methodists and the Church Missionary Society (CMS), who were later joined by the Baptists and the Roman Cath-olics.[25] The CMS opened its first house in Lagos in October 1852 and built its first school in 1853. By 1855 their missions had spread throughout Yorubaland and beyond. The introduction of Christianity came with occasions for pub-lic outings, which increased the demand for clothes. Demand also increased in response to the initiation of uniforms in mission schools and colleges. In some cases, tailors were employed by the missionaries to sew uniforms and dresses for the students and workers in their institutions.[26] To meet demand, tailoring and dressmaking were taught in some of the vocational schools run by missionaries. The Christian Yoruba wardrobe was filled not only with "Sunday dresses" but also with "school uniforms or colonial uniforms sewn in European style" (Ajayi 1965, 160). In addition to imposing uniformed dress sewn in European style, at some point the missionaries also enforced uni-forms made of wax print fabrics. For example, Tunde Akinwumi's 1981 study shows a certain primary school in Bonny in 1909 where pupils dressed in uniforms sewn in wax print (187). What is striking, from a photograph of the uniformed pupils in Akinwumi's study, is the manner of sewing that deviated from the European-style shirt and shorts. The sewing style seems to reflect local preferences and dynamics, embodied in their style of wax print wrap-pers and blouses.[27] This is remarkable and strongly resonates with the ubiquitous use of similar wax prints and perhaps styles of sewing for present-day *aso ebi*. Similarly, Akinwumi observes that in 1950 the Sunday uniform of St. Andrew College students were *Oyala* and *Sapara*, indigenous Yoruba hand-printed textiles. Akinwumi suggests how the students' regular appearance in the dress during their visits to the townships could have influenced the spread of uniformed fashion among Yoruba youths. By the early twentieth century, the Anglican churches in Lagos and its environs commissioned uniformed fabrics for members during important church events, such as anniversaries (Akinwumi 1990; Akinwumi and Renne 2008, 126–45). Based on these examples, one can surmise that there was a strong relationship between the spread of *aso ebi* and a growing ethos of modernity among converts. In turn, this might have encouraged the spread of *aso ebi* among friendship associations that emerged in early twentieth-century Lagos, as I will now show.

By the 1950s many Yoruba age groups had deployed *aso ebi* as group uniforms (Bascom 1951, 490–95). Women's associations were distinguished by their colorful *aso ebi*. *Aso ebi* had already started forging various forms of solidarities and senses of purpose aimed at community development and progress. *Aso ebi* had also manifested within the virtue of comradeship that originated in the pairing of Yoruba *Gelede* masquerades.[28] In Yoruba there is a local epistemology that drives the practice of two partners who reach a pact, adopt a common secret name, and dress alike, a practice that is sometimes misinterpreted as twins. Again, fraternal love in Yorubaland is epitomized by an often-embodied twin-like intimacy that insinuates same parentage (Micheli 2008, 70).

The European merchants and missionaries played an important role in the spread of uniformed dressing through the importation of sewing machines and the establishment of tailoring businesses in Lagos. Some of the earliest available evidence suggesting the existence of tailoring activities in Lagos is a descriptive analysis of the social and economic life of Yoruba society by W. H. Clarke during his visit to Yorubaland between 1854 and 1858. Clarke describes the craft of dressmaking thus: "The females never cut or sew garments but sell all articles of merchants. . . . Conversely the males use the needle entirely but never or at least, very seldom engage in the art of selling."[29] From this, Clarke's allusion may not directly suggest the use of sewing machines but rather the dressmaking activities that immediately predated them.

The sewing machine was invented in Europe in 1830, and the first of them were designed for factory use. It was only in 1851 that the first Singer home sewing machine was patented in England, and it could not have spread to Yorubaland as soon as 1854 when Clarke was writing. However, by 1867 the first trained tailors in Yoruba were beginning to return from abroad to practice in Lagos and other Yoruba towns. This was the period when twenty boys taken to Whydah during slave trade in the mid-nineteenth century returned to Lagos from Bouffarick, near Algiers, from where they received training in different handiworks, including tailoring.[30]

By 1889 the tailoring innovation had become widespread in Lagos colony.[31] In 1891 there were as many as 524 tailors and 30 seamstresses in the colony of Lagos.[32] By 1908 sewing machines had become popular among missionary schools and training centers in Lagos, where they were used in training seamstresses and for sewing uniforms.[33] Many of the newspaper reports of wedded couples recorded in, for example, the *Lagos Observer* and the *Lagos Standard* of the late nineteenth century constantly made reference to *aso ebi* dresses. The mention of *aso ebi* also featured prominently in local reports to colonial authorities and Christian missionaries, where members raised concerns over its inherent contentions. Some of these contentions no doubt will lend insight into the exact origins of *aso ebi* in the city of Lagos.

ASO EBI: OF DISPARATE HISTORIES AND FRIENDSHIP NETWORKS, 1840–1980

The examples cited in this section are by no means comprehensive; however, they do provide some historical pointers as to the ways *aso ebi* was used among Yoruba organizations. Since, to the best of my knowledge, there is no systematic documentation of *aso ebi* use among friendship associations in precolonial, colonial, or postcolonial periods, I have pieced together disparate records that may help articulate the importance of *aso ebi* over time. What I attempt here is much like a seamstress trying to stitch together odd pieces of cloth in order to form something akin to a complete and well-sewn robe.

Historically in Yoruba society, friendship was usually invoked in age groups and associations in the form of what is known as ẹgbẹ́, a word that literally translates as "association" in Yoruba. By the nineteenth century many ẹgbẹ́ included both women and men, with separate officers for each, but during the colonial period some became single-sex associations. In Ikaleland, for example, an eastern Yoruba community, women's ẹgbẹ́ emerged in

1900 under the auspices of the Christian churches, while in Aiyede, another Yoruba province in the present Ekiti State, female ẹgbẹ́ merely organized dances at festivals in the 1930s (McIntosh 2009, 210).

By the late colonial era, however, women's associations were found throughout Yorubaland. Marjorie Keniston McIntosh specifically states that an ẹgbẹ́ was formed in Ikaleland in 1900. It is possible that the provenance of other ẹgbẹ́ might date before McIntosh's 1900 following Deji Ayegboyin's record in his study of the Baptist Women's Missionary Union (BWMU) in Ogbomoso in the 1850s. Ayegboyin demonstrated how the Baptists deliberately used the traditional institution of ẹgbẹ́ to create similar female age-grade associations in their churches. In Ogbomoso, the center of Baptist mission activity from the 1850s onward, there were five women's groups––the ẹgbẹ́ Iya Sioni, ẹgbẹ́ Iya, ẹgbẹ́ Esteri, ẹgbẹ́ Mimo, and ẹgbẹ́ Irawo Kekere–– comprised of grandmothers, mothers, young married women, young girls, and infants, in that order. Ayegboyin notes that in the breakaway African churches, however, adaptations manifested themselves even more strongly. The United Native African Church, founded in 1891, represented the first thoughtful endeavor of Yoruba Christians to construct a theology that supports the embodiment of local cultural aspirations and the sentiments of Nigerian Christianity (1991, 50–58). Its main debate centered on polygamy as a necessary basis for a peaceful, conservative, and stable society. During the 1930s women were the catalysts behind the significant progression and institutionalization of Aladura churches that emerged in Yorubaland in the 1930s (Peel 1968). The sect approached evangelization through conciliatory and eclectic ideas that were demonstrated in the benefaction of worshippers (Denzer 1994, 1–39). It is possible that if the Baptists could import the traditional institutions of ẹgbẹ́ into the church as far back as the 1890s, perhaps ẹgbẹ́ could have dated back before the nineteenth century. However, while not in the context of ẹgbẹ́, 1890 proved significant in tracking the origins of *aso ebi* in Lagos during the late nineteenth century. Photographic records of the 1890s missionary photo archive in Lagos have revealed that some chiefs clothed their wives in *aso ebi* uniforms. Through these photographs, high fashion for housewives heralded similar fashion sensibilities among Christian women. While this uniformed trend was regarded as the chiefs' prerogative in the late nineteenth century, it provoked early twentieth-century women to challenge masculine tradition that would not allow them to claim new fashion statuses for themselves as their male counterparts did. Once they did that within the ambit of the church missionary societies, they assumed new social status as church leaders and fashion pacesetters, contrary to their life-style in pre-Christianity Lagos. One can argue here that *aso ebi* opposed male subordination of wifely sartorial modernity. It was clear that church affiliation was coterminous with social status, which found ultimate expression in dress. Competition in fashion among women was already in place within the church societies that used uniforms, and this propelled the popularity of *aso ebi*. Carolyn Marion Keyes (1993) had remarked that the *aso ebi* craze of early twentieth-century Lagos "swept Southwestern Nigeria and catapulted women to the forefront of Nigerian fashion" (325).[34]

There are more veritable extrapolations to further locate the origins of *aso ebi* in the late nineteenth and the early twentieth centuries Lagos. For example, Ayodeji Olukoju demonstrates the connection between culture and economic vicissitudes in his article on the post–World War I maritime economy and society of Lagos (2006a) He argues that "the *aso ebi* culture (as distinct from aṣọ *egbe*, pioneered by Egbe Kila) in Lagos and Nigeria started only in the context of the stupendous and unprecedented accumulation occasioned by the post-war boom of 1918–20" (2006b, 10).[35] In effect, he debunked received wisdom of a distant antiquity of this "wasteful practice" with verifiable evidence that it did not exist before 1920, although his assertion may have been countered by Keyes's photographic evidence mentioned above. Writing on the influence of maritime trade in Lagos in the aftermath of the First World War, *West Africa* magazine in 1920 notes how "new buildings are springing up all over Lagos" and how the infrastructural transformation promises an imminent renewal of the city.[36] This unexpected opulence, according to Olukoju, instituted a new culture of dress known as *aso ebi*, "a uniform dress that had been traditionally worn as an indication of co-operation on festive occasions" (2006a, 123).

Olukoju notes how *aso ebi* has become ubiquitous in Lagos. This novelty received an unequivocal condemnation from the *Nigerian Pioneer* because "it is not the custom as handed down to us by our forefathers."[37] The newspaper stressed the "waste and debt which are associated with it" as sufficient reason for opposing the practice. The recklessness of spending wealth that accrued from the trade boom became a source of concern to perceptive observers of the time. For example, in a thought-provoking editorial titled "Whither Are We Going?" the *Lagos Weekly Record* condemned the careless spending among Lagos inhabitants and attributed this to the "increased prosperity occasioned by the greater demand and higher price paid for produce of late years." The *Record* further, noted that "the feverish desire to make a show of our wealth has got a firm grip on our people."[38] This observation is critical to an eventual rationalization of future *aso ebi* practices as an unfortunate social malady that is discernible through its economic dissipation.

Olukoju's claims that *aso ebi* was part of a culture of conspicuous consumption occasioned by the post–World War I boom of the early twentieth century may find support in reports in some Lagos newspapers of the nineteenth century. For example, the *Lagos Standard* of February 24, 1915, expressed contentment over the abated extravagance in Lagos weddings occasioned by the Lenten season. The publication further noted that the pageantry mostly occurred in marriages and wasre exacerbated by "the custom of aso ẹbi, the expense of which increases every year."[39] The writer concludes with: "At this point, one is inclined to ask will this foolish extravaganza cease?" Similarly, in the "Letter to the Editor" section of the *Nigerian Chronicle* of April 10, 1914, a writer identifying himself as Aiye K'oTo writes, "I must invite your attention to the caption of my letter viz. 'Aso Ebi.' The practice is taking hold of the people and appalling as it is, it is most obnoxious as a custom. This has only recently come to existence and perhaps the Doctor might tackle and nip it in the bud ere it is late. It is sickening and I know your hands are full but [I] feel sure you will not keep silent over such a degrading and worthless custom."[40]

A most veritable indication of *aso ebi*'s emergence in early twentieth-century Lagos was the writer's mention of the fact that "aso ebi has only recently come to existence," suggesting that it was a recent phenomenon, or that even if similar practices existed in precolonial Yorubaland, the phraseology of "*aso ebi*" might not have been in use then. The phrase "*aso ebi*" must have been coined by Lagos residents of the early twentieth century who perhaps deployed it to its complex context. Further corroboration of *aso ebi*'s provenance in this period is evidenced from Tunde Akinwumi, who observes that "*aso ebi*" seems a corrupted version of "*aṣọ -ti-ẹbí-da-jo*," meaning the various clothes contributed by family members as grave goods for the dead in precolonial Yorubaland. Akinwumi's findings indicate that *aso ebi* is a Lagos concept that emerged only in the early twentieth century.[41] Citing one of his informants, Akinwumi (1990) notes that a certain type of Yoruba cloth known as *ashigbo* was deposited on the grave of the deceased and also worn as uniforms by members of Sashere and Olowo families. These clothes were apparently never called *aso ebi*, as conceived by the Lagos people. In an issue of the *Lagos Daily News* from 1930, *aso ebi* was interpreted as "uniform mourning outfits which many people strove to have and wear as a mark of respect for the dead." This source further indicates that *aso ebi* is associated with funerary events such as "Third Day," "Sitting Sunday," and "Church Going." (cited in Akinwumi 1990: 171, 173) Basing his judgment on this and other indices, Akinwumi connects *aso ebi*'s origins with funeral services in Lagos churches in the early twentieth century.

Tunde Akinwumi and Elisha Renne (2008) observe that the Anglican Church in Ondo State became one of the earliest churches in southwestern Nigeria to adopt commemorative uniforms for church members. The church's 1925 cloth was the first church commemorative cloth in Ondo, and it coincided with the introduction of the new fashion of wearing *aso ebi*.[42] Akinwunmi and Renne note that *aso ebi* fashion was encouraged by the importation of cheap, mass-produced dress materials produced in England at that time. Reverend Sodake proposed that the Anglican Church should have its own uniform (*aso ebi*) cloth, to be used as a church anniversary cloth that would be worn by all church members, a proposal that was unilaterally accepted by the church members. This innovative use of cloth to mark a church anniversary was the first of its kind in Ondo. The cloth Reverend Sodake decided upon was *luboleguneitan*, a cloth handwoven in Ondo, which was considered to be among Ondo's finest cloths. That the Reverend Sodake advocated its use, and the women's decision to use it in their own right, would suggest that *aso ebi* was not imposed, as it were. However, what can be established at this point is that colonialism and/or missionary activities influenced the emergence, and the popularity, of *aso ebi*. Since the nineteenth century, these social contexts in which *aso ebi* was deployed continued to expand in new forms of Yoruba ẹgbẹ́.

The evidence above strongly indicates that *aso ebi* originated between late nineteenth- and early twentieth-century Lagos. Contestations in Lagos newspapers regarding the crises caused by *aso ebi*'s importation into 1920s Christian churches, as suggested by Akinwumi and Renne, needs to be historicized as part of a new wave of ẹgbẹ́ that emerged in Lagos in the early twentieth century.

By the 1920s there was an increasing importation of clothes from Britain and as well as an increasing interest in the money economy, with Britain deemphasizing the barter trade. This process stimulated a great interest in the social uses of cloth, especially in *aso ebi* by Nigerians. In fact, the booming textile import in this period occasioned the subversive materiality that *aso ebi* was beginning to gather.[43] Improved transportation also served to stimulate economic growth and led to concentration of commercial activity and progressive differentiation between port sites according to their suitability for land/sea interchange. By the beginning of World War I, the first phase of railway construction in West Africa had been completed. Indirect European contact had been replaced by well-defined colonial territories that were increasingly called upon to be economically self-supporting.

After the war, the rail link with the Niger River had extended to the hinterlands, stimulating economic growth between Southern Nigeria and Lagos. From 1926 onward the port facilities were greatly extended, particularly to handle the ever increasing cloth import. It was through Lagos, the first port the British gained in Nigeria in 1861, that the majority of textile materials were imported, which draws attention to the importance of Lagos in the practice of *aso ebi*.[44] However, ẹgbẹ́ in the late twentieth century took a different turn, and so does its accompanying *aso ebi*.

Important functions that the ẹgbẹ́ provided in the nineteenth century included assistance to members during burial ceremonies (McIntosh 2009, 210). When a family member died, a woman would be assisted by the rest of the ẹgbẹ́. They helped her accomplish required tasks and galvanized the social ceremonial that accompanied the event. During the colonial period, the ẹgbẹ́ and other women's associations were centered on diverse common interests. While they occasionally bear different names such as "clubs," "societies," or "unions," their social functions never deviated from certain basic ẹgbẹ́ organizational structures such as the wearing of identical uniforms. This uniform was called *aso ebi*.

By the 1940s *aso ebi* was believed to have spread from the Christian associations in Lagos to the Muslims; it also traveled as far as Ilesa in western Yorubaland. It was banned by the colonial authorities in 1946, by which period it had reached Osogbo. By 1950 the colonial ban caused a decline in the practice. The mid-twentieth century saw a proliferation of women's associations that comprised boundless categories, such as market women, craft women, and other church associations. Categories became so fluid that one association could fulfill multiple roles. For example, McIntosh notes that in 1956, Mabel Aduke Williams of Lagos was delighted when her fellow Obalande market women turned up for the party she threw for her fiftieth birthday, complete with several live bands. The women were all dressed in "raki raki—a type of purple woolen wrapper and headties . . . and how impressive they looked while dancing!" (2009, 11). That all the women were dressed in a similar type and color of dress needs further exploration, as this could only imply the uniformed code known as *aso ebi*. The similar mode of dress suggests that Williams's friendship network already had an *aso ebi* dress code that identified members.

Members of an ẹgbẹ́ association come together during celebrations, be it a funeral, a naming, a chieftaincy, or a house warming, and it is a common feature for members of an ẹgbẹ́ to dress uniformly on such occasions. The wearing of similar clothing or *aso ebi* apparently serves to heighten the positive good feeling of individual association (Moloye 2004). In most of these friendship organizations, the use of *aso ebi* was already popular. For example, a show of solidarity was seen among the friendship network of Miss Mojisola Olowu of the Bata Shoe Company in Lagos during her twenty-third birthday anniversary. A photograph of the party—which took place on April 23, 1966, at 68 Tokunboh Street, in Lagos—shows that Olowu and her colleagues were dressed in the same design and color of *aso ebi* uniform.[45]

In another example, on Saturday, August 16, 1965, officers and other members of the Oshodi Tapa Descendants Union gave a party in honor of Mr. Abiola Oshodi on his appointment as director in the Federal Ministry of Housing and Surveys. A photograph published on page six of the *Daily Times* newspaper on August 21, 1965, shows that guests were dressed in the same uniform. Furthermore, "It was already becoming fashionable to dress in such unique *aso ebi* if one desired one's 'celebration' to appear in some of the few Dailies published in the 1950s. That was when people competed with such attires as aṣọ *ebi*" (Aderemi 2011).

By the 1950s Lagos had become a nexus of mobility, and social and cultural changes were brought about by its new status as the capital of Nigeria. Prominent aspects of these changes were Western education and increasing levels of Christianization. Further influences included colonial administration that supported the activities of the missionaries and helped them establish primary and secondary schools based on government guidelines. Mission schools education was coterminous with the religious aspirations of the missionaries and thus was designed to train men as personnel in different capacities within the church. By this period, sartorial politics were becoming intertwined with anticolonial nationalism. In the early 1950s opposition to colonial rule was beginning to manifest in the abandonment of Victorian attire and a passionate commitment to local Yoruba dress. What was happening throughout British West African colonies, including Nigeria, was a symbolic subordination of African-styled tailored clothes by colonial authorities, although African dress would eventually become incorporated into discourses of high fashion (R. Ross 2008, 128). The only way I have been able to gather evidence of the use of *aso ebi* among associations during this period is through some of the photographs in newspapers and the mention of "uniform dressing" by the writers, who interestingly did not invoke the phraseology of *aso ebi* within their narratives of uniformed dressing. For example, one of these numerous women's associations whose photographs reflected the use of *aso ebi* in the early twentieth century was the Abeokuta Women's Union (AWU), formed in 1946.[46] The AWU's president was Mrs. Funmilayo Ransome-Kuti, who by then had developed a nationalist consciousness that had made her dress only in Yoruba attire since the 1940s.[47] Ransome-Kuti's position did not affect her sartorial attitude; instead she sought equality with the people she represented through dress and language. Her dress was always made up of Yoruba style, consisting of *gele* (head-tie), *iro* (wrapper), and *buba* (blouse). During her dealings with colonial authorities on behalf of the AWU, she spoke in Yoruba and her words were translated into English. The AWU's policy on dress suggests that its leadership wanted to visually reflect internal unity and oneness, two qualities to which *aso ebi* wearers aspire. It was the organization's policy to use a cheap uniform of ordinary white cotton, stipulated for use by everybody as an *aso ebi* uniform.

The aim of this cheap material was to discourage elaborate and expensive clothes, and it would not require added expenditure. Judith Byfield (2004) remarks that photographs of women at AWU gatherings show that all wore the same article of Yoruba dress. She observes that the aim of moderate dressing through cheap uniforms helped to achieve certain levels of uniformity. Again, in addition to imbuing the women with a sense of sartorial equanimity, it blurred the class distinction through visual sameness. In this context *aso ebi* could be seen as something that is imposed when an organization decides to adopt a particular style, and the sewing of a uniform was an antidote to social class and divisions instituted through Western dress during colonialism.

Commenting on this gesture by the AWU, Phyllis Martin remarks that "during the colonial period, some women might wear European dress in public but developing a uniform dress code among the association's members was one way in which women blurred divisions and helped to empower themselves collectively" (2004, 228). This does not mean that the same perspective applied to other friendship associations or other organizations. Indeed, the manner of usage varied, as an organization or association might choose a particular color and allow members to buy different textile materials and sew the uniforms in their different styles. One slip in Byfield's article (which has continually recurred in most other studies on Yoruba social issues) is an obvious circumvention of the phrase "aṣọ ebì." This has no doubt contributed to a process of dehistoricization of a crucial aspect of *aso ebi* in Yoruba dress history. The fact that the photo to which Byfield refers had hundreds of members of the AWU clothed in the same color and fabric of head-tie and dress material and yet did not receive the mention of *aso ebi*, again suggests that authors do not recognize *aso ebi* as worthy of study.

The example of the AWU illustrates an important dimension to the use of *aso ebi*. In this context, *aso ebi* is underlined by a sense of unity and equality through a compulsory enforcement of the same quality and design of dress materials for everyone. In this way, moderation helped the members not only to nurture unity but also to remind them of their shared goals and aspirations. Contrary to this, the present usage of *aso ebi* allows members, in most instances, to invent their own designs. In doing so, differentiation, inequality, and competition are now increasingly invoked.

What can be observed from the above records is that *aso ebi* was more manifest among women's organizations or ẹgbẹ́. Given the examples to this point, it may seem as if *aso ebi* was an exclusive practice for women and not men. That is not the case. As O. O. Familusi (2010) observes, buying *aso ebi* is not essentially gender driven, despite the fact that women were more predisposed to appear in uniform than men.

In 1960, with the fervent passion for cultural renaissance that came with anticolonial nationalism, *aso ebi* blossomed, reaching a zenith during the oil boom era in the 1970s. In the late 1970s, an ẹgbẹ́ usually started as a small informal group of friends from the same neighborhood, of the same age, sex, and religion. A person's closest friends often constituted members of the same ẹgbẹ́. Some of these developed into more formal organizations, with a name, a larger membership, and elected officials. These ẹgbẹ́ held regular meetings, arranged dances, and chose a particular type of cloth as their uniform during religious festivals and rites of passage. By the late 1970s, increasing urbanization occasioned by the oil boom gave rise to a new type of ẹgbẹ́ that was known as *occupational* ẹgbẹ́. By this time in Ogbomoso, for instance, there were over thirty of these organizations, covering both market trade and the crafts and ranging from tailors' and photographers' associations to cloth sellers and the makers of local soap. It is within this new emergence of ẹgbẹ́ that McIntosh again identifies forms of what she calls "contemporary *egbe*" (association) in the cities. While McIntosh mentions "uniformed dressing" in her 2009 book, she does not emphasize its precise role. She writes, "When an *egbe* went out as a group, its members generally wore distinctive attire—the same fabric or colour of clothing, the same style of dress, or at least a similar head tie—to demonstrate the size and standing of their association. (See the cover illustration for a recent example)" (211). It is remarkable that McIntosh directs readers to the cover of her book (see fig. 3), which has a photograph of women dressed in *aso ebi*, but she does not use the common Yoruba name for the practices. This omission notwithstanding, the contemporary signification of her study shows how the ẹgbẹ́ provided an "outlet for the Yoruba love of sociability, eagerness to gain group identities, and pleasures in wearing fine clothing on special occasions" (210).

Under the new conditions of *aso ebi* practices today, such notions as a "Yoruba love of sociability" might not be appropriate if imported into the modern city phenomenon of *aso ebi*. I have explained elsewhere how the practice of *aso ebi* is identified more closely with Nigerian culture as a whole than with Yoruba culture per se in contemporary Nigeria. Again, I shall seek to clarify my use of terms such as "Yoruba" in this study. The present practice of *aso ebi* in urban Lagos has transcended ethnic boundaries. While I deploy the concept of "Yoruba" in tracking the *aso ebi* genealogy in some ways, I do distance it from older anthropological frameworks of ethnicity in approaching a much more widespread city practice.

It is important to observe that, as in the early twentieth century, there are other forms of associations where *aso ebi* was employed. These groups were formed by extended family members and town or ethnic groups who have moved to the city. The latter are commonly known as "hometown associations" (Trager 2001, 3).[48]

CONCLUSION

The image of Lagos that emerges from this chapter might differ from the image put forth in certain literature of nineteenth- and twentieth-century explorers, missionaries, colonial administrators, and anthropologists. Whereas the latter might offer (albeit with a few exceptions) the popular mental images of colonial domination and native submission, the chapter presents far more complex relationships that are evident from the sartorial stylistics of Lagos life.

In this chapter, cloth is manifested as a form of politics in colonial Lagos. It has also served as a critical commodity of an emerging modernity. For example, by the nineteenth century, the *oba*'s wardrobe had become supplemented with foreign elements such as satins, velvets, damasks, and silks. These fabrics came through trade deals between the *oba* and European merchants. Jane Guyer and Samuel Eno Belinga's remark that "in the eighteenth

Figure 3. Marjorie Keniston McIntosh's book cover with women dressed in *aso ebi* (uniform), 2009. © Indiana University Press.

and nineteenth centuries a great deal of imports in slaves and 'legitimate trades' came in uniform manufactured goods in large lots [including clothing materials]" (1995, 119) is suggestive of why the subsequent *oba's* wardrobe became neither "African" nor "Western."[49] While the Christians emulated the Europeans in dressing, the non-Christian locals expressed their repudiation of Christian influence by retaining their local dress. As illustrated, there is varied sartorial agency, with some locals retaining their indigenous robes, and the slaves returning from Brazil and Sierra Leoneans inventing a new wardrobe through imitation and borrowing.

An identification of *aso ebi* use among Lagosians during different periods in the twentieth century provides a fresh vantage point for the subsequent investigation of *aso ebi* in Lagos. Whereas written texts are few on the subject of *aso ebi* I have attempted to maximize these and other potential sources for uncovering its past. Few possibilities come to mind. For example, from the 1920s through the 1950s and 1960s, *aso ebi* had already become so influential that it formed a subject of contention on the pages of such newspapers as the *Nigerian Pioneer*, the *Daily Mirror*, and the *Daily Times*, among others.

By the mid-twentieth century, the AWU deployed *aso ebi* cloth as an instrument of nationalist struggle. Again, by the early twentieth century, different Yoruba ẹgbẹ́ had adopted *aso ebi* as their dress code. In my attempt to (re)construct *aso ebi's* history, one suggestion points to the impact of Christian missionaries (as suggested by Keyes, Akinwumi, and Renne) and colonial administrators through uniforms. A most plausible validation of *aso ebi's* history is the existence of newspaper commentaries during the early twentieth century in Lagos that mentioned, and suggested, how *aso ebi* was a new practice then. Another suggestion points to the 1920s post--World War I accumulation that opened importation and consumption opportunities for textiles as suggested by Ayodeji Olukoju.[50] In addition to faster sewing methods with sewing machines, these textiles likely facilitated the production and use of *aso ebi* among increasing friendship networks in the rapidly urbanizing Lagos. However, while this chapter merely opens up these possibilities for possible (re)consideration in approaching the history of *aso ebi* in Lagos, the next chapter undertakes a detailed and specific genealogy of how the textile economy has intensified the spread of *aso ebi* in Lagos.

CHAPTER 2

Cheaper Clothes in a Fluctuating Economy, 1960–2008

On December 6, 2010, Chidi Ogbu, a butcher in the popular Lagos butchery located at Egbeda, a sprawling suburb in Lagos, came to the Balogun textile market to buy *aso ebi* fabric for his upcoming wedding. Ogbu, an Igbo from eastern Nigeria who had resided in the predominantly Yoruba Lagos for most of his life and now was regarded by his Yoruba friends as one of them, had been planning for his wedding to be held on December 31, 2010, at the CKC Catholic Church Egbeda. My relationship with Ogbu started around early December 2010, after we had a long conversation during one of my visits to his butchery. Our mutual seller/customer dialogue resulted in my receiving an invitation card to his wedding. I engaged him in some discussions regarding the choice of *aso ebi* for the event. He told me that he would do *aso ebi* during his wedding and that his wife-to-be had given him the color of the textile to be bought. When I insisted on accompanying the couple to the market on the day they would purchase the *aso ebi* material, he accepted. Ogbu, his fiancée, and I arrived at one of the shops at the Balogun textile market, where a great variety of foreign and locally made materials abound. The owner brought out different types of materials with different prices. Ogbu, being a low-income worker, initially demanded to see the cheapest ones. The seller brought out one light material she called *ankara*, referring to it as "China *ankara*." She also brought out others specified differently as "Akosombo Ghana *ankara*" and "Nigerian *ankara*." The seller revealed that China *ankara* sells for five hundred naira, Akosombo Ghana *ankara* sells for one thousand naira, and Nigerian *ankara* sells for two thousand naira. When I asked the woman to explain the difference between China, Akosombo, and Nigerian *ankara*, she told me that the Nigerian type is stronger in terms of the quality and therefore more expensive. But Ogbu's fiancée, inevitably for economic reasons, demanded that they go for the China *ankara*. Part of the reason why she chose the China *ankara* is that the price would allow them to purchase enough for the thirty friends of the family who would wear the *aso ebi* uniform. The more expensive Nigerian *ankara* would not have afforded Ogbu the opportunity to purchase enough for the thirty persons who would eventually buy from them.

On another textile market outing, I came with another friend, this time Ola Oguntade, a banker and my close friend since the 1990s. Oguntade too was preparing for his own wedding on January 8, 2011. But he had decided to come with his proposed wife so that she could select the material and color that suited her and her friends.

What transpired between Oguntade's fiancée, Chidi Ogbu, and the cloth seller exposed disturbing contradictions about original and fake materials for the rich and the not-so-rich. Oguntade's fiancée said, "I don't want all those useless Chinese textiles that don't last." The seller confessed that different categories of buyers demand different qualities and that Oguntade's fiancée belongs to those who desire good and expensive quality. She chose the Nigerian *ankara* and another foreign lace for the head scarves. But for the not-so-rich like Ogbu, the quest to engage in *aso ebi* can invoke an expedient desire to go for "cheap" textiles. Considering the latter, in the cultural codes of commodified sartorial practice like *aso ebi*, authenticity and a sense of belonging can be attained only by copy and inauthenticity, and the very idea of originality comes from copying.

One could argue that since China became a major economic power, especially in the production and export of cheap textile materials into Africa, *aso ebi* practice invokes the crisis of fake/original among different groups within the city. By bringing into sharp contrast these discourses, the quest for an *aso ebi* outfit clearly illustrates how fashion has fueled the rise of capitalism.[1] By 2015, when I went back to the Balogun textile market, there seemed to be an outright elision of Nigerian *ankara* from the entire market. Uche Idike, an apprentice at the Dano Textile Shop in the market said, "Oga, there is no Nigerian *ankara* here again o! everything you see in this market is China *ankara*. They will not tell you the truth. Even all the labels you see written 'Made in Nigeria' and 'Made in Ghana' are lies; all of them are made in China and printed 'Made in Nigeria.'" (Idike 2015). It is possible to argue that while the Chinese presence in the Nigerian textile industry offers some consumers the democracy of aesthetic self-expression, for others it is a form of bondage to the consumerism that fuels expansion of an economic system beyond people's control. Delving into the above banal, everyday transactions in the Balogun textile market fundamentally exposes the logic of an economic system that impacts mundane living. The instabilities witnessed in the textile industry cannot be dissociated from the unstable political system in Nigeria. To understand how *aso ebi* has changed over time, one needs to contextualize these political changes from the urbanization that took place in Lagos after the first quarter of the twentieth century, precisely after World War II. This will assist in understanding how population influx affected the textile economy and the eventual transnational dealings in a type of textile fabric known as *ankara*.

The political changes in Nigeria after the Second World War were accompanied by sociocultural as well as economic changes. The urbanization that came with colonial rule exploded in the 1950s to unprecedented levels. For instance, Lagos, which had an estimated population of 126,000 in 1931, expanded to over 274,000 by 1951, and by 1963 to over 675,000 people. As in previous decades, people flocked to cities for employment and other economic activities, but cities offered more than just hope for jobs. Cities became cosmopolitan centers, where people and cultures from all over Nigeria, West Africa, and other parts of the world converged, learned from one another, and drew on one another's experiences. New migrants came to Lagos and participated in the many aspects of the city's life (Falola and Heaton 2008, 155). Urban experience was beginning to be encountered in more self-aware terms. People became conscious not only about their family, social, and friendship networks but also about the corresponding sartorial outlook that accompanied these networks. There is no doubt that *aso ebi* was at the core of this sartorial outlook.

However, while Nigeria gained her independence in 1960, the country was still far from being economically independent. The government's development planning initiative of the postwar era did achieve sustainable development for Nigeria. Very little industrial development had been undertaken, and the industries that did exist were still largely owned by European companies.[2] As seen in chapter 1, colonial relations were not rewarding for the Nigerian economy, and neither did they empower the indigenous population. Whereas colonial development plans were overwhelmingly interested in increasing agricultural output to boost the export economy, the independent government of the 1960s was far more concerned with the development of manufacturing industries. The question here is, How did *aso ebi* thrive amid the vagaries of a postcolonial textile economy? This chapter investigates the changes that attended *aso ebi* practice through a careful examination of local and foreign textile transactions. This is possible because textiles have proven a veritable archive for investigating social history. An account of the experiences of some textile merchants in the Oshodi and Balogun textile markets in Lagos serves to illuminate some blurred interstices. In exploring the impact of this textile economy, I start by tracking a brief history of locally made textile materials—such as aṣọ òkè and *adire*—for *aso ebi* and then examining the impact of imported foreign materials such as *ankara, lace,* and *george,* among others, on *aso ebi*.[3] In doing this, the chapter explores the relationship between culture and commerce and argues that the reason for the spread of *aso ebi* may not be explained only in terms of the expression of agency. One may need to recognize the ubiquity of cheaper textile materials resulting from late global capitalism.

The history of Nigerian textile traditions cannot be discussed outside the larger histories of textile merchandising in West Africa. This history provides a departure from narratives of dark Africa that span the mid-ninth century BC. Textiles discovered at Igboukwu have been dated to 2500 BC. Historical accounts of human activities in such a remote Africa were also about, as John Picton (1995, 12) notes, "people leading successful lives making and using art, about production and patronage, about constantly revised design agendas thereby maintaining a contemporary relevance. It is about an ability to thrive in competition with all manner of rivals in Africa that is not all about civil war, corrupt politicians, starving people and infectious diseases." Although the political history of nineteenth-century Africa seems to present Africa as a defeated voice, such one-sided narratives of power have not enabled an appropriate recognition of Africa's agency in world sociocultural history. It is assumed that local textile traditions such as aṣọ òkè and *adire* may assist us to explore Nigeria's major role in these sociocultural histories.

AṢỌ ÒKÈ

Aṣọ òkè is a short form of aṣọ *ilu oke,* meaning "clothes from up-country" in the Yoruba language. It is a special locally made fabric/textile with different designs. Aṣọ òkè is one of the earliest forms of handwoven textiles—among the Yorubas of southwestern Nigeria—used, among many other things, for *aso ebi*.[4] Picton defines weaving as a simple process of interlacing a set of thread (warp and weft) at right angles to form a web or fabric (1988, 99–

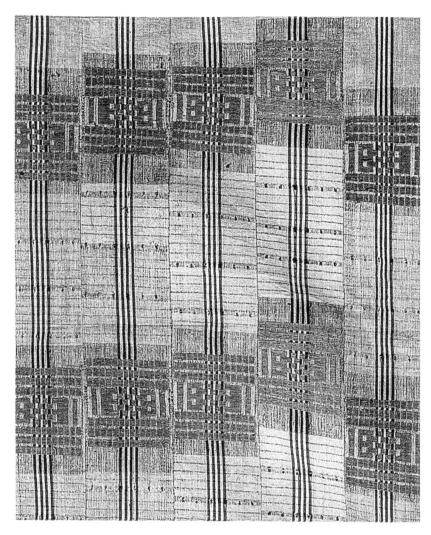

Figure 4. Narrow-strip textile (aṣọ òkè) cotton with supplementary weft float design. Yoruba, Nigeria, twentieth century. Collection of Peter Adler.

102). The aṣọ òkè fabric can be either warp-striped or designed in weft-faced patterns (see fig. 4). Many factors go into the design and weaving of aṣọ òkè, which, although not within the purview of this book, depends upon three variables: the nature and color of fibers employed; the kinds of relationships between the warp and the weft, which may be affected by the loom; and the possible methods of embellishing a fabric after manufacture.

There are three major aṣọ òkè types--*etu*, *alaari*, and *sanyan*--with many variations that are achievable with the use of an extra weft brocading technique. These variations are identifiable by their patterns and color, which in effect inform their uses at designated traditional ceremonies. Aṣọ òkè is generally believed—especially among Yoruba women—to be a clothing material reserved for special occasions where dignified dressing is required.[5] Yoruba women use aṣọ òkè as girdles (oja) to strap babies; wrappers (iro); head-ties (gele); blouses (buba), and shawls (ipele), or iborun, which are usually hung on the shoulder of the user.

Yoruba men used aṣọ òkè in ancient times as work dress on their farms as well as for social, religious, and traditional ceremonies. They wore a complete dress consisting of sokoto (trousers), buba (top or blouse), agbada (large embroidered flowing gown) and fila (cap). In the 1960s and up until the 1990s, aṣọ òkè was valued both as a wedding gift and as a special gift for dignified people. Aṣọ òkè was also used for aso ebi. For this use as aso ebi, the variations of material and stylistic repertoires have transformed since the 1960s.

The attainment of independence in Nigeria in 1960 was marked by a rising urban middle class, most of whom were concentrated in Lagos. As the population of Lagos increased with the state's flourishing economy, aṣọ òkè came to define the emerging sartorial modernity of a new Lagos middle class. Aṣọ òkè was widely interpreted as a symbol of wealth, ethnic pride, and conspicuous accomplishment, occasioning wide patronage and a boom in the aṣọ òkè economy (Perani and Wolff 1999). Wealthy Lagosians were less concerned with the exorbitant prices of aṣọ òkè than with its fashionable, social, and religious resonances. In fact, by this period aṣọ òkè's survival rested on its social significance as an expensive product.

From the late nineteenth century until the mid-twentieth century, aṣọ òkè weaving and distribution were controlled by family-based networks. For example, Aderonke Ojo, whose family was one of the earliest weavers of aṣọ òkè in Surulere, said that in the 1960s the workforce of her aṣọ òkè business consisted of her family members, which lowered the cost of production given the huge commissions they received (Ojo 2011). She also said that they relied on many outlets to get commission, including individuals who used aso ebi in traditional weddings. From Ojo's explanations, I observed that the production and marketing of aṣọ òkè in Lagos was restricted within small-scale producers. At present most aṣọ òkè producers in Lagos use a mechanized loom, and the commercial prospects have significantly declined. Most weavers I interviewed produce for some individuals who engage in aso ebi and other social events.

Shola Akande is a young university graduate who started producing aṣọ *òkè* after she completed her education in 2010. She set up a small loom and a workshop with two male weavers around the Egbeda area of Lagos. She told me that her clients are mainly women who prepare for *aso ebi* during traditional marriage ceremonies. They often demand it in large quantities. She first arrives at a design with them, goes to buy the raw materials, and then comes back to work with her weavers. She said that many of her clients who use aṣọ *òkè* for *aso ebi* are still considered rich. Akande said that aṣọ *òkè* is, in fact, seen as a "prestigious cloth" by those who still use it (Akande 2011). I discovered that prestige is the ultimate visual signature of family and ethnic pride in the Yoruba fashion world. *Aso ebi* practice is thus celebrated within this ethnic pride. Therefore, any *aso ebi* group dressed in locally woven aṣọ *òkè* immediately exudes affluence, demonstrated in both the overflowing comportment of the aṣọ *òkè* dressing itself and the exuberant prosperity that characterizes Yoruba ceremonies. A recent transformation has affected the meanings of aṣọ *òkè* as an embodiment of Yoruba ethnic cloth, thus locating it within modern sartorial style as street fashion that is commonly used for *aso ebi*.

REINVENTION OF AṢỌ *ÒKÈ* FOR *ASO EBI*

In very recent times, aṣọ *òkè* has undergone significant transformation as a hip style and is generally economically restrained as only head scarves and shawls for women and as *fila* (caps) for men. Akande told me that, depending on the choice of the client, whole outfits are sewn in some *aso ebi* commissions, while some demand only a cap or head scarves, sometimes numbering about one hundred or more for a particular event. Although it has been reinvented through modern weaving technology, in present-day Nigeria, aṣọ *òkè*'s existence has remained somewhat marginal.[6]

In fact, by the early 2000s, aṣọ *òkè* became less popular for use as *aso ebi* because it was replaced by *ankara* and lace materials imported from China. Individuals began to recreate aṣọ *òkè* styles into Western-styled designs: women's blouses and skirts were restyled, men's styles were transformed into short-sleeved coats and straight sewn pants and a host of other different styles. The introduction of English-styled sewing made aṣọ *òkè* more attractive to the younger generation. It was no longer seen as a static, unchanging practice but as something that transforms with the changing times. Recently, women who use aṣọ òkè for *aso ebi* have mixed reactions: while some define it as "traditional," old-fashioned, and provincial, others see it as a reinvented high fashion of urban modernity. For the latter group, to be fashionable in an *aso ebi* group, one can wear tailored aṣọ òkè sewn in European style—distinctive creations from fashion designers using a combination of aṣọ òkè dress materials and recently imported textiles. I traced aspects of these changes in aṣọ òkè used for *aso ebi* textile materials and dress designs over the years through the visual archive of J. D'Okhai Ojeikere's photographs in Lagos, to which he allowed me access in 2009. I compared the 1960s *aso ebi* photographs with those of the present day, and the variations in uniformity and choice of fabric were revealing. While the majority of the *aso ebi* groups in the 1960s favored a combination of lace and aṣọ òkè, by 2008 *aso ebi* practitioners preferred *ankara* fabric and lace. The explanation for this could lie in the changes in the textile economy and late capitalist commodification. For example, figure 5 shows *aso ebi* in the early 1960s with its fabric comprising aṣọ òkè (for skirts and head scarves) and lace (for blouses). Figure 6 also shows *aso ebi* style of the 1960s with the celebrant flanked by her three family members. Friends and family members do not wear the same color nor, sometimes, style of dress in *aso ebi*. This must explain why the woman in the first row in figure 6 appeared in a different color of lace material.

In figures 5 and 6, all of the *aso ebi* outfits, except for the *pele* (shawl), include all the parts of a supposedly "complete" *aso ebi* attire--namely, *gele* (head-tie) *buba* (blouse), and *iro* (wrap-around skirt), without which some individuals usually assume that *aso ebi* is incomplete (Omolara 2010). A remarkable difference in all the figures here is the style of sewing: while the women in figures 5 and 6 wear more elaborate long sleeves made from lace with their skirts tied in the form of wrappers, the women in figure 7 wear blouses made from *ankara* with attenuated hands and free-flowing skirts also made from *ankara*. Figures 5 and 6 reveal *aso ebi*'s significance as a form of fashion even as it was in the 1960s. It is arguable that although *aso ebi* is seen as a form of "cultural" practice, its 1960s styles might also suggest that fashion was loosening the "grip of *culture* which *aso ebi* has on the body."[7] *Culture* and cosmopolitanism were becoming deeply intertwined. In these photos, the styles of sewing deserve proper analysis. Figures 5 and 6 indicate that in the 1960s there was a somewhat rigid adherence to *aso ebi*'s uniformity of style. This might suggest that perhaps sartorial individualism was not rigidly applied as it is in the present context. Individual dress designs in figures 5

Figure 5. Lagos ladies in *aso ebi* in 1960. © J. D'Okhai Ojeikere.

Figure 6. *Aso ebi* in the 1960s. © J. D'Okhai Ojeikere *aso ebi* photos, Lagos 1960. (Reproduced with permission of the photographer.)

Figure 7. Four women in *aso ebi*. Lagos, January 1, 2010. Photo: Okechukwu Nwafor.

and 6 do not differ markedly as they do in figure 7. In figures 5 and 6 the women maintain a somewhat uniform body posture, as can be seen from their hands, which stretch downward with their handbags, unlike in figure 7, where they stand in a less self-conscious pose. In figure 7 all the elements vary significantly, such as the colors of the handbags, the head scarves, and styles of sewing. While this may not represent entirely the contemporary styles of *aso ebi*, it points to one thing: the evolving contestations of the material and moral uniformity that historically defined *aso ebi* practice. Influenced by the technomedia world, *aso ebi* uniformity is radically being reimagined in line with the attendant instabilities that came with late global capitalism. Friends arrange for *aso ebi* even through social media and suggest colors of the dress to be bought. In the ensuing entanglements of these textile and media transformations, aṣọ òkè use for *aso ebi* has gradually been replaced by the imported *ankara* and lace textiles.

ADIRE

Adire was among the popular fabrics used for *aso ebi* during the 1980s. While *adire's* origin has not been adequately established, it was thought that some Egba women who relocated to Abeokuta from Ibadan in the late nineteenth century brought the technique with them. *Adire* employs indigo (*oro*) in a process of resist dyeing and is produced through an elaborate procedure that involves sewing the fabric, and then wrapping and tying it before dyeing. The process parallels similar techniques employed in the production of Japanese *shibori*, and Malian and Ghanaian indigo, among others. A type of *adire* called *adire alabere* is produced by sewing the fabric with raffia or other type of stitching before dyeing and untying it after the process to reveal the design. In another type, known as *adire eleko* (fig. 8), the fabric is painted with cassava starch before dyeing, and in *adire oniko* the fabric is tied with raffia before dyeing. The introduction of a broader color palette of imported synthetic dyes in the second half of the twentieth century enabled the label "*adire*" to be expanded to embrace a variety of other hand-dyed textiles using wax-resist batik methods to produce patterned cloth in a glittering arrangement of dye tints and hues (Picton 1995).

Adire's prototype was tie-dyed *kijipa*, a handwoven cloth dyed with indigo used for wrappers and covering cloths. Yoruba women deployed the *adire* technique to many uses, including redyeing faded clothes and dyeing yarns. By the first quarter of the twentieth century, *adire* became popular across West Africa, commanding huge patronage from Ghana, Senegal, and the Congo (Byfield 2004; Eades 1993). During this period merchants traveled as far as Senegal to purchase thousands of *adire* wrappers from Abeokuta women producers (Byfield 2002, 114).

With an increasing regional economic recession in the 1930s, the *adire* craft suffered a significant decline that almost caused its disappearance by the 1940s (Byfield 2004; Keyes 1993). This decline was further aggravated when Europe banned export goods to West Africa during World War II. In the 1950s *adire* production was adversely affected by the influx of European, Asian, and African textiles into the Nigerian market. Its economic prospect was further undermined due to its increasing distaste by urban dwellers who dismissed it as "a poor people's cloth" (Byfield 2004, 212–18) despite its popularity in the rural areas.

By the mid-twentieth century, the importation of cheap, colorful printed

Figure 8. Uchechukwu Ezemo. *Adire eleko, olokun* design on 100 percent cotton fabric using natural indigo color from plant leaves.

textiles by the British posed a challenge to the *adire* industry. The dyers gradually abandoned the expensive handwoven cloth and made use of imported white cotton. Being soft and smooth, the imported white cotton offered a convenient surface for decoration and diverse creative manipulations that were better than the rough *kijipa* cloth, leading the women dyers to embrace it. This ample creative promise of the cloth also enabled the women to make specific patterns using the tie-dye method. This is in addition to the use of raffia yarn to achieve an elaborately patterned *adire alabere* through the stitch-resist method. The smooth-surfaced cotton also aided the development of *adire eleko* through hand-painted starch-resist. Although Abeokuta historically remains the center of *adire* production and trade, Ibadan had a number of women artists who had championed the hand-painted *adire eleko*. A popular wrapper design from Ibadan was known as Ibadandun (meaning "the city of Ibadan is sweet"). The designs on the wrappers most often adopted a repeated scattered pattern that lacked a primary focus.

The late 1960s marked a turning point in *adire* production, especially with readily available chemical dyes from Europe, thus sparking an innovation in *adire* color and techniques (Keyes 1993, 38). These imported dyes dried faster than indigo, enabling many Nigerian fashion designers to appropriate them in the production of high-quality cloths and other decorative and utilitarian materials (Eicher 1976, 76–77). In the production of multicolored *adire*, a simple technology was deployed to mass-produce a cheaper type of *adire* known as *kampala*.

Kampala became popular during the Kampala Peace Conference to settle the Biafra War in Nigeria. It was manufactured by locals who had no prior knowledge of dyeing, such as farmers, clerks, petty traders, and the jobless (Picton 1995, 17). *Kampala* bears close similarity to the batik fabric thought to have originated in Indonesia, in which fabric is dyed, painted, or stamped with a tough paste, usually derived from cassava, before dyeing. Sometimes hot wax or paraffin was used to replace the cassava paste as a resist agent, while designs were achieved by simple techniques of tie-dye, folding, rumpling, and haphazard sprinkling or splashing of the hot wax onto a cloth before dyeing. With an increasing demand and an emergence of professional *adire* dyers, a block-printing technique to apply the hot wax was developed and largely displaced stenciling (Picton 1995, 17). This distinct production process resulted in the fabric's multiple colors and high capacity for dye retention. It is important to note that all traditional *adire* are dyed in indigo (monochromatic colors), while fabrics dyed in multiple colors are more commonly known as *kampala*.

Adire eleko and *kampala* possess a uniqueness in their stenciling technique that is lacking in other fabrics of the Nigerian region. The stencils are carved on wood or recycled tin cans, while the cloths are painted with peacock feathers. Sometimes stencils are created to commemorate an important event, such as the silver jubilee of King George V and Queen Mary in 1935 (Borgatti 1983, 16)), while instances abound where designs reflect local Yoruba repertoires. In recent times contemporary styles of *adire* and *kampala* designs have entered the international market because of their superior quality and unique design. For example, *adire* and *kampala* fashions have been worn by such prominent figures as Michelle Obama, dressed by Maki Oh, and Lupita N'yongo, dressed by Busayo. Nike Davies Okundaye, a Nigerian textile artist has championed the production of contemporary styles of *adire* for many decades, recording an unprecedented recognition internationally for her numerous works. She runs an *adire* workshop in her center, the Nike Center for Art and Culture, with locations in Abuja, Ogidi, and Oshogbo, which gathers women and other learners from across Nigeria and beyond. By the late 1970s, foreign textile materials, mainly imported illegally into Nigeria, would eventually pose a threat to *kampala*, *adire*, and aṣọ òkè. A brief examination of the impact of foreign textiles will enable a deeper understanding of the nature of proliferation that attended *aso ebi* in urban Lagos.

A BRIEF HISTORY OF FOREIGN TEXTILE MATERIALS IN NIGERIA

Foreign textile materials have a long history of Western trade that was also tied to colonialism and imperial hegemony. European textiles have been traded in West Africa since at least the fifteenth century (Steiner 1985; Sylvanus 2007). One of the earliest accounts of this trade was in 1469, when Benedetto Dei, a representative of the Portinari firm in Florence, arrived at Timbuktu, where he aspired to barter his Lombardian cloth for the gold of the Sudan. From this period henceforth, and through the next five centuries, textiles became an important trade commodity in the "trade by barter" for gold, kola nuts, and even slaves (Steiner 1985). By the seventeenth century, a thriving textile merchandising business between Europe and Africa was enabled through the Dutch West India Company, the Royal African Company, and the Compagnie du Senegal (Hopkins 1973). Informal trade channels were also opened through the coast of Guinea, where the Dutch fleets of the East India Company anchored at the ports. Among this trade was the exchange of Indian and Javanese batik cloths, the precursor of the wax print. This batik cloth was the main cloth worn by the thousands of slaves who returned to Africa from Java after they were freed from the Dutch East Indian Army in the nineteenth century.[8]

The nineteenth century was characterized by a trade scramble in Africa between the British manufacturers of the dull-colored, coarse-grained fabric and the Indian companies that produced the brightly colored, lightweight materials (Evenson 2007). African consumers preferred the Indian textiles. This came to the attention of Manchester textile producers, who became especially interested in meeting the aesthetic and practical demands of their West African clientele.[9] From the 1780s, a sense of finesse and taste among African consumers—made up mainly of the British middle class—was concomitant with the Industrial Revolution, and this impacted the creative output of textile manufacturers (Edwards 1967, 47). Almost a century later, this taste and refinement was reflected in the textile business between Europe and Africa.

In 1885 Governor Alfred Moloney, who was governor of Lagos from 1886 to 1890, was specifically interested in addressing some trade issues in the cotton market among the Yoruba and West Africans.[10] He remarked that durability, quality, among other attributes, had to be of paramount importance to the British manufacturers in order to transcend the competition posed by the native weaving industry. The native weaving industry that Moloney refers to includes the aṣọ òkè industry (Johnson 1974b, 181–82). By the 1870s, European manufacturers were "well aware of regional preferences to which they paid careful attention" (Spencer 1982, 81–82). The European-African textile market had already become established, and, contrary to previous notions, it was apparent that Africans had a taste for high-quality fabric, just as the Europeans did. The issue of quality print was one of the most important determinants of the textiles produced for the African market in the nineteenth century (Sylvanus 2016; Steiner 1985, 53–55).

Governor Moloney saw to the implementation of a policy that enabled European cloths to surpass the limits of the competition. It was evident that the quest for quality materials could not be compromised in the Euro-African textile trade, and this attracted wide interest in European textiles. The African climate, which is characterized by high temperatures, dust from the dry landscapes, and dirty sludge after rains, also informed the preference for European cotton textiles due to the case of laundering and its colorfastness. The laundering of indigenous cloths usually washed off the dyes, while European cloths retained the dyes longer (Cordwell 1979). By 1895 there was a general perception that the European textile trade had disarmed African textile weavers and reduced the indigenous cotton production to the scant cultivation of the cotton species of *Gossypium punctatum*. Writing to the governor general of French West Africa in a letter dated November 2, 1895, L. Mouttet, who was the director of the Interior, summarized this perspective quite well:

> The introduction of European-manufactured cloth, as similar to the most beautiful textiles of the country [Senegal] as possible, has led to a decline in native cloth production; a decline which has rapidly prompted the extension of our [Euro-African] trade. . . . At present, weavers produce exceedingly few fabrics made of indigenous cotton. Cotton fields are neither vast nor regular; they occupy insignificant corners of village perimeters. (Steiner 1985, 94)

As the prices of imported cloth skyrocketed with the formation of ad valorem taxation in the early 1900s, Mouttet's portrayal of a perfect space for the advancement of European imperial commerce began to change. M. Levecque wrote in his *Rapport politique du Senegal:*

Since the increased price of textiles, which render our fabrics almost inaccessible to the natives of the interior, the latter have taken to cultivating cotton once again; a task which they neglected while they were able to purchase inexpensive textiles in our shops. Around the villages today, we notice numerous fields of cotton, and the weaver's loom has reappeared in many marketplaces. Indigenous cloth, which [for a time] was considered too expensive, has come into favor once again, and business is now idle in the shops of our merchants who are well stocked with imported European goods. (Steiner 1985, 94)

Beneath the competition that existed between European textile manufacturers and African weavers is a design tension caught between homogenous African and hybridized Eurocentric aesthetics. While the above transactions took place during the colonial period, when Nigeria was subsumed under the West African colonial administration, recent textile trade relations between independent Nigeria and the rest of world have changed significantly and thus occasioned a new style in *aso ebi* fashioning.

In recent times, lower-priced *ankara* from China, while affordable, tended to be lower in quality. Daniel, a Nigerian businessman who has lived in China for more than fifteen years, said, "If you make quality cloths and send to Africa not everybody will buy it, but if you have cheap ones, people will rush to buy it."[11] Quality aside, Chinese-produced *ankara* opened the possibility for greater numbers of people to partake in the *aso ebi* practice. It is necessary to see how, in making their choices of *aso ebi*, these greater numbers of people were influenced by the variety of colorful textiles that were enabled through the larger textile economy between Nigeria and the rest of the world.

TEXTILE ECONOMY, STRUCTURAL ADJUSTMENT PROGRAMME, AND *ASO EBI* SINCE 1960

By the time of independence in 1960, Nigeria had a moderately thriving commercial class, which had developed since the late nineteenth century, despite discriminatory colonial policies. After independence, nationalist ethos swept across all segments of society and produced a counterculture that saw to the enthronement of a new sartorial modernity through native attire. In most wedding events or birthday parties, *aso ebi* made from aṣọ òkè and *adire* defined the cultural moment of post-independent sensibilities. Revelries where *aso ebi* and other native attire like *agbada* were worn became a central enchantment of Lagos urban life of the 1960s. A new group of people with the sobriquet "Lagos Boys" were leading the fashion course. Women adopted colorful, light fabrics, such as *adire* (*kampala*), "lace," *agbada*, and *ankara*. Aṣọ òkè was also modified into novel colors and in Lurex and worn mainly as *aso ebi* in festive occasions. This cultural renaissance in native dress reached a zenith in 1970 when the *agbada*, for example, not only became the fashion of aspiring middle-class women but also entered into the discourse of political ambitions for men.

It is important to note that the rise of Nigeria's commercial and industrial bourgeoisie in the 1960s and 1970s was a result of the rising Nigerian economy. Nigeria's economy expanded rapidly in the 1960s and 1970s, powered by the discovery and export of rising volumes of oil, the price of which soared by 1973, a period that was commonly referred to as the "oil boom era." During this period there was huge growth in the Nigerian government's physical infrastructure, commercial services, and industrial bourgeoisie as the country's rapidly rising oil exports made foreign currency exchange freely available for imports (Kraus 2002, 398–99). During this period of economic boom there was also increased demand for foreign textiles from Asia, Europe, and other parts of the world. The year 1978 marked an abrupt shift in the economy due to Nigeria's loss of foreign exchange and as low industrial productivity triggered a government ban on the importation of lace and other elite materials.[12] An unexpected and positive outcome was that foreign textile producers began to partner with their Nigerian colleagues, and production shifted from outside to Nigeria. The weak implementation of the textile ban did not stop the importation of lace and *george*, two essential cotton and synthetic garments from Indonesia and England that constituted fabrics of choice of the elite society at the time. The poor, however, adopted less costly damask, brocades, and *ankara* wax prints.

From the mid- to late twentieth centuries, the Nigerian fashion industry was tied to the global market economy. By this time *adire* had become less fashionable for Lagos urbanites and was replaced by *agbada* and *ankara* prints. Aṣọ òkè was increasingly a cloth for special occasions for the well-to-do only. Acclaimed international designers from Europe, such as Gucci, Versace, and Christian Dior, made enormous sales from the urban nouveau riche in Nigeria and other booming oil nations. Expensive materials imported from the West were appropriated in the production of most locally worn apparel, including the "wrapper."[13]

By the 1980s there were more than 140 thriving textile companies in Nigeria, making it the second-largest industry in Africa after that of Egypt. As the second-biggest employer after the Nigerian government, in the 1980s the textile industry employed over a million workers with an output income accruing to more than one billion naira.[14] The textile industry supported millions of Nigerians in an artisanal economy. By 1986 a ban on the importation of clothing and high import duties on all textiles and textile fibers by the military government once again encouraged local textile production. There was an increase in *adire* dyers and aṣọ ọ̀kẹ̀ weavers, and the number of tailors who specialized in locally made fabrics swelled in the city of Lagos. *Adire* became more affordable than the exorbitantly priced foreign textiles, and more individuals embraced it for *aso ebi*. In fact, the 1980s was the height of the *adire* boom because the country's Structural Adjustment Programme (SAP), introduced in 1986, encouraged many individuals who were economically disinherited to embrace local entrepreneurship in the fashion business.[15] This move to entrepreneurship was enabled by the passage of the 1987 National Open Apprentice Scheme (NOAS), which promoted job creation through self-employment. NOAS was perhaps most successful in the areas of cloth weaving, dressmaking, and tailoring, which were attractive to primary- and secondary-school graduates.

By late 1991, most local fabrics, such as *adire* and aṣọ ọ̀kẹ̀, were gradually replaced by *ankara* for *aso ebi*. According to Carolyn Marion Keyes, "By the end of 1991, *ankara* had taken over *adire*'s position as a mid-range mid-priced cloth" (1993, 183). The rise of *ankara* was phenomenal, and up to the present day it has remained one of the most preferred fabrics for *aso ebi*. *Ankara* wax prints imported from China were of lesser quality and cheaper, while those made in Nigeria were of better quality and more expensive. As observed by Chidimma Ogbonna (fig. 9), some customers know the difference between the *ankara* made in Nigeria and that made in China and Ghana and can make specific requests for either foreign or locally made *ankara* (Ogbonna 2010). "As at the late 1990s when I started selling in this market," remarked Jumoke Shubayo (fig. 10):

> the number of people that come to buy these materials are always very few because then you see we only sell lace, damask, velvet, and Hollandais, but since this *ankara* started coming in large quantity, my brother, I can tell you that in a week people come in groups to buy traditional in bulk. For example, just yesterday two groups came and bought five hundred yards from me because they are preparing for a wedding and a lot of people are going to wear it

Figure 9. Chidimma Ogbonna, Balogun textile market. Lagos, November 29, 2010. Photo: Okechukwu Nwafor.

as *aso ebi*. In fact, even most other people who used to sell other brands have switched to *ankara* because many people come to buy it for *aso ebi*. (Shubayo 2010)

While the Nigerian textile sector became close to moribund, *aso ebi* practice seems to have flourished. One major example for understanding this growth is through some accounts of individual merchants who sold textiles in large quantities in the Balogun textile market. According to Shuaibu Danjuma, a merchant in the market, in November 2003 he sold five hundred yards of London wax for *aso ebi* to more than twenty customers for special occasions while in December 2009 he sold five thousand yards of *ankara* materials to about one hundred customers who used the materials for *aso ebi* in just weddings alone (Danjuma 2011). Danjuma's record of business transactions revealed that the number of people who bought *ankara* for *aso ebi* for weddings alone in just one month in early 2009 equaled the number of all those who bought other materials for *aso ebi* in more than six months in 2003. The astronomical rise in *aso ebi* practice, despite the virtual absence of Nigerian-

Figure 10. Jumoke Shubayo, Balogun textile market. Lagos, April 9, 2010, Photo: Okechuk-wu Nwafor.

made wax prints used for *aso ebi* during this time in 2008, was rather para-doxical. Danjuma, however, confirmed that the Nigerian textile industry pro-duced original wax-print cloth that was different from the imported cloth. Chidi Ibenegbu, another textile merchant in Balogun, who came to Lagos in 1999, sold Hollandais-brand cloth first and told me that on average, two peo-ple a week came to buy Hollandais from him for *aso ebi* in the year 2000, but by 2009 more than fifteen people came every week to buy *ankara* textile for *aso ebi* for their weddings and other ceremonies (Ibenegbu 2011).[16]

From these accounts, it is evident that while the collapse of the textile industry was a misfortune for the employees and their dependents, it was a positive development for those engaging in *aso ebi*. For example, Busayo Ola-jumoke (2010) notes that Nigerian wax-print cloth is of a higher quality but more expensive, while the Chinese wax cloth is cheaper and more colorful but of lesser quality. In fact, Uche Idike, an apprentice in the Balogun textile market, told me that "almost all the fabrics sold in Balogun are Chinese. Hun-dreds of people come here every day to buy the China *ankara aso ebi* for their wedding or funeral" (2015). Most textile marketers in Balogun sold in larger quantities and on weekends recorded the highest sales. The aggressive trade import in foreign textile by Nigerian textile merchants led to an explosion in local tailoring businesses in Lagos. Both local and established designers appropriated local and foreign design elements into their Nigerian fashion.

The tailors who emerged in the 1990s in Lagos strove to meet the demands for weekly *aso ebi* uniforms used for regular weekend parties. They also struggled to meet the needs of the increasing number of Nigerians who had turned to the use of the so-called *ankara*, also referred to as "traditional dress," in almost all social activities. The use of these "traditional" outfits, however, was not only noticeable in social gatherings but could also be seen in official settings, such as the Nigerian parliament, where 90 percent of members wore "traditional attire," often known as *agbada*.[17] But much more attention was focused on how the urban tailors disseminated the styles of these clothes and their use of popular magazines as their sources of inspiration.

By the late twentieth century, the popularity *ankara* grew as the new material of hip fashion enabled a new interpretation of *aso ebi* outside its meaning when aṣọ òkè and *adire* were the sole textile paraphernalia used. Aṣọ òkè and *adire* fell out of favor with the rich who used them for *aso ebi*, because their fashionability as an urban style was becoming increasingly challenged by the sartorial fads that came with late global modernity. As in the late 1990s, some friends, close acquaintances, and relatives purchased and gave aṣọ òkè and *adire* to individuals as *aso ebi* for upcoming ceremonies, with the tacit understanding that the recipients would pay for the materials whenever they could.[18] Many celebrants desired large crowds adorned in *aso ebi* during their weddings. Some celebrants preferred that individuals participate in their *aso ebi* and pay them for the fabric at their convenience, months or weeks after the wedding. This was when many individuals could not afford the *aso ebi* fabric. "Now almost anyone can solicit for an *aso ebi* group and get immediate response because almost everybody can afford *ankara*," remarked Chidimma Ogbonna, a textile dealer of *ankara* at the Balogun textile market (fig. 9). From Ogbonna's assertion it can be inferred that life itself was cheapened by a proliferation of mimetic commodities, a logic supported by Leslie Rabine who rightly notes that the affordances of the new global economy facilitate mass consumption of fashion through mass production and mass distribution (Rabine 2002). *Ankara*, which is imported mainly from China, and sometimes Europe, subscribes to Rabine's description of "mass production," which begets mass consumerism in *aso ebi* practice. This process seems to blur the gap between culture and commerce, thereby subverting the meanings of *aso ebi* culture to consumers.

If the majority of the textiles used for *aso ebi* in present-day Nigeria come from China, then one could argue that *aso ebi* has defied the meaning of "culture" and branched into the signifying logic of industrialized economy. In effect, global production, export, import, and consumption of cloth have altered the significance of fashion in Western high streets and in open-air urban markets in the third world, further underscoring the reality of consumption goods as those that transcend the boundaries of culture and geographic space (Tranberg 2004). Here culture framed in the context of cloth in this sense is subject to multiple readings. It is indeed no longer the business of the locals to determine its trajectory.

If local consumers contribute to breaking Western hegemony in fashion by inventing local design styles, they also contribute to reinforcing this hegemony through their dependence on Western textiles. There is an appropriation of the local and the global in the bid to invent a universal language for clothing, perhaps in the logical phrase of what Arjun Appadurai describes as "global localities" (Appadurai 1996). *Ankara* seems to subscribe to global locality because it is imported from the West but reinvented by the locals for *aso ebi*. The use of *ankara* changed the meaning of *aso ebi* as more individuals began to associate *aso ebi* with high fashion instead of its initial link to "tradition" when aṣọ òkè was used. Many participants see it as an occasion to sew the latest fashionable cloth and also partake in the city's sartorial contest. The question here is, How did *ankara*, and indeed other foreign textiles, come into Nigeria to constitute this global locality that seems to reinvent the meanings of *aso ebi*?

ASO EBI AND THE PARADOX OF "TRADITIONAL DRESS"

At this point some attention to the activities of China in the Nigerian textile market is warranted (Renne 2015).[19] This may help shed light on how and why *aso ebi* practice is intensifying in urban Lagos. By 2010 an estimated 80 percent of imported textile fabrics in Nigeria came from China (Olatunji 2007). The increasing production of lesser-quality textiles from other Asian countries pushed many European producers of wax prints out of business with only Vlisco in the Netherlands and the Chinese-owned A.B.C. in England surviving (Sylvanus 2016).

Before the introduction of neoliberal policies—such as open access to foreign investors—in Nigeria in the 1980s, the textile industry engaged in foreign export of its excess products. By 1994 President Bill Clinton introduced the African Growth Opportunities Act (AGOA), which ushered in a preferential textile quota for Africa. This development occasioned a radical shift in the Nigerian textile market with much impact being felt by the emergence of some Chinese firms into the Nigerian textile industry. For these Chinese firms, the onus lay in the exploitation of the auspicious business opportunities in Nigeria and other African countries offered by AGOA (Ndubuisi 2007). In Lagos a state-of-the-arts Chinese shopping complex called Chinatown was established under the government's preferential textile quota law. Chinatown started full operations in 1998 but within a few years was indicted by the Nigerian textile workers and other groups. One of those groups is the Manufacturing Association of Nigeria (MAN), which along with Nigerian textile workers, leveled some allegations of misconduct against Chinatown management and their cohorts. One allegation centered on unlawful copying of local designs, which were taken to China for mass production. The allegations did not end at the level of mass production. The Chinese were also accused of stamping the textiles with stolen Nigerian tags, printed in China, and imported back into Nigeria. Not only that, but these textiles were also re-exported from Nigeria to the United States in order to derive optimal benefit from the United States' preferential textile quota for Africa (Idun-Arkhurst and Laing 2007).

In a nutshell, China was seen as reaping the fringe benefits intended for indigenous manufacturing firms in Nigeria when, ostensibly, the manufacturing firm was located in China. Within this system, it is assumed that China was engaged in illicit exploitation and that their rhetoric of business collaboration under the neoliberal policies of Nigeria was only lip service. In light of the allegations, Chinatown became notorious for contraband and fake textiles and for the accumulation of cheap, low-quality Chinese textiles in the Nigerian market. Mass production and the supply of cheap and low-quality textiles in Nigeria are key issues here. This is important in subsequent discussions, especially in providing explanations for the mass of people who have embraced *aso ebi* in recent times. Both "mass production" and "cheap textile" might become apt metaphors for the "mass" of people who engage in, and the expansion of, *aso ebi* practice itself.

In October 2007, in an attempt to resuscitate the dying textile economy, the Nigerian Senate summoned its federal government to revisit the current import privileges in relation to the polyester filament yarns manufactured locally. The federal government urged the Senate to address the issue and demanded that the Nigerian customs services initiate an extensive anti-smuggling campaign and invoke the import prohibition list of 2004. This, however, was rejected (Jimoh 2007). The Senate's rejection marked a major setback in the enactment of expedient measures to curtail the excesses of the Chinese merchants. The significance of the Senate's move is that more than 80 percent of the textile materials used for *aso ebi* are imported from China.[20]

While the majority of all cloth material used for *aso ebi* is imported from China, most often the popular narrative lexicon surrounding *aso ebi* uniforms is framed by most Nigerians under the term "traditional" dress. Frank Osodi attributes the ubiquity of multiple textile materials in Nigeria to the common weekend celebrations where *aso ebi* is the dominant dress style (2009). In this respect, it is important to recognize that there is a system of bricolage taking place in Nigeria, a re-signification as imported textiles are reconfigured to suit local demands (O. Nwafor 2011). In terms of stylistic choice in dress, Karen Tranberg Hansen observes how ideas "have moved beyond the idea of emulation to embrace notions of bricolage, hybridity, and creolization" (2004b, 372). In a sense, the understanding of capitalism may compel one to see this practice in terms of the relationship between culture and commerce, as suggested by John Fiske. The appropriation of imported textiles for *aso ebi*, if I may borrow from Fiske's paradigm, means that "users don't simply passively consume commodities; they actively rework them to construct their own meanings of self, social identity and social relations." So while one can argue that there is a continuing economic base in the capitalist mercantile network of imported textiles, there is also a rival cultural economy in the circulation of commodities in terms of "meaning and pleasures" (Fiske, cited in Docker 1994, 160). The meanings attached to these imported textiles have been largely located within the dexterity of the urban tailors and designers who merge "tradition" and "modernity" while their end products are interpreted by the locals as "traditional." Although the quotidian garments in urban Lagos may comprise "Western" dresses, important public occasions like parties or church services are seen as moments for the display of one's latest style in "traditional" attire. A new kind of growing clientele also desires clothing sewn in the local style to be worn as everyday dress, too. Ninety percent of the people I spoke to in Lagos between 2010 and 2016 discussed *aso ebi* dress styles and materials in terms of "traditional" national or ethnic identity. None felt that the blending of *aso ebi* dress style with Western dress materials in any way diminished the impact of the meanings of "traditional" and the characteristics it possessed. I can argue that "traditional" is a popular slogan that explains the wider implications of post-structuralism in the use of language—this time one can speak of the popular production of meaning—as seen in a postcolonial context. The use of the phrase "traditional dress" could allude to a constant rejection of Western prescriptions of dress culture by the locals who hanker for a word that would carry the baggage of "tradition" as a constant reminder of their "Nigerianness." In fact, in popular understanding, "traditional dress" is a dress style devoid of external mediation. As something that has entered into a popular language mainstream used to describe *aso ebi* in Nigeria, "traditional" dresses could approximate an anti-language and could also translate to "culturally contingent code" (Barker and Galasinski 2001, 11). However, if the ubiquitous market established by the Chinese textile network in Nigeria could be described as hegemonic, then the appropriation of these textile materials for *aso ebi* could be considered an opposition to the influence of Western dress culture seen through a rejection of European suits and style of garments for most public outings by Nigerians.

Considering the impact of *ankara* fabric in the expansion of *aso ebi* practice, Pius Adesanmi believes that "the democracy of *aso ebi* is evident in its trans-class dimensions" (2011). It seems that what Adesanmi refers to when he mentions "trans-class dimensions" is the fact that there is an impartial and ultimate democracy of sartorial uniformity that pays no heed to the class of individuals who wear it: "Rich or poor, people are united by the debt of weekly appearance in *aso ebi* in weekend celebrations." While Adesanmi seems to suggest that uniforms might become a good metaphor for the dissolution of class boundaries, he might have also ignored the costs of individual uniforms as another means of enacting class division.

What may have come out of Adesanmi's submission is the need to interrogate more critically the history of subjectivity in the postcolonial context. There is a need to question certain postcolonial attitudes such as the switch by Nigerians to the use of *ankara* for *aso ebi* in the 1990s. This attitude may be seen as something that was not informed by the singular desire to assume sartorial agency but instead could be articulated within the broader context of the economics of Chinese textile exploits in Nigeria. That Nigerians abandoned the use of Western dress, which before the SAP constituted more than 70 percent of cloth materials worn in weddings and other social events, may be seen as a clear manifestation of the logic of economic necessity. Not only did the market expansion in the textile industry destroy the indigenous manufacturing firms, but it also gave rise to a redefinition of the *aso ebi* practice in accordance with new economic realities of *ankara* fabric.

CONCLUSION

In this chapter, the decision by a growing part of the Lagos urban populace to embrace the *ankara* textile fabric for use in *aso ebi* aligns with Georg Simmel's idea of fashion as a "sense of stylistic change—as in late-nineteenth-century Europe—characteristic of the increased tempo of urban life created by a capitalist mass consumption economy" (1997, 187). While his European referent might speak to nineteenth-century industrialism in Western Europe, Simmel did not envisage the progression of the late capitalist economy of the present time and Nigerian context.

Aṣọ òkè was initially used for *aso ebi* but soon replaced by *ankara* fabric imported from China and elsewhere. By associating *ankara* with local and national cultural values, the meaning of *aso ebi* became transformed as more individuals identified *aso ebi* fabric and its tailoring as both "traditional" and high fashion. It is rather paradoxical that while the local textile industry declined, *aso ebi* practice blossomed. This is a result of the emergence of China as an economic superpower whose impact continues to shape the cultural and political economy of sartorial practices in Africa.

As a leading economic power in Africa and as the most populous Black nation on earth, Nigeria seems to be a better country to assess the nature of "culture" and capital, especially through the impact of foreign textiles in Nigeria. It could be said, therefore, that capitalism intensifies culture. If capitalism has succeeded in reorienting all of human existence to its own ends, then the current notion of *aso ebi* as an unmediated cultural phenomenon may be questioned.

This chapter challenges one to rethink the processes of consumption under late capitalism and then ponder Vincent Miller's worries of consumer culture and its impact on the concrete practice of life or the French philosopher Henri Lefebvre's fears of the devastating effects of capitalism on everyday life (Miller 2005; Lefebvre 1991, cited in Gardiner 2000). From the experiences of Chidi Ogbu and Oguntade, this chapter has demonstrated that the vicissitudes witnessed in the Nigerian economy were among the major contributors to the evolution of *aso ebi* practice. It shows that culture could be defined by market possibilities and that there is a need to refrain from taking certain cultural practices as given.

Thus, I conclude by arguing that *aso ebi* fashions represent a somewhat organic expression of market desires. This chapter attests to the masking effects of commercial and global industrial capitalist networks. In particular, the invasion of foreign textiles into the Nigerian market reveals an essentially complex dynamic in the unstable process called *aso ebi* "tradition." While this chapter might have demonstrated that the influx of cheaper textile materials explains why a greater number of people, and indeed lower-class members of society, have joined the *aso ebi* practice of dress, in the next chapter I seek to investigate why both the middle class and other members of the Lagos society desire large numbers of people in *aso ebi*. It seems that this desire goes beyond the cheaper prices of textile materials as suggested in this chapter.

CHAPTER 3

Coloring Wealth, the Crowd, and Class

The second democratic government phase after independence, Nigeria's Second Republic, which commenced on October 1, 1979, under the presidency of Alhaji Shehu Shagari, was born amid great expectations. Oil prices were high and revenues were on the increase. It appeared that unlimited development was possible. Unfortunately, the euphoria was short-lived, and the Second Republic did not survive its infancy. By 1981 the economic hopes and dreams of an optimistic era embodied in the virile democracy of 1979 and the oil boom era of the early 1970s were challenged by the uncertainties of declining oil revenues and political instabilities.[1] The GDP, which rose 10.5 percent in 1971, declined by 4.8 percent in 1981. The country slid into recession, went borrowing on the Euro-dollar market, and succeeded in economically disempowering the majority of the populace. The environment was already conducive for the military to justify their entry, and in 1983 they seized power for the second time since Nigeria's independence in 1960. Economic uncertainty, quite pervasive in this age of panics, engendered the city dwellers' introspective attempts to recreate a diminishing public image in the embattled social spaces. For these city dwellers, large gatherings with colorful *aso ebi* served as expedient sites for financial reaffirmation and self-reinvention. It is likely that increased signs of desire for *aso ebi* would reassure the public of the celebrants' salience in the affairs of things. The question I ask in this chapter, then, is, How does *aso ebi* evoke the desire for visibility among city dwellers? The aim of the chapter lies in the understanding of how a large followership dressed in colorful *aso ebi* could build a public image of visual spectacle and well-being amid personal and collective economic instability, postcolonial urban crisis, and political impasse.

Some of my fieldwork itineraries across Lagos between 2010 and 2019 resulted in my attendance at more than one hundred weddings and participation in more than fifty discussion groups with those who either organized or were about to organize weddings or birthday parties in Lagos. Most often my interviews revolved around *aso ebi*. In one of my encounters, Abiola Ogunlana, a staff member of Zenith Bank in Nigeria, who in 2010 was preparing for his wedding with Vera, his fiancée, narrated how *aso ebi* became the most discussed item in his wedding list. Abiola said Vera's sister, Titi, visited their house in Lagos Island almost four times to help them choose their *aso ebi*. Notably, Titi came with photographs of a rich family from a wedding she had attended in the Lekki area of Lagos and showed Vera how beautiful the *aso ebi* looked. She attempted to convince Ogunlana and Vera to buy the same color of *aso ebi* fabric. Vera, however, told me that her sister was always interested in copying colors and designs of people's dresses.

Ogunlana said they bought three different sets of *aso ebi* colors and designs for their wedding. He said that displaying different colors of *aso ebi* dresses in a wedding is an indication of one's wealth and a criterion for assessing a successful wedding: "Different colors of *aso ebi* are important in weddings; they make your guests stand out in class," he remarked. "If you visit *aso ebi* websites and Nigerian wedding Instagram photos, you will fall in love with the unique colors of *aso ebi* styles there," said Vera.

These kinds of spectacular evocations of colors in social media underscore the complex interplay of aesthetic and visual culture relations surrounding *aso ebi*. This includes the translation of a simple act of seeing into nuances of class and prestige. It also shows how individuals depend on *aso ebi* websites to fashion themselves. Vera's emphasis on the colors of *aso ebi* shows that the processes undertaken to arrive at a particular selection of *aso ebi* involve a more complex procedure of visualization than merely the simple practice of going to purchase the fabric.

Colors have become one of the greatest selling attributes of *aso ebi*.[2] Many of the fashion websites offer online lectures on how *aso ebi* colors can be combined. For example, there is a full lecture titled "The Art of *aso ebi* Colour Picking" provided on the *AsoEbiBella* website, where ideas resonated around public spectacles evoked through ideas of color and how *aso ebi* colors can actually provoke desires to purchase *aso ebi* fabric by friends. Almost every website that advertises *aso ebi* places great emphasis on colors. There is also a presumptuous attribution of wealth and class to the number of colors of *aso ebi* on display during one's wedding. Different colors translate to multiple materials and increased costs, which many couples and their guests may not be able to afford. While this act of visualizing is conveyed most imperceptibly through sensory devises that are not easily endorsed in the regimented exercise of academic theorizing, subsequent chapters reveal more explicit means of, and the formally endorsed act of, seeing *aso ebi* through photography, social media, and magazines.

During Ogunlana's traditional wedding, three sets of *aso ebi* uniforms were worn, each differing in color. His family members and friends of Vera wore a blue and white *ankara* that cost him N6,500 per five yards (which is enough for only one person) just for the introduction ceremony. In the same ceremony, Ogunlana and Vera each wore a deep brown lace material that cost him N22,000 per yard. During his engagement ceremony, a gold and brown *ankara* was chosen for the party for guests, while a lace material of blue and green was selected for themselves. The costs were estimated at about N7,500 and N46,000 respectively. According to Abiola, the number of people who wore *aso ebi* for both their introduction and engagement ceremonies totaled one hundred, and this constituted the expensive dimension of *aso ebi*. He said he also provided food, drinks, and gifts for all the participants.

During Ogunlana's wedding proper, apart from his suits, which cost N120,000 and Vera's wedding gown, which cost N350,000, for the church ceremony, Ogunlana and his parents wore an amber with brown and gold lace materials for the ceremony as well as sky blue and white *aṣọ òkè* for the reception, totaling N120,000 and 150,000, respectively. "So what I spent for *aso ebi* alone was about N800,000," remarked Ogunlana. In US dollars N800,000 amounts to about $2,000 being the amount spent only on *aso ebi* cloths.

In Nigeria, money has always been perceived as a central image in the discourse of self-realization. While this same idea could be seen as a generic perception, the attribution of money to cloth and wealth draws a historical import from the days of the slave trade, where textile materials became critical commodities of an emerging capitalist transaction (see chapter 1). In contemporary Nigerian society, where the sociocultural dynamics of celebrations are driven by the self-aggrandizement of the "big man," the same textiles and money have served as expedient means of glorification, which is quite evident in *aso ebi*. The fact that many individuals wear *aso ebi* ascribes a sense of financial cost to the number of cloths worn, thus rendering a subtle gesture to the wealth of the celebrant.

Ogunlana's friends and relatives bought *aso ebi* from him and Vera. He sold the *aso ebi* to them at a price higher than what he bought it for and therefore recouped some of the money with which he bought wedding gifts he gave to those who bought *aso ebi*. "In this way we did not incur much expenses buying the gifts; the wedding was crowded, and in fact my in-laws were so excited about the whole ceremony that they believed our wedding was the most expensive and the best among the recent weddings they have attended," said Ogunlana.

One major point to note here is how Titi, Vera's sister, was swayed by the design she saw from one of the affluent weddings she attended. More than 80 percent of those I interviewed during my research in Lagos said they visited *aso ebi* fashion websites or Instagram during their wedding preparations primarily for the purposes of selecting not just designs but colors of *aso ebi* fabric. This is emblematic of how colors evoke imitation and desires to copy.

My interview with a family friend of the Ogunlanas, Rose Oyelami, whom I met during their wedding in Lagos, revealed instances where friends and family members disagreed over colors of *aso ebi* dress: "Sometimes my friends invite me to the market, where we select the colors of the *aso ebi* dress, and I can tell you that is always one of the most difficult times for me during the preparation for *aso ebi*; there is this idea that multiple colors of *aso ebi* uniforms displayed during a wedding makes that wedding prestigious" (Oyelami 2010). Ogunlana and Vera's wedding was marked by an array of *aso ebi* colors during different stages of the wedding. These different *aso ebi* color displays have become part of the engaged efforts by Lagosians to rise above the invisible self that was hitherto eclipsed within the gloom of the post–oil boom economy in the late twentieth century. In fact, the Ogunlanas' experience is a very important case study to navigate around issues of shifting identities in the event of Nigeria's economic decline after the oil crash. It reveals the multiple ways that *aso ebi* functions in the collective imagination and the multiple meanings it embodies. It also examines the conditions that gave rise to, and the consequences of, new ways of creating and visualizing *aso ebi* identities around class, wealth, and public salience.

ASO EBI: PUBLIC SALIENCE AS PUBLIC VISIBILITY

No doubt, the Ogunlanas' experience serves to show that colors are remarkably significant in defining *aso ebi* as a visually instigated practice that is also implicated in discourses of wealth. Across different segments of the Lagos society, multiple cases abound in which similar desires to achieve visibility are expressed either modestly or ostentatiously through *aso ebi*. What is remarkable is that each group uses colorful *aso ebi* uniformity to evoke the spectacular. Vera told me how some of her friends have declined to purchase *aso ebi* of other friends because the colors, as they argued, were not "colorful" enough. Since each *aso ebi* encounter is expected to add to women's wardrobe after the wedding, each participant desires to make an aesthetic statement that will endure after each wedding. As the photos of *aso ebi* dress designs enter into fashion magazines and fashion websites, there is always a tension between individual dress practices and collective fashion imagery. Every woman's dress is a conscious effort in experimentation, shapes, and design, while the array of *aso ebi* displayed during the wedding reveals a collective participation in open fashion competition. Bearing this in mind, individuals preparing for a wedding invest sustained attention to colors in order to attract participants. If the colors are not attractive, some friends may decline to participate and there is more inclination to describe the wedding as dull.

PURCHASING *ASO EBI*

In recent times, there has been an unresolved public dilemma that comes with the purchase of *aso ebi* textiles. In some weddings of rich individuals, *aso ebi* has been sold to the public for reasons that are connected with expansion and, in certain cases, the quest to make illicit money by certain unscrupulous individuals connected to the rich. This is where purchase primarily defines the criterion for participation in *aso ebi*. It is noteworthy that individuals who purchase *aso ebi* also expect a return gift at the wedding venue. Apart from colors, many reasons have been attributed to why individuals either accept or decline to purchase *aso ebi* (see chapter 4).

Part of *aso ebi*'s embodied morality rests on the punitive purchasing power of individual participants. The Ogunlanas' friends and relatives had to purchase the *aso ebi* cloth from them in order to qualify for participation. Buying oneself into an *aso ebi* social group entails visibility of some sorts, and this does so many things for one's persona: it connects the material insignia of colorful uniformity to needless ostentation and wealth; it also elevates the hidden persona to a public persona because the images of *aso ebi* participants, in most instances, enter into the social spaces of Instagram and fashion websites, where they become desirable models of taste and raw materials for design experimentation and emulation.

In other words, in purchasing *aso ebi* from friends, one aspires to be initiated into a fashion trend and a dress practice displayed as personal styles but subsumed into the psychosocial network of colorful performers. There are examples where *aso ebi* has been described as a form of social investment in people and wealth and as something worthy of emulation. In fact, this is a popular metaphor when discussing *aso ebi* in Nigeria. Titi attempted to foreground this idea when she believed that Vera, her sister, could emulate the cloth of the "wealthy" family in *aso ebi*. Wealth translates not only to money but also to "the things people imbue with value" (Guyer 1995, 83). Fabrics and the individuals who wear them foreground the narrative of value here.

Aso ebi fits into the Yoruba popular belief of cloth as a "thing" used to achieve public salience (Barber 1995).[3] In Yoruba, *aso ebi* has served as one of the expedient avenues through which wealth manifested in bodily spectacles that attracted more of an entourage to an individual. *Aso ebi* is a metaphor for both cloth and people. This double incarnation has survived since nineteenth-century Yorubaland, where, for example, Oba Oyekanbi (1861–1877), a nineteenth-century Yoruba king of the Okuku community, was greeted: *Alamu labuta ore / Lanihun baba lo waa regbe bora bi aso* ("Alamu possessor of many friends / Lanihun the father has companions to wrap himself with like a cloth") (Barber 1995, 214). In the social dressing of *aso ebi*, there is an evocation of a process of self-investment through clothes. In Yoruba, the dignity of the rich has been magnified through the construction of an imposing personality of distinguishing bodies metaphorically referred to as "colorful cloths." Cloth metaphors have often been used to represent multiple layers of people as well (215). Ogunlana's friends and relatives fashioned his public figure and expanded his family's prominence by purchasing and wearing his *aso ebi*. *Aso ebi* is thus used to convey the impression of prestige into public space, embodied through colorful, elaborate, and sumptuous uniformed attire worn by his friends and relatives.

That *aso ebi* could be described as multiple layers of people could be attributed to the idea of control that the rich have exercised over multiple numbers of people. By purchasing *aso ebi* from Ogunlana, each individual's physical body is socially transformed by investiture with uniformed costumes. Each individual is represented as investing (and investing in) themselves through clothing. There is a double moral charge to this investment that rests in the idea of reciprocity. Each buyer of *aso ebi* believes that their turn will come when the same people clothe themselves and constitute into their own solidarity. The inevitable demand for *aso ebi* in weddings and other social events in Nigeria suggests that every individual has the capacity for inventiveness and an aversion to invisibility and sartorial inadequacy, an indication that everyone has the potential for self-aggrandizement in the social spaces in which they find themselves.

In fact, Nigerians' engagement with *aso ebi* in recent times derives from its specificity as a phenomenon linked to modernity in which clothing was subject to fixed sartorial color codes, through which prestige and distinction were distributed according to rank. However, among the lower-class members of the society, this distinction is sought differently, as will be discussed in chapter 4. In present-day Lagos, *aso ebi* cloth has been used to signify wealth and public visibility, especially through public sale of the fabric. A typical example was illustrated in the wedding of Wale Adenuga's daughter, Bella. Wale Adenuga is one of the richest men in Nigeria and the owner of the mobile network Globacom. Before Bella's wedding, *aso ebi* was put up for public sale at the cost of N350,000, an equivalent of USD$1,000. Some of the participants, who were not connected to the Adenuga family, told me that no specific individual was restricted from purchasing Adenuga's *aso ebi*. It was assumed that anyone who could afford this amount was rich and would be recognized during the wedding. Jide Ogunleye, a reporter who attended the wedding, said that a piece of *aso ebi* fabric was sold to each participant from Adenuga's family and their guests at the sum of N350,000 while the groom's family bought it at the cost of only N180,000. Despite this exorbitant price, all of the cloth was sold off (Ogunleye 2010). What is notable here is the huge amount of money that was invested in *aso ebi* and how the purchase of the fabric was used to enable group solidarity. Social solidarity and a sense of belonging are determined by the ability of the individual to purchase *aso ebi* no matter how expensive, a practice that also promotes an individual's visibility in the society. The moral economy of *aso ebi* lies in the fact that the piece of cloth serves only one person in a wedding that lasts for just few hours. The heightened urge to appear in Bella's *aso ebi* suggests the general understanding in Lagos that "all the attendees will feature in the richest news media platform in Nigeria and beyond" (Okon 2010). Most photographers, event management groups, and fashion designers were available to cover everyone and launch them in their various media platforms, including elite magazines, fashion websites, and fashion TV shows, among others. Again, part of the motivation for the increased rush in the purchase of Adenuga's *aso ebi* was likely the speculation that anyone who bought the *aso ebi* would automatically receive a gift of an iPad during the wedding reception (S. Adeleke 2010). In Nigeria, media outlets have served as avenues through which salience is sought, and most individuals depend on their visual images to fashion their *aso ebi*, just as could be seen from Titi, who brought the picture of a rich couple's wedding.

There are examples where despite the fact that individuals bought *aso ebi* from a public sale, they were excluded from the wedding. A case in point is the wedding ceremony of Tosin Saraki, the daughter of Nigerian Senate president Bukola Saraki. The initial notice that announced Tosin's wedding appeared in many news dailies in Nigeria. Tosin is the first daughter of four children of the Senate president and was married in Lagos on October 28, 2017. She studied at the London School of Economics and received a bachelor's degree in law and anthropology. She also has a master's degree in international legal practice from the University of London. It was reported that the invitation to her wedding was highly sought after. Invitation cards were accompanied with a free *gele* (head-tie) or *fila* (cap). However, *aso ebi* fabric was put up for public sale at the cost of N200,000. Azeezat Kareemannounced that "*aso ebi* is now available for [those] who can afford it" (2017). There was no restriction to who could buy the fabric, and many individuals indeed purchased it. However, a dramatic twist occurred when many of those who purchased, sewed, and turned up in *aso ebi* that day were denied entry into the arena. It was reported that more than one thousand individuals in *aso ebi* were denied entry, as there was an anxiety that the crowd in *aso ebi* could constitute a security breach. While this is a peculiar case of how purchasing could result in misrecognition, purchasing *aso ebi* has allowed many individuals to locate themselves within a certain network that amplified their quests for self-aggrandizement.

Aso ebi unveils a fruitful interplay between social conspicuousness of the big man and the surrounding gaze of praising adherents. It is also a good paradigm of social mobility, albeit temporary, with cloth serving only as a symbolic form of such recognition. First the celebrant sees money as something that can bestow prestige upon the wedding and views expensive *aso ebi* as a means through which this money could be exhibited. It follows, therefore, that the ability of one to afford such expensive apparel launches one into the rich social network of the celebrant, just for that occasion. The fact that human bodies become sites of possible pecuniary investment—in the form of expensive *aso ebi*—by the big man might compel one to think of Karin Barber's remark that "a big man's money was manifested in bodily display and conspicuous expenditure which attracted more people to his entourage" (1995, 215). This is akin to Peter Wollen's remark which, drawing on Thorstein Veblen, notes that "within the new system of fashion, wealth rather than rank as such became important, but also the ability to deploy wealth, through fashion, as a form of symbolic capital, one that attracted both attention and envy, as well as respect" (Wollen 2003, 133). *Aso ebi* in this respect affirms the capacity of the commodity to confer meaning and status (as a form of commodity fetishism); it expresses a particular kind of image that is tied to an inherent utopianism and steeped in pecuniary investment.

However, rather than such pecuniary investments translating into purely economic remunerations, they may satisfy socially acceptable assumptions of aggrandizement in the current context. Despite the high cost of Adenuga's or Saraki's *aso ebi*, the materials were highly sought after. Could it be assumed, in this instance, that fewer people could have purchased their *aso ebi* if it were less expensive?

Adenuga and Saraki might have invested their personhood with an image of money using expensive *aso ebi* cloth and the spectacular image of the crowd. This investment surely begot recognition of their self-worth by supporters, who bought expensive *aso ebi* dresses. There is, however, a certain contextual ambiguity in the concept of individual largesse in such a way that the big man in Adenuga and Saraki did not seem to "recruit" supporters but "attracted" supporters. One can argue here that *aso ebi* serves as both people and money and, as argued by Karin Barber, "people and money are inseparable and were in fact the joint constituents of social well-being" (1995, 213). The fact that Ogunlana's relatives and friends contributed money for his *aso ebi* which assisted him in raising money to purchase the gifts explains the inseparable connection between *aso ebi*, people, and money. In contemplating these three links, the use of the words "recruit" and "attract" serves to explain how certain individuals deploy each to serve the purposes of *aso ebi*.

The use of the word "attract" is suitable in addressing the transaction that took place in Adenuga's case. In other contexts, such as the case of certain politicians (as will be explained subsequently), the "big man" needed to "recruit" supporters to wear *aso ebi* because individuals may restrain themselves from his *aso ebi* except when money is pictured as an attractive gesture of this *aso ebi*.

ASO EBI, MONEY, AND ATTRACTION OF THE CROWD

In August 2010, Chief Uche Ibekwe, an Igbo businessman, had organized a reception party to mark his daughter's wedding in Lagos. Ibekwe owns a business conglomerate with facilities in Lagos and Onitsha, in Eastern Nigeria, where he imports many wares from China and elsewhere. During the wedding reception, more than five hundred people who attended received free *aso ebi*, cloth which he bought and donated to his family network and beyond (Ibekwe 2010). Chief Ibekwe was motivated to purchase *aso ebi* material for all of his employees at his Ibex Technologies company in Lagos because he wanted the wedding to look grand. The daughter remarked, "My friends were very happy to attend. In fact nobody spent any money on *aso ebi*. You just come and check your size and take." I received an *aso ebi* textile because I attended the wedding as one of the friends through another friend of mine. During the wedding reception, everyone was served food, including those in *aso ebi* and those not dressed in *aso ebi*. I received a free gift of an umbrella because I appeared in *aso ebi*, but those not dressed in *aso ebi* did not receive the umbrella gift. Ibekwe's daughter's wedding was very much discussed in terms of the number of people dressed in *aso ebi*. Many people who attended described the event as successful.

What could be suggested from the above is that there was a desire on the part of Ibekwe to command a large crowd through *aso ebi*. The success of the wedding, in popular estimation, was determined by the number of individuals who attended and dressed in *aso ebi*. In a popular Igbo slogan that addresses this success, an attendee exclaimed, "*Mmadu abia ka,*" meaning "The crowd was overwhelming." The fact that about five hundred *aso ebi* participants ate, drank, and received a free gift of an umbrella from Ibekwe readily explains why a large crowd dressed in *aso ebi* immediately conjures an image of wealth of the celebrant in any event. Speaking about a similar tendency, Patrick Cole notes how the elite expanded their social persona through a dependent crowd. He observes that "emphasis was placed not only on how much an individual had but also on how much of it he was ready to redistribute as largesse among his 'followers' and others around him" (1975, 199). The largesse was a step above the general display of hospitality expected of all in the society and also went beyond the usual demonstration of generosity. It was given by a socially superior person to others below his social category in order to maintain the idea of his goodwill. The recipients of such benefaction more often than not constituted the followers of the big man, and they were useful in the process of social advancement. Their support and admiration for him bred more aggrandizement and support for him from a wider populace. From Chief Ibekwe's experience, the concept of "big man" and wealth conflated notions of a large *aso ebi* crowd as supporters. What was ascertained from Chief Ibekwe's example is that such largesse was extended to free *aso ebi* clothing, free umbrella gifts, and free food.

In his article on a prominent Action Congress (AC), Toyin Anisulowo, a senatorial aspirant in Ado-Ekiti, the Ekiti state capital, in Western Nigeria, noted how a mammoth crowd adorned in expensive *aso ebi* outfits ushered politician Dele Alake into the state. Alake, who had just declared his intention to contest for the Ekiti central senatorial seat in 2011, pulled in a crowd that gave him the grandeur and splendor needed to boost his prestige and elevate his status. In the image of a politician, the crowd is seen as a very strong force—not just the crowd, but a crowd that wears *aso ebi* outfits. Among Alake's crowd were party supporters and leaders drawn from all the fifty-two wards that constitute the Ekiti central senatorial district. The crowd even obstructed traffic movement as they sang and danced to the admiration of the passengers and onlookers (Anisulowo 2010).

Aso ebi is one of the many processes through which "big persons" visibly extend themselves beyond their bodily boundaries by organizing the acquisition and distribution of *aso ebi* fabrics for their followers (Ferme 2001, 171).[4] This draws a parallel with the Yoruba saying "*Bo lomo ogun boo lomo ogun wehin re wo*"—(A leader can only ascertain his level of followership when he looks back.) In this context, the celebrant may not truly be a leader of any kind but is understood to be leader of the moment by virtue of being the one celebrating an event and who has requested people to buy the fabric that is meant for the occasion. In fact, when it is time to dance, that celebrant leads while well-wishers follow. This implies that any celebrant who, despite the fact that they have chosen a group uniform and yet people refuse to buy and identify with that celebrant, could be a social misfit. Therefore, there is a sense of esteem on the part of celebrants who are so honored. This point is buttressed in another Yoruba saying: "*Eniyan laso mi,bi mo ba boju wehin timo reni mi, inu mi adun ara mi a ya gaga*—my people are clothes" (Familusi 2010, 2). Although people cannot be worn, their presence or willingness to identify with a celebrant by virtue of wearing *aso ebi* is a cover for them. This suggests that not being identified with a large number of people is synonymous with nakedness. Also it is usually said, "*Karin kapo lo yeni*," meaning that the crowd conjures a befitting aura.

These expressions enunciate the importance of *aso ebi* cloth and its ensuing followership. They also underscore the relevance of wealth in the conceptualization of clothes and people in Nigeria. Possession of wealth alone does not elevate one socially but a display of such wealth is through clothes and

people who wear them. If traced from the above examples, then the significance of the crowd becomes even more evident in the contemporary Nigeria's
sociocultural milieu. The people, often commonly known as the big man's
crowd, may provide ample room for a further critical interrogation of the
concept of crowd and wealth. Jane Guyer deploys the concept of "wealth-in-
people" to encapsulate the nature of studies of wealth in precolonial African
societies. Some studies on wealth in precolonial Africa have touched on "the
techniques by which pre-colonial war-lords built up, motivated and remunerated their followings," especially given the fact that the concept of followership is broad enough to apply to, for example, "wives, children, clients, political followers, religious acolytes, titled associates, occupational apprentices
and so on" (1995, 89). Prior to Guyer, Suzanne Miers and Igor Kopytoff (1977)
had developed the concept of wealth-in-people in the 1970s to exemplify the
centuries-long conditions of human-thing evaluation in Africa. Miers and
Kopytoff's wealth-in-people concept draws an unmistakable link to a Marxist
term of "social accumulation" as well as African kinship and religious and
political clientelism (Smith 2001). While Miers and Kopytoff applied the idea
to slavery and other relations of dependency relationships, Caroline Bledsoe
(1980) was one of the first to use it prominently to describe marriage and
social networks in Sierra Leone. While Sara Berry does not invoke wealth-
in-people as a concept, she reviews processes of maintaining powerful social
institutions as an instrument of resource control and access to wealth. In fact,
for Sara, "control over capital goods—cattle, granaries, gold—was also often
based on social identity or status" (1989, 42). Joseph Calder Miller (1988)
and Jan Vansina (1990) both use wealth-in-people as an uninterrupted standard within an evolving social history of equatorial African societies as they
embrace geographic and mercantile modernities.

In short "the neo-Marxist insight has been universally acknowledged to
provide a compelling body of interpretation. Guyer suggests that the users of
wealth-in-people abandoned the Marxist intellectual agenda while conserv-
ing some of its framework—in particular, the focus on control and accumulation (1995, 107).

Indeed this concept of wealth-in-people, I must say, is considered in my
present context of *aso ebi* as a symbolic show of clout, wealth, and control.
My present use of wealth-in-people in *aso ebi*, as has been shown from the
examples of Ogunlana, Ibekwe, Saraki, and Adenuga, could actually serve as
an allegorical import of Miers and Kopytoff's form of control. Looking at the
four hundred individuals who wore Ogunlana's *aso ebi*, or the five hundred

people who wore Chief Ibekwe's daughter's *aso ebi*, the more than one thousand people who bought and wore Saraki's *aso ebi* and then were excluded from the event, or those who wore numerous *aso ebi* of Adenuga and Dele, the politician, in one way or the other demonstrates a symbolic form of power. And this gives the individual an illusive sense of control.[5]

These few case studies show that *aso ebi* is popularly perceived in terms of wealth, status, and the crowd. Some previous studies have proved this fact more convincingly. For example, William Bascom's study of early Yorubaland deals with, among other things, the issue of clothes, wealth, and ownership of property, which, as he argues "are not in themselves sufficient enough to win prestige and social status" (1951, 8). Those "aspiring to such exalted positions must not only possess wealth and own properties but they must also spend the money (*na owo*) on clothes and people." Bascom notes that the person must "spend on his clothes so that he can be well dressed." He remarks further:

> A person spends money so that people will know him and so as to attract a
> large number of followers. One of the important measures of social position
> is the number and rank of the individuals who associate with him and partic-
> ularly who accompany him when he goes about town. No man of high rank
> would be seen in the streets alone, while an ordinary individual invites the
> members of his club (*egbe*) to his house for food and drink at the time of a
> religious ceremony, funerary, wedding, or any other important event, so that
> he may have a large crowd dressed in fine clothes following him when he goes
> in the streets. (1951, 8)

Bascom succinctly captures this inseparable link between cloth, wealth, and human followership. Yoruba clubs employ distinctive uniformed dress that serves as group identification. By mentioning *aso ebi* as the uniformed dressing in Yoruba *egbe* adorned by about forty to sixty members to honor their members or guests, Bascom stands as one of the earliest scholars of Yoruba to recognize the phraseology of *aso ebi* as a potential source of scholarly investigation.

My interviews across Lagos with different respondents who had used *aso ebi* in one way or the other resonated with Bascom's account and the very notion of "purchasing *aso ebi*" as a criterion for visibility in most social outings. Take, for example, Ogunlana's experience where the wish to purchase *aso ebi* by friends was overwhelmingly expressed. Again, the multiple fabrics and colors of *aso ebi* that Ogunlana's *aso ebi* group changed into strangely signify a wealthy, flamboyant outing.

Vera, Ogunlana's wife, said that during her friend's child-naming ceremony, the friend demanded that Vera invited her own friends to buy *aso ebi* from her in order to increase the number of *aso ebi* wearers (Ogunlana 2010). Vera's friend "needed these fake friends to make her child's naming ceremony 'colorful and rich,' and anyone beholding such [a] large crowd around her would not doubt her wealth" (Irabor 2010). To Vera's friend, attracting a lot of friends connotes an impression of wealth and a successful naming ceremony, a consciousness that resonates with popular criteria for judging a successful event. To achieve this, Vera's friend embarked on a friendship hunt. "Most parties you attend [a] large crowd dresses in different colors of *aso ebi* and you might not know any of them outside your own group," remarked Vera. Chioma, one of their friends, notes that "most often the celebrants no longer care who buys the *aso ebi* because they believe the more people that wear *aso ebi*, the more colorful and the more the party gives an impression of wealth" (C. Okoye 2010).

A very significant point that runs through the above narratives is the propensity to increase the number of *aso ebi* wearers: Vera's friend demanded that Vera's own friends purchase *aso ebi* even though she did not know any of them (but this was part of Vera's friend's ploy to give her party color and create an impression of wealth). In these cases, the criterion for inclusion in *aso ebi* was no longer familial recognition but a desire to expand the crowd. Inclusion is no longer driven by true friendship or family network but by a socially imposed competitiveness that borders on sheer number. It therefore follows that inclusion has been redefined to accommodate expressions of wealth as shown through clothes and a large followership. This propensity for the crowd in *aso ebi* is consciously desired across different classes of people, bringing the issue of class as an important area of investigation in *aso ebi*.

ASO EBI CLOTH AND CLASS

Individuals in the postcolonial city of Lagos have experienced some forms of social (in)visibility that derived from class and inequality. *Aso ebi* dress has served as one of the avenues through which these social (in)visibilities are advanced. This is because dress has been used to distinguish the elites in social events in Nigeria. But the nature of contemporary Nigerian society makes it difficult to pursue such arguments around class. Given the nature of capitalist commodification, it is rather a tough task to discuss the explicit theoretical implication of "class" as an analytical category in the study of dress in contemporary Nigeria. Jonathan Haynes and Onokome Okome, writing about Nigerian video films in 2000, observed that the crucial incongruity, flexibility, and infiniteness of social groups in Africa complicates a contextualization of class using the European model (2000, 78). They noted that in Nigeria the class situation is further destabilized because of extreme underlying economic instability, the possibility of rapid mobility for a limited few, and nearly universal aspirations for individual advancement, which tends to inhibit the formation of class consciousness. Haynes and Okome recognized one of the signs of the incomplete process of class formation as the aspiration by almost everyone to rise socially by imagining their inherent potentialities in spite of the seeming unlikelihood. This compelling worldview constantly and fundamentally imagines an elite lifestyle as a realizable achievement of anyone who is propelled by hard work and has a dint of luck. Stories abound in the hinterlands of Nigeria on how Lagos city holds a huge promise in the realization of such imaginations, an imagination that has been explored in many literary and creative works.

It is possible to identify some parallels in the Nigerian video films and the practice of *aso ebi*, for "images of lavish wealth," which are paradigmatic of the videos, in some cases might have become the motivation for the spectacular display seen in the *aso ebi* dress. These images of the video films and of the spectacular *aso ebi* crowd are sometimes interpreted as both visions of aspiring middle-class seekers and the "desired dream by, and for, the masses" (Haynes and Okome 2000, 79). However, while Haynes and Okome's observation applies to a great extent in this study, the relationship that *aso ebi* has with class and status in Nigeria is worthy of further study in order to understand clearly the context in which *aso ebi* is being used in certain quarters in Nigeria. As discussed in chapter 2, in the event of Nigeria's independence in the 1960s, aṣọ òkè was often used as *aso ebi*, especially in Western Nigeria, to distinguish the rich from the poor.[6] Aṣọ òkè was eventually phased out because of the impact of the Chinese textile market, which also affected the nature of *aso ebi* practice. In recent times aṣọ òkè is still being used but on very few occasions, and it is still seen as a mark of class.[7]

While it is important to acknowledge the existence of a huge literature on class in Nigeria spanning the sociological, historical, anthropological, and political disciplines, it is necessary to stress that for the convenience of this study, class will be considered only in relation to *aso ebi* cloth.[8] The question is, How do *aso ebi* clothes mark social class? In purchasing Saraki's daughter's *aso ebi*, for example, I was informed that the more than one thousand women denied entry into the venue did not purchase *aso ebi* from the source that sold it at two hundred thousand naira. They purchased from another source that sold the same color of material at a less expensive rate and thus did not have the permit and emblem that could allow them entry into the venue. This information contradicts the reason reported by the mainstream news media as to why the women were denied entry.

In Nigeria, class is most visible through symbolic and subtle distinctions of wealth, such as cloth and *aso ebi* during social events. In weddings, funerals, and other ceremonies, rare and elaborately produced garments that include *aso ebi* produce a symbolic stratification of accomplishment that is based on the rich and not-so-rich (Lawuyi 1991, 257). It is important to note that ostentatious amounts of clothes as a symbol of status and wealth in Yorubaland appeared on chiefs and wealthy men long before capitalist networks availed the commoners of such exclusive opportunities (Cordwell 1983).

Aso ebi embodies a sense of class within the vast sartorial uniformity of its textile paraphernalia. In chapter 2 it became evident that *aso ebi* practice was socially delineated through its identification with expensive aṣọ òkè dresses. Very rich people adorned expensive lace or aṣọ òkè with their family members, while the not-so-rich wore cheap Chinese products as *aso ebi*. Indeed, the fetishization of material culture through *aso ebi* uniforms in Lagos belies the neoliberal insistence on the declining significance of class. The nature of exclusion instituted with expensive *aso ebi* of, for example, Saraki's daughter invokes a curious revelation of how class is implicated in the quest by the rich to invest their body with expensive and gorgeous robes. Money and its purchasing power rationalize the subtle references to the rich and poor among *aso ebi* practitioners.

Understanding class in relation to *aso ebi* again brings the notions of the "elite," in the Yoruba context, to the fore. The definitions of the elite in traditional Yoruba thought emphasizes the possession of *ola* (Adeboye 2003, 283). *Ola* translates as "honor," and while the ultimate in individual social advancement in precolonial Yorubaland was to attain a position of *ola*, there were several mediating social categories in between the masses and *olola* (possessor of *ola*). These categories included the *Borokinni/Gbajumo* (celebrities), *oloro/olowo* (men of wealth), *ologun* (powerful warriors who came to attention in the nineteenth century), and *oloye* (titleholders). In terms of individual social advancement in the traditional Yoruba society, there was more inclination for the pursuit of power than wealth, a passion for a "total state of sufficiency and command over their social environment, a state called *ola*. *Ola* is [a] complex, composite, shifting and sensuously realised concept. . . . [It] is ultimately the capacity to attract, command and retain the gaze of other people" (Barber 1991, 203).

Ola is greatness of splendor that transcends all that is mean, poor, obscure, or inadequate, and above the inhibition of powerlessness or low esteem. It is simultaneously self-assured and magnificent. The essential point here is that in certain respects, the concept of elite in Western philosophy corresponded to the notion of *olola* (and *ola*) in traditional Yoruba thought. Underlying both concepts are the same principles of high class, social influence, social superiority, and public acknowledgment. Due to the dynamism of the elite category, values associated with it are often modified and appropriated within its limits as a response to changing times. In the case of Adenuga, for example, elements of self-sufficiency, social command, and public acknowledgment in *ola* were accompanied by the splendor that is in *ola*. Similar features are seen in the Ogunlanas' wedding (Mann 1985, 284).

In colonial Lagos, those who constituted the elite comprised several categories. There were the chiefs whom we could call the "traditional elite," wealthy individuals who corresponded to the "commercial elite," and the first-generation educated intelligentsia whom we could call "educated elite." During the decolonization period, a new set of individuals acquired elite status. These were the politicians (284). Although educated, their ticket to elite status was more attributed to the leadership role they played through modern political parties in the country. There were also elites among religious leaders in traditional religion, Islam, and Christianity. The meaning of *ola*, therefore, for the elites in colonial Lagos involves the flamboyance that accompanied the *olola*, which was very much evident in their dressing. In part, their *ola* derives from the dignity bestowed upon them by the presence of the number of well-clothed individuals around them. Many of the prominent individuals in Lagos had numerous wives and thus children whom they had an obligation to robe in *aso ebi* at every special social occasion (S. Adeleke 2010). Although polygamy was a common practice in traditional Yorubaland, it acquired a wider appeal to the nouveau riche in the twentieth century. Part of the maintenance of a big polygamous household involves clothing family members during important events to form a visual impact of *aso ebi*. How does the crowd robed in *aso ebi* reflect the visual impact of wealth? (Cole 1975, 63). *Aso ebi* exemplifies the profound making of the crowd in contemporary Nigeria social events and strongly resonates with expressions by many Nigerians that the crowd is indeed the driving force of *aso ebi* culture (Adesanmi 2011).[9]

CONCLUSION

Watching different groups of people dressed in different colors of *aso ebi* fabric at a particular wedding (in the case of Ogunlana or Adenuga, Chief Ibekwe or Dele Alake) one sees multiple negotiations that define the singular code of *aso ebi* uniformity. As such, *aso ebi* positions the human body as a site of multiple political contests and an object of public gaze within the context of wealth and public salience.

Ogunlana expressed his pleasure at having spent less amount of money in buying gifts for numerous people who wore *aso ebi*, while his parents were very happy that, in their thinking, the party was expensive and thus the best among the recent wedding parties they had attended. The paradox of *aso ebi* plays out here in a very interesting manner. A suggestive way of explaining this could be that Ogunlana's parents were able to enjoy the attendant glamour evidenced from the large number of people in *aso ebi* while Ogunlana was delighted that the proceeds made from selling *aso ebi* enabled him to offset the incurred expenses of the gifts offered to the same large number of people.

This chapter has demonstrated that *aso ebi* dressing is conceived in terms of large followership as a yardstick for measuring wealth. The chapter demonstrates that large followership manifests in *aso ebi* through some individuals in the city who believe that prestige and wealth do not automatically translate to people robed in *aso ebi* but in getting a sizeable number of people to attend an event. In order to signify salience, this number of people must approximate a crowd. While opening up issues around *aso ebi* and notions of hierarchical ordering of society in certain social events in Nigeria, the chapter shows that *aso ebi* is a sumptuous type of paraphernalia employed for the objectification of rank and the elaboration of class. Almost approximating a social convention, *aso ebi* employs its material accoutrements to construct a discourse of the haves and the have-nots in social events in Lagos. In other words, in the process of the whole public display, it invokes imitation and a desire to multiply the number of people who wear *aso ebi*.

CHAPTER 4

Fractured Materiality and the Political Economy of Intimacy

The preparation of Kemi's wedding in Lagos revealed certain visual enchantment from the elite's *aso ebi*. Kemi first visited the popular BellaNaija website, where she intended to select unique styles and colors of her *aso ebi*. She saw numerous design styles and colors that were so attractive that she found it difficult to make a choice. However, her entire choice would dramatically change when her mother-in-law-to-be visited her house in Lagos with a prearranged style and color of *aso ebi* fabric for Kemi and her fiancé. Her future mother-in-law showed them a photo she brought of an *aso ebi* group from their village. She said the design was introduced by a photographer who took the photo of the couple at a wedding in Lagos. She said everyone she showed the photo loved it and that it was the best *aso ebi* attire they had ever seen. She insisted that Kemi should adopt the color and design of the fabric in the photo. Kemi's enchantment with the BellaNaija fashion website was overwhelming and would not allow her to take a second look at her future mother-in-law's *aso ebi* photo. BellaNaija is dedicated to the promotion of *aso ebi* design styles. The site not only serves as a space where numerous ideas of *aso ebi* dress designs are disseminated; it also serves as a site where the fractious materiality of *aso ebi* is interwoven into unending debates over the dilemma of seeing and being seen in beautiful dresses. Kemi disagreed with her mother-in-law-to-be over the choice of color and dress design. It almost caused a strained relationship between them, but Kemi's fiancé became an umpire and resolved the dispute. Kemi adopted the color of the material brought by her fiancé's mother but got design ideas from the BellaNaija site. The resolution of this situation underscores the exigency of *aso ebi*'s perplexing dimension: how the material and visual culture of *aso ebi* practice is interwoven with urban life. The paradox is that "the material culture of urban life, although constantly engaged with, is little noticed by its practitioners, an often taken-for-granted norm that living in the city is, as [Michel] de Certeau argues, about the practice of everyday life" (Wells 2007). *Aso ebi* in itself is about the practice of everyday life in urban Lagos.

However, the fracas for Kemi was not totally resolved. She announced to her friends that she had bought the fabric for *aso ebi* and that they should come and buy from her. She also asked her friends to bring along their own friends to buy. Kemi bought the *aso ebi* fabric, a Hitarget foreign material, at six thousand naira but sold it to her friends at twelve thousand naira. One of her friends, named Juliet, declined to buy because of the high price. She complained that she could not afford it. Kemi told me that "Juliet is stingy and that she does not always support her friend's *aso ebi* and that people will not support hers too" (Kemi 2015). Another of Kemi's friends, Omo, asked Kemi to drop off the fabric at her house and let her know the price. Kemi sent someone who dropped it off at her house. Later in the evening, Omo sent her younger sister to return Kemi's *aso ebi*, informing her that the price was too high and that she did not wish to participate in the *aso ebi*. Apart from Juliet and Omo, who declined to purchase, more than thirty of Kemi's friends bought the *aso ebi* at twelve thousand naira and also sold to their own friends, who bought at the same price. Kemi did not know most of her friends' friends who bought the *aso ebi*. This transaction is necessary for an understanding of a theoretical analysis of the moral economy of intimacy being the core message of this chapter.[1]

During Kemi's wedding, which I attended, I had the opportunity to interview a number of her friends who eventually participated in the *aso ebi*. About ten of those revealed that the virtuous materiality embedded on the surface of the human body was beginning to gather fractious burdens of a moral economy. Their verdicts were overwhelmingly supportive of the implicit discord embodied in *aso ebi*'s uniformity. Most of them were unanimous that my questions were very good, with some expressing their gratefulness on how I was raising the issue. Some of the respondents—including, for example, one of them named Uju—said she knew that the price of Hitarget is not more than four thousand naira but that she just wanted to support her friend Kemi because she understood that Kemi would use the profit to buy gifts for her guests. "Although I don't like it, but what can I do?" Uju said. Another of her friends, named Buki, said, "Most of us live a fake life; I know she wants her *aso ebi* to look more beautiful than others she has seen. Everything is about show-off. The worst thing is that those people who did not wear *aso ebi* did not receive any gift here, if you noticed it." Another friend, named Mary, complained that she was "tired of this *aso ebi* thing," that it compels her to spend a lot of money almost every weekend to buy *aso ebi*, and that "if you don't buy, your friends will misinterpret it as being wicked." "Everyone wants to be seen as the best; that is the problem," Mary argued.

What came out of these interactions was that Mary complained that she had attended so many weddings where she was not friends with the brides, yet she was part of their *aso ebi*. She was not friends with Kemi either, but she bought the *aso ebi* fabric from a friend of Kemi who sold it to her to support Kemi and her fiancé: "I have even lost some friends because of this, and I think this *aso ebi* thing should just be voluntary and not by force as many people now believe." The above narratives point to one salient objective: the quest to be seen as beautiful and the best.

While chapter 3 explored the apparent desire for large numbers of people in the practice of *aso ebi*, this chapter interrogates the meanings and types of solidarities forged by this increasing number of people in *aso ebi*.[2] One cannot divorce these questions from the issue of the fluctuating Nigerian economy, which to some extent redefined the meanings of friendship in *aso ebi* practice. This is because, by the year 2000, it became obvious that in order to effectively contain the huge expense of catering for large numbers of people in *aso ebi*, one needs to possess enough financial resources. *Aso ebi* became highly commercialized, as suggested by Kemi's experience. Celebrants now purchased textile materials intended for use as *aso ebi* and sold them to their friends at exorbitant prices. Kemi's *aso ebi* and her friend's concerns fundamentally reveal the great contention I attempt to resolve in this chapter: the proceeds from the sale of the textile materials help celebrants to offset the expenses incurred from hosting a large crowd during a party. While it is assumed that the crowd at some points constituted themselves as friends and forged solidarity for the celebrant, this chapter seeks to uncover the politics of love that fuels the act of seeing and being seen. It analyzes how the material insignia of *aso ebi* and the crowd can reveal the power relations that characterize urban life. The chapter offers a framework for analyzing material culture in the city and how the study of fashion and ways of seeing can contribute to unraveling the reification and fetishization of urban life. The chapter is grounded in a dialectical understanding of commodities as both things and social processes.

Is there a moral peril attached to the failure of material transaction in *aso ebi*? I aim for a careful analysis of the conflicts surrounding the social life of *aso ebi* within the bounds of individuals' interpretations and valuations of "things." *Aso ebi* as a "thing" may lead to a conflicting social life such that the meanings people attach to it may not harmonize. The quest to uncover the differences between individual attitudes toward *aso ebi* and whether *aso ebi* as a "thing" embodies a different set of expectations and actions among its practitioners remains a major task of this chapter.

In the bid to clarify the dialectical discourses of "cheap friendship" within the social dilemma of *aso ebi* solidarity, I seek to problematize prevailing views of *aso ebi* that place emphasis on solidarity and conviviality. By challenging the moral economy of intimacy, I show that *aso ebi*'s solidarity is constructed along bodily attire rather than along its purported belief in "real" friendship. The chapter also shows that *aso ebi*'s type of solidarity entails the subtle enforcement of an indirect social power that is fundamentally exclusionary. Its exclusionary tendencies may well have been informed by a social convention that recognizes uniform as the only yardstick for measuring solidarity, friendship and oneness.

In this chapter, therefore, I first address the issue of the "oneness" that *aso ebi* wearers profess. The question that I ask is how oneness manifests itself through the artificial material signifier of uniform (*aso ebi*) among people of different cultural, ideological, and sometimes political affiliations. Second, the meaning of friendship is interrogated as a discourse among groups of friends (in the city) who use *aso ebi* to show support to their friends in events such as weddings, birthdays, and naming ceremonies, among others. The definition and redefinition of friendship among these groups prompts my analysis of whether all those who wear *aso ebi* are truly friends. Finally, the chapter makes use of Marcel Mauss's "the logic of gift" to raise questions about the gift that is meant to accompany *aso ebi*.

INTERROGATING *ASO EBI*'S ONENESS

Aso ebi symbolizes togetherness and a sense of solidarity (Moloye 2004, 18). Among most categories of clothing, uniforms embody less ambiguous meanings and most conspicuously reflect an avenue through which the most powerful individuals impose their will. One of the most distinctive features of uniform is its ability to distinguish between "them" and "us." The functions of uniforms are also contradictory. In certain quarters, such as schools, in the nursing profession, and in many other institutions, "uniforms simultaneously enforce uniformity and demonstrate difference" (R. Ross 2008, 108). Beyond the reference to institutional aspects of the use of uniforms to enforce difference, it is possible to see how such paradigms have also manifested in the social use of *aso ebi* uniforms to enforce difference among friends in Nigeria.

In their endless pursuit of solidarity, *aso ebi* wearers constantly enthrone differences. Friendship transactions among particular groups of friends entail enforced conformity in dressing and behavior during social events in Nigeria. This has ruptured relationships that ordinarily would have been kept intact without *aso ebi* uniforms. In her study of the Mande people of Sierra Leone, Mariane Ferme (2001) explores the aesthetics of power through *aso ebi* dress. Although, according to Ferme, the "visual impact of the *ashobis* at large gatherings is striking," (169) it cannot resolve the notions of difference that inhere in *aso ebi* uniformity. In Lagos, for example, such differences are manifested in the design stylistics of individual dresses. Sophistication in "designs of clothes and quality of textile materials used for each *aso ebi* distinguishes women whose clothes were sewn by professional tailors from those whose clothes were sewn by amateurs" (O. Nwafor 2011, 15; Ogunyemi 1996, 10). Ferme also identifies such differences among the wealthy, who add expensive embroidery and extra layers of cloth to distinguish themselves "within the general colour uniformity of *aso ebi*," (169) and from others who cannot afford a whole outfit and who add only matching tops and head coverings. Apart from this type of difference, which is scripted on individual dresses, other forms of differences extend to broader human relations, which I address below.

Before 1930, *aso ebi* had started attracting what appears to be the first wave of condemnation from well-meaning Yoruba people. This condemnation became so ubiquitous that the church management in Lagos convened a Christian interdenominational committee in 1930 on the issue of *aso ebi*. The committee, which met at the Lagos CMS Girls Seminary in Lagos, was spread across the Methodist, Catholic, Baptist, and Anglican missions. According to Marion Johnson, one of the Anglican delegates to the committee:

> The committee after their deliberations agreed that the craze for aṣọ *ebì* in many homes was on the increase; that many married women unreasonably participate in aṣọ *ebì* thereby worsening the financial crisis of their various families. The women also destabilize the peace of their families by constantly extorting clothing allowances from their husbands[,] who barely manage to

feed the family. Some of them also got aṣọ ebi on credit from the celebrant[,] who usually distributed the cloth to well-wishers expecting their husbands to pay eventually. (Cited in Akinwumi 1990, 175)[3]

The committee's unilateral resolve was that aso ebi was a threat to the unity of the church and families. Incessant aso ebi debts stretched the husbands beyond their financial reach, as their wives participated in an average of four aso ebi events per month and incurred corresponding bills. The findings also observed a contributing factor to this vice: the cloth merchants who gave out aso ebi textile materials on credit to women, thereby increasing the cycle of indebtedness. The findings indicated that the church would not be held responsible for this mad rush for aso ebi and recommended that while the aso ebi tradition should not be banned, they advised practitioners to demonstrate moderation. Moderation in all aspects of the Christians' life, including aso ebi, seemed to form the core of the churches' subsequent sermons.

In early twentieth-century Lagos, the pace at which aso ebi provoked urban fashion sensibilities, especially among women, was also the same pace with which it generated household crises. Aso ebi became a sort of social menace in urban Lagos in that girls began to demand it as part of their engagement presents, thus instigating the colonial government and the Ijebu to ban it in 1940.[4] In 1946, many young women deceived young men into purchasing expensive dresses for their engagement and eventually disappointed the young men and left them in debt.[5] Some further criticisms of aso ebi appeared in the 1940s newspapers where, for example, one critic alleged that the church encouraged aso ebi patronage during its harvest and bazaars and that the children who attended the church mission schools were compelled to pay for festival cloth levies. This critic argued that as long as aso ebi was associated with Christian religious worship, the solution would lie with the church.

In the *Nigerian Outlook* of June 13, 1960, Jude Reke remarked that aso ebi was threatening to tear the unity of families apart. A similar sentiment was echoed in the *New Nigeria* newspaper of December 28, 1975, which read, "Aso ebi has never been a good aspect of our culture. Instead of the unity it was supposed to foster it separates families because husbands and wives battle over aso ebi money. I know extended families who have become enemies because one did not provide the other with aso ebi during an important ceremony" (Uwem 1975).

The same opinion of division did not stop at the family level but extended among friends who disliked the manner in which aso ebi was becoming an object of discord among them. For example, Edith Thomas told how her companionship with her best friend broke up because she could not afford to pay for her friend's *aso ebi* during the friend's wedding in 1999. "It is not just about friendship," Thomas remarked. "It is about making money and claiming to be the best *aso ebi* in town. I can tell you that you can only know your true friends when it comes to *aso ebi*. If you tell your friend you don't have money to buy her *aso ebi* you can become her permanent enemy. And you must buy it at her inflated price" (E. Thomas 2010). Some of these statements are earlier forms of opposition that were beginning to reshape the spaces of sociality around *aso ebi*. They set the precedents for articulating subsequent forms of discord that would threaten *aso ebi's* aspiration toward oneness.

From the 1960s it was obvious that *aso ebi* was already becoming a fabric textured by complex and controversial social relationships. It is no surprise, therefore, that in expressing present-day solidarity in *aso ebi*, friends and family members sometimes show conflicting interests and strong emotional reactions that may result in enmity. During Kemi's wedding, some individuals were denied food: "I was not served food here by the waitress because I did not dress in *aso ebi*," said Bisi, one of the recruited friends. "Other people around me were eating and drinking, but I was left without any food except a bottle of malt, so when I demanded the reason, one of the guests behind me said it's because I did not wear the *aso ebi*. . . . I was also not offered any gift. The gift sharers ignored me. It is unfortunate that *aso ebi* is becoming a big issue in Lagos weddings these days" (Olukoya 2011). In some social events the cost of *aso ebi* determines the kind of gift one receives such that, for example, "a fifteen-thousand-naira lace begets a gift of rechargeable lamp while five-thousand-naira fabric attracts a thermal cup or laundry basket, and higher priced *aso ebi* may even fetch one an iPod, depending on the amount of wealth on display" ("*Aso ebi* Wahala" 2011, 20). Antonia Nweke and her friend Bunmi Oke were expected to join a colleague of theirs for Nweke's father's seventieth-birthday celebration. Both Nweke and Oke and their colleague work at a shipping company in Lagos. The birthday party was in the Ilupeju area of Lagos. Meanwhile they had no idea of an initial plan by their colleague's family to sell *aso ebi* to any interested guest. This is because their colleague did not inform them of any such plans. The occasion, according to Nweke:

> was like a carnival, and almost all the guests were dressed in one color of aṣọ ebì or the other except us. Our friend was busy inside the inner room and we could not see her. We discovered that the people sharing the food never

wanted to come to our table. As one of them carrying some plates of food and drinks came across our table, I called him but he ignored me. Another guy came and when I asked him to give us food, he said that all food has finished and that the only thing remaining is Coke. In fact he gave us the Coke. But, lo and behold, we saw some other waiters carrying food and passing us. I think they instructed them not to give food to those not dressed in any of the *aso ebi*. The waiters had clearly been instructed not to serve us. Some women on a table beside us didn't find this funny and were raising their voices at the waiters, saying loudly in Yoruba, "What kind of party is this?" (A. Nweke 2011)

This means that the exclusionary narratives of *aso ebi* are not about boycotting friends or family members per se, but those (whether friends or not) who do not adorn themselves in *aso ebi* uniform. This concept offers one a space to see uniforms as a disciplinary construct that admits, permits, and allows one to develop a sense of security and confidence among a group. This is not applicable only to *aso ebi* but uniforms in a wider sense as well: military uniforms, a security organization's uniform, police uniforms, and others.

We can understand such expressions of solidarity "as a set of shared expectations that constitute a context of meaning central to a group's self-understanding" (Dean 1996, 15). If one may question further why Bisi was excluded from gift recipients, then it may be helpful to understand the implications of *aso ebi* as a system of mutual obligation such that one who buys *aso ebi* from a friend or relative hopes to be reciprocated by the same gesture of buying in one's future event. This mutual dialogue seems to sustain the cycle of the transaction and is often heightened by fear of isolation. In Bisi's case, she violated the mutual obligation of not appearing in *aso ebi*. We could justify this, however, by suggesting that Bisi was a stranger and thus did not require reciprocation, yet it endorses the fact of uniform that is restrictive of outsiders. The rewards and punishments are clearly spelled out in *aso ebi* in the form of remuneration and denial, respectively.[6] They further reinforce my analysis of *aso ebi* as exclusionary rather than inclusionary. They link *aso ebi* to more intangible and amorphous—but equally powerful—anxieties about attending social events in Lagos as a persona non grata. The above example illustrates a profound disjuncture separating the perceptions and realities of *aso ebi* practice, largely articulated as an abiding sense of ostracism, unfriendliness, and division. Ultimately, Lagosians are unable to reconcile the experiences of *aso ebi* costs with competing and shifting notions of friendship and solidarity.

Wedding gifts have also been used, according to Bisi, to enforce difference. Underlying this attitude is the fact that solidarity operates within a
notion of membership that is both exclusionary and repressive. It shows that
solidarity is an "exclusionary norm." *Aso ebi* solidarity seeks to shore up the
unity of the group in advance through buying the dress from the host days
before the event, sewing it, and dressing in it for the actual event. Whoever
lays their hands on the dress before that day, and by whatever means, receives
the gift on the day of the event.

In exposing such contradictory power of uniformed solidarity, "uniforms
are also open to appropriation and modification by outsiders who manage to
lay their hands on them" (Nathan 1986, 74). This system forbids any attempt
to challenge problematic aspects of uniformity in *aso ebi* solidarity on the
day of the event. This is because there is a common assumption that it is only
close family members and close friends who are allowed to have access to
the *aso ebi* uniform of a celebrant. But as will be shown in subsequent discussions, this is not always the case. In certain instances, such types of close
relationships did not exist and were flexible and porous. Some *aso ebi* relationships were indirectly forceful and revealed lines of alienation and exclusion in friendship. The way the materiality of a fabric is assimilated into local
understanding of friendships suggests how the human body is constituted as
a space of contested meanings. The covering of the human body with *aso ebi*
uniforms indicates emerging forms of social relations in which individuals
sacrifice their differences by conforming to the rules of uniformity, which are
sometimes coercive and totalizing.

However, it must be noted that within the imposed solidarity of uniforms,
there are divergent twists to the plot. Much is hidden under the façade of
uniformity: foes masquerade as friends and vice versa. The difference that
inheres in *aso ebi* uniformity lies in the fact that uniforms may not change
the character of an individual; rather such uniformity can only serve to level
everyone under the rhetoric of solidarity. Difference (and status) are the con-
notative languages spoken through most uniforms, including military uniforms, which ordinarily do not offer any uniformity within their insignia of
ranks. Timothy Parsons (2006) has suggested that while a member of a uniformed group cannot pursue a personal or political view by altering an established uniformed code, individual variations still exists within the assumed
fixed code. What can be inferred from Parsons's observation is that within
the terminology of uniformity, class differentiations are enacted through

individual styles. In *aso ebi* the establishment of social class often manifests in the real ceremony, where women and men display their styles of *aso ebi* dress. Within such perceptions of uniformity among *aso ebi* groups, aṣọ ọ̀kẹ̀ is sometimes used to mark status (Lawuyi 1991). Such practices unveil the ambivalence of oneness, especially when the space of the ceremony is used to distinguish the "elite" from the poor "through viewing some lace materials as rich while some are seen as poor" (259).

Considered in this light, there is always a show of symbolic solidarity that also speaks of dominance and hostility among social ranks during the ceremony. There could be no "oneness" in individuals' manner of social stratification, in which, for example, the distribution of food served at an event is deployed to demarcate high-status individuals from those of the rank and file. It is therefore not surprising that women walk the nooks and crannies of the city searching for an adept who could invent a unique design. Metaphorically, one can liken communal solidarity to the colors of *aso ebi* dress, which are usually matching, and then liken disagreements in *aso ebi* practice to individual designs, which usually differ (Ogunyemi 1996, 10).

The protestation of Kemi's friends who refused to adorn themselves in *aso ebi* produced an inverse reading of *aso ebi*, a reading whereby friends were denied both food and wedding gifts because they refused to adorn *aso ebi*, and enemies who did dress in *aso ebi* may have received food and wedding gifts. In other words, this example shows that subversion is embodied in *aso ebi* uniformity itself. It also suggests that uniforms transform foes into friends and friends into foes. It has become evident that *aso ebi* is a mechanism used to transform potentially distant relations into imagined friendliness. It shows that *aso ebi* solidarity is based on thin, ephemeral robes rather than thick, resilient bonds.

In Yoruba, hometown associations' notions of "love" and "friendship" are evoked as a way of showing people's affinity. Lillian Trager notes that "an Ilesa chief, A. O. Lamikanra, once stated in an interview that 'we love ourselves abroad more than we do at home'" (2001, 3).[7] Studies in several African countries and among a variety of ethnic groups have emphasized the importance of social networks among families and kin, spanning multiple locales; they also note the reliance on such networks both for those at home and those who migrate.[8] Although links to family and kin networks play an important role in the migration process in some parts of the world, connections to the home community as a community could be much more important in West Africa than elsewhere. What may be necessary to identify here is how some of these social connections deploy notions of oneness that may be rhetorical and have far-reaching objectives in the ways they invoke *aso ebi*.

INTERROGATING *ASO EBI*'S FRIENDSHIP

A report in the *Lagos Standard* of February 24, 1915, lamented the increasing cost of *aso ebi* in Lagos weddings. The report stated how parents of the bride invite the female friends of their daughter to buy *aso ebi* from them at a cheap price and how what it described as "marking up" increased the price of the *aso ebi* from its initial five shillings to thirty shillings.[9] The writer dismissed *aso ebi* as a material of "a light and flimsy nature, and chosen more with reference to gay colouring, so that the dress, as a rule, is only fit to be worn on that single occasion, and is quite unsuitable for ordinary wear." The writer further worried over the introduction of *iborun* (a piece that covers the shoulder) and a silk handkerchief that "swelled the already considerable expense of the *aso ebi*" (4). This report is an indication that during the first decade of the twentieth century, *aso ebi*'s contestations were framed in terms of monetary disagreements.

The above example constructs a picture of an affair that was gradually transforming into an illicit pecuniary transaction as early as the second decade of the twentieth century. This transformation, quite modest in this period, is quite brazen in recent times, as *aso ebi* is sold to strangers for monetary gains: "strangers who have nothing in common with the celebrant wear the same *aso ebi* uniform to weddings" (A. Okoye 2009). Shifts of meanings that redefine solidarity in *aso ebi* are seen through differences occasioned by fluid constructions of friendship in present-day social networks in Nigeria.[10]

One of the main reasons why individuals detest *aso ebi* is because many cannot afford the exorbitant prices their friends tag on it. In the beginning of this chapter, Juliet and Omo declined Kemi's *aso ebi* because of economic reasons. While some people have other reasons why they do not like uniforms, it seems that most complaints are linked to the high price tag.

The question that may arise here borders on how such categories as "friends" and "family members" are construed in the present context of *aso ebi* practice. The puzzle of *aso ebi* friendship lies in the fact that Kemi invited remote friends of her own friends to buy *aso ebi*, and Mary confessed she does not know Kemi, yet she bought and participated in her *aso ebi* through Kemi's friends. While this takes the discussion of the dialectics of friendship into a wider perspective, it begs a critical inquiry into how, and why, friendship is constituted in the *aso ebi* practice. That *aso ebi* is premised on individuals' belief in the institution of friendship begs a critical interrogation of the concepts of friendship in academic scholarship. As an interstitial institution,[11] friendship offers new avenues through which to explore the nature of companionship in *aso ebi* practice.

In modern Western scholarship, Michel de Montaigne is regarded as one of the earliest and most influential proponents of an ideal position on friendship. In his essay "Of Friendship" (1972) he regards emotional attachment as an essential constituent of friendship. His emphasis on "real" friendship, however, is drawn from particularities expected of friendship from Euro-American societies. Nevertheless, an exploration of such friendship features might provide a prefatory footing and an overview of initial formulations of concepts of friendship in academic scholarship. While it may not relate directly to my case, it could still offer an insight into my further interrogation of various models of friendship construction in *aso ebi*.

According to Montaigne, friendships are informed by a sense of volition and choice, they are optional and altruistic, with a private rather than social motivation. They are also characterized by a certain form of affinity and unpretentiousness quite uncommon in other relationships. Most importantly, they are realized among persons inspired by a similar spirit of equality. Measured against the *aso ebi* limitations discussed above, Montaigne's relationships would be somewhat flawed. Mary was not a close friend of Kemi, yet she received an invitation like every other close friend to wear *aso ebi*. This attitude removes friendship from Montaigne's view as a "personal affair" to a social affair. In *aso ebi*, Montaigne's theory is defeated by Mary's concerns about her remote relationship with Kemi yet being obliged to support her *aso ebi* through Kemi's own friend (Obiekwe 2010). Again, in *aso ebi* friendship at times is not voluntary as proposed by Montaigne. Friendship could be subtly coercive, and a lot of societal impositions remove the trait of voluntariness from *aso ebi* friendship. However, Mary suggests that "*aso ebi*, should be a voluntary thing." This type of oblique imposition of friendship that pertains to the present-day practice of *aso ebi* might have been an import from similar occurrences among earlier age-grade organizations in Yoruba society.

ASO EBI FRIENDSHIP AND THE "LOGIC OF GIFT"

In chapter 1, where I traced the antecedents of friendship associations that use *aso ebi*, there was no mention of gifts in any of the uniformed groups discussed. In other words, gifts are possibly a recent manifestation among *aso ebi* wearers. There is still a need for deeper historical inquiry regarding when gift giving was introduced in *aso ebi* practice. In recent times, gifts are offered as a form of compensation to those who buy *aso ebi* from the celebrants. Most often, during the event, the sharers of such gifts are instructed not to offer gifts to anyone not dressed in *aso ebi*, especially when the gifts are counted (Dike 2010). Such gifts usually range from little household objects, such as metal plates, cups, and plastic bowls, to expensive items such as wristwatches, umbrellas, trinkets, and phones. However, it is always assumed that only rich people can afford expensive gifts, especially when their *aso ebi* is very expensive.

It therefore logically translates that the cost of *aso ebi* either parallels the costs of the gift or contributes to the buying of the gifts. This comes with an increasing public criticism that the gifts are mere trivialities compared to the cost of the *aso ebi*. The cost of the *aso ebi* fabric determines the brand of gifts or souvenirs one receives. A gift hierarchy can range from fifteen thousand naira worth of *aso ebi* lace material that begets a rechargeable lamp; a five thousand naira *aso ebi* fabric attracting a gift of a thermal cup or laundry basket; while a three thousand naira *aso ebi ankara* may get one a branded pen and a handkerchief decorated with the faces of the bride and groom (Udobang 2011). However, a very expensive *aso ebi* could even attract "electric kettles and even iPods, depending on the amount of wealth on display" (Udobang 2011). From this gift hierarchy, it is evident that each *aso ebi* guest receives a gift commensurate with the price of the material they purchase. In this vein, it is assumed that *ankara*, which in one case received the least valued item of a pen and a handkerchief, remains the lowest priced.

When I visited Theodora Dike at her residence in the Ojuelegba area of Lagos, she showed me numerous gifts that she had accumulated from the many *aso ebi* events in which she participated. Theodora, a tailor, who has also been active in the *aso ebi* fashion business, has sewn a lot of *aso ebi* for numerous clients, through which she has built her own network of friends. She said it is difficult for her to recount how many *aso ebi* she has participated in. She took me into her kitchen, where she showed me different kinds of gifts she received while participating in *aso ebi* and which, according to her, now constitute her kitchen and household utensils (fig. 11). However, Theodora told me that one of the expensive gifts she received was an electric pressing iron (fig. 12). The iron gift was distributed only to friends who bought the particular *aso ebi* that was shown in her photo in figure 13. Theodora remarked

Figure 11. Theodora Dike's *aso ebi* gift items. Lagos, December 6, 2010. Photo: Okechukwu Nwafor.

that the photo was taken at a wedding of one of her friends whose husband is rich. She had the opportunity to appear in one of the soft-sell fashion magazines because her friend's husband invited the members of *Today's Fashion Magazine*, who photographed and interviewed her and some other people she happened to be among. She noted that the *aso ebi* was very expensive at N25,000 and could be afforded by about ten of them, who received the gift of a pressing iron. Others, who bought a cheaper *aso ebi*, were offered the gift of trays and plates (Dike 2010).

She explained her unbounded joy when she saw herself in *Today's Fashion Magazine* and felt like a celebrity (see fig. 13). The magazine gave her the opportunity to also speak about her fashion business. However, expensive gifts mark a rupture in the solidarity that *aso ebi* purports to uphold. Theodora's statement shows that the economy that underlies the *aso ebi* gift is a complex one such that a transaction would have taken place before the day of the event. On the day of the event, the idea of the "gift" manifests itself only as the outcome of a behind-the-scene transaction.

"Gift" as a word does not offer any semantic ambiguity when read from its simple dictionary definition as "something given voluntarily without pay-

Figure 12. Theodora Dike with her iron gift item. Lagos, December 6, 2010. Photo: Oke-chukwu Nwafor.

ment in return." Even within its nuanced exegesis, one does not discover any situation where this meaning has been supplanted with a contrary view. It is against this apparent straightforwardness that I interrogate the notion of the gift as offered in *aso ebi* transactions.

There is a growing feeling among Nigerians that *aso ebi* is gradually dissolving into a system of reciprocal transaction between the guests and the hosts with gifts and *aso ebi* as two contingent fragments of such transactions. While the guest bought *aso ebi* from the host, the host compensated the guest with a gift in return. However, such correspondence has been attacked by some critics who believe that the gains are weighted toward the hosts who sell the *aso ebi* at a higher price and use part of the proceeds to purchase cheap gifts. The hosts have been criticized for offering gifts that are in no way commensurate with the price of the *aso ebi* bought by the guests. A counter-argument holds that the guests gain by adding to their wardrobe through the *aso ebi* while at the same time receiving a gift. It therefore follows that in this system, gifts are not offered as "gifts" but as a form of recoupment for those who bought *aso ebi*.

THEODORA DIKE...

Theodora Dike is a young designer whose profile has been on the rise lately. She was one of the most sought after fashion models a couple of years back. She was then the master of lighting the runway with her catwalk which was skillful. After getting to the peak of her modeling career, she decided to re-invent herself and moved into fashion which was what led to the launch of her fashion label 2 years ago. And since she came one board, her new career has been soaring high. Her fashion label coined from her name, *"Theodora"* has a unique perspective. She creates fabulous one-of-a kind works of art that reflects a sense of style that is youthful, with a hint of classical, rock and glamour. Recently she unveiled her new *Ankara* designs with a theme called *"Ankara Fever"*. She created looks that were powerful and feminine using typical African prints that range from *Ghana* prints to *Woodin*, *Akosombo*, aso *Oke*, *George* e.t.c, which were combined with lace and organza. What inspired her designs were the materials, their color, texture and pattern. Her designs are characterized by simple feminine layered cuts with delicate textured fabrics in vibrant colors. It's contemporary for every *African* woman for all age.

- Bola Akinboade

Figure 13. Theodora Dike, *Today's Fashion Magazine*, April 2005. Photo: Okechukwu Nwa-for.

Perhaps in the everyday language use of such words as gifts one may need to invent a new term for such transactions. In most events in Nigeria, celebrants believe they exhibit forms of altruism by extending a gift gesture to people who buy and wear *aso ebi*, but on the other hand, the denial of gifts to those who do not purchase *aso ebi* may have found empirical validation in the statement that "reciprocity in itself is a principle of exclusion" (Douglas and Isherwood 1979, 152). The underlying contradiction here, therefore, is that the quest for gift giving seems to destabilize the notion of unity for which *aso ebi* friendship yearns. The gift as offered in *aso ebi* transcends its purported gesture of generosity, perhaps in line with Marcel Mauss's own contention that "although gifts are fundamental to friendship connections, they are informed by a sense of obligation and economic self-interests" (1990, 1, 73). In this theoretical invocation of the "logic of gift," I can argue that expectations of a return (conscious or unconscious) underlie every *aso ebi* gift.

In most events in Nigeria, celebrants believe they are rationally extending a gesture of friendship to people to wear their *aso ebi*. However, at the same time, and according to popular criticism, their choices are often guided by inclinations toward enrichment. It means that social life is structured along an essential logic of "give-and-take." The gift betrays multiple threads that weave social fabric together. It becomes a "total social fact" that, in the case of *aso ebi*, challenges individual and collective conceptions of familial brotherhood. While it is established that gifts essentially contribute to solidarity, it is also recorded that increased familiarity heightens expectations of reciprocity.[12] In fact, in reality, gifts conform to a basic moral dictum that is premised on repayment. Mauss refutes any established practicality in voluntary gift exchanges; rather he argues that just as (pure) gifts are not freely given, they are also not really disinterested and mainly represent total counter-services that aim at repayment and profitable alliance, one that cannot be rejected. "It is one that is both mystical and practical, one that ties clans together" (1954, 73).

Mauss was influenced by Bronislaw Malinowski, whose own research reveals the rule of "give-and-take" or reciprocity as the bedrock of social order in the Melanesian societies he researched. This encouraged Mauss to establish the foundational framework of traditional ceremonial gift exchanges.[13] Mauss's gift economy has opened a lot of debates around the actual motives of friendship, especially the idea that in many societies friendships are socially constructed and cannot be revoked without severe social or ritual penalty (Cohen 1961). The above remarks are very striking in that what is obtainable is *aso ebi*, which, following Mauss, is "socially constructed" and comes with severe penalties in the form of social exclusion, as could be seen from the *aso ebi* transactions where some friends were denied gifts and food.

In *aso ebi* practice, friendship is not detached from social, economic, and political incentives, contrary to a particular paradigm espoused by nineteenth-century European romantics that has, to some extent, persisted in some industrial and postindustrial societies. Anthropologists maintain that inasmuch as homologies of friendship exist in nearly all human societies, archetypes of friendship differ significantly, thus posing a challenge to any proposition of a marked, all-embracing definition of friendship with a capital *F* (Bell and Coleman 1999, 4). Anthropologists have also warned that Western presumptions of affections, seclusions, and emotional attachments should not be taken as a universal benchmark to measure friendship.[14]

Often seen as a product of modernity, friendship in Euro-American societies has been the object of important historical and sociological works.[15] In contrast, there is a paucity of major studies on the subject of friendship in postcolonial societies where kinship is made to encompass the entire field of sociality. Here friendship appears as a subsidiary relation. Some authors argue that friendship would barely thrive in societies that are still inhabited by strong kinship networks.[16]

Two models of friendship traits have been defined by both Yahudi Cohen and Eric Wolf as inalienable and instrumental friendships, respectively. The difference between these two authors' theories lies in the social contexts in which these models of friendship thrive. According to Cohen, inalienable friendships tend to manifest in closed societies, mainly collective lineal groups, where deeply organized kin groups, physical closeness, and domestic life engender notions of strong social togetherness (1961, 354, 314). In contrast, according to Wolf, instrumental friendships flourish in open communities, where people can mobilize ties of both kinship and friendship to widen their spheres of social relations (1977, 174).

Even though multifarious friendship models exist, friendship may be determined by erratic social structures and circumstances. It is regrettable that many authors have neglected what Gerald Suttles describes as the "situational elements of friendship" (1970, 100). Undoubtedly, greater philosophical and sociological approaches have often accepted friendship as a given, especially when they juxtapose the dynamics of friendship with other social relationships.[17] Their descriptive analyses of models of friendship in many societies suggest likely emotive and expedient obligations expected of friendships, but they ignore the social situations that have informed particular forms of friendship.

In the postcolonial context, especially Africa, formations of friendship networks in the city have not been adequately explored by authors because, as I mentioned earlier, kinship relations are still thought of as the underlying bedrock of affinities in Africa. Cities in Africa have not yet been thought of as reconstituting a change in African kinship systems. In *aso ebi*, forms of friendship are established beyond the boundaries of one's own family and immediate friendship groups and even beyond the boundaries of visible human sociality. There emerges a context informed by social situations of "imitations." It is this imitation that engenders constructed friendships with their peculiar characteristic of importance attached to bodily markers of uniform rather than any tangible essence of friendship.

Aso ebi models of friendship unveil a stasis between free will and obligation, individuality and generalization, altruism and malevolence, and responsiveness and aloofness. *Aso ebi* friendship seems akin to "instrumental" friendships (Wolf 1977, 172). In this manner they are generally entered into as a system of fluid constructions, sometimes as eminently social relations, often governed by artificial sanctions. They are not totally altruistic but they fulfill unrealistic societal objectives: acquisition of dress materials, fake solidarity, and competitive show-off. Despite their instrumental character, however, uniformed solidarity continues to be an important ingredient in the relation, so much so that if this trait is absent, it must be contrived lest a celebration is thought less important.

In Nigeria it has become evident that *aso ebi* does not constitute a fixed, universal relationship but "takes its shape and form from the specific context in which it develops" (Spencer and Pahl 2006, 40).[18] Under the present context it is assumed that *aso ebi* could have produced a different kind of friendship that is informed by economic reasons whereby some celebrants actually intend to raise money through conscription of nonexistent friends. *Aso ebi* has proved that the terms "family" and "friends" do not have shared or stable meanings and that any explorations of contemporary social life must take into account the basis of different kinds of solidarity rather than simply rely on categorical labels.

ASO EBI: THE RHETORIC OF POLITICAL SOLIDARITY

On October 19, 2010, a crisis erupted between the supporters of Alhaji Olasunkanmi Salami; the chairman of the Oluyole Local Government Area of Oyo

State, Nigeria; and a few members of the People's Democratic Party (PDP) in the Local Government Area. The trouble started at the motor park when supporters of the PDP, of which the chairman is also a member, gathered at the motor park for a trip to Abuja to visit the president. Attempting to enter the bus procured for the trip, a few members were denied entry for not wearing the *aso ebi* uniform prescribed for the trip. Those denied entry into the bus accused the chairman of giving the cloth only to those within his camp, ostensibly to deny them access to the Abuja trip. Ademola Babalola reports the incident further: "According to a reliable source, all the party supporters were said to have been directed to wear the *ankara aso ebi* uniform as the ticket for the trip, but many suspected to be opposed to Salami's leadership style were allegedly denied the attire" (2010, 6). Some of the people who were denied the *aso ebi* were not only refused entry into the bus, but they were also beaten up at the motor park by thugs believed to be loyal to the president and who believed that those who were not wearing the *aso ebi* uniform were working against the interest of the president's reelection ambition.

The above scenario aptly captures the nature of politics that has invaded *aso ebi*'s solidarity. The activities of the politicians could be the point at which *aso ebi* is most susceptible to misuse. The politicization of *aso ebi* indicates the manner in which Nigeria's corrupt politicians appropriate the essential assumption of brotherly pledge to bastardize the culture of *aso ebi* by transforming it into one of the items used to win support in the context of Nigeria's perverted political culture (Adesanmi 2011).

In another similar event, a meeting convened by the Nobel laureate Professor Wole Soyinka to resolve the lingering crisis between the governor of Ogun State, Otunba Gbenga Daniel, and the former president of Nigeria, Olusegun Obasanjo, witnessed a situation where *aso ebi*'s purported solidarity was only a hoax and a political tool. The supporters of the governor had hired a group of women and students and dressed them in *aso ebi* for the sole purpose of disrupting the meeting. This is because they had perceived the conveners of the meeting as anti-governor elements. The women were purportedly lured into this situation with a promise of a handsome reward in cash. The *aso ebi* was therefore bought and sewn many days before the meeting and kept while attempts were being made to gather a considerable number of women to wear it. When a good number of women were gathered, they were given the *aso ebi* with specific instructions to disrupt the meeting (Adesola 2011).

The meeting, which took place at the Henry Townsend Hall of St. Peter's

Cathedral, Ake, Abeokuta, Ogun State, on December 18, 2010, was well attended by important personalities in Nigeria. Debo Adesola reported that Soyinka attempted to berate all parties involved in the crisis of the state. However, when Soyinka turned attention to the governor's party, these groups of women and students in *aso ebi*, numbering more than two hundred, became unruly and rancorous. They were uncontrollable and caused chaos, which brought the event to an abrupt end.

To demonstrate the ambivalence of solidarity implicit in *aso ebi*, Adesola said that hours after the meeting, the women were seen a small distance from the venue in an unruly encounter with the governor's party. They held the governor's kingpin hostage for not paying them the exact amount promised to them for wearing *aso ebi*. The process was marred by a series of violent clashes that left a number of the women heavily battered.

This is a remarkable incident that serves to illustrate the nature of solidarity that attends *aso ebi* not just in the political arena but in other aspects of Nigerian existence as well. It suggests that there is an increasing trend of dressing in *aso ebi* to express political support. To outsiders, the women and students in *aso ebi* appeared as genuine supporters of the governor, while to the likes of Adesola, the *aso ebi* had become a necessary tool needed to woo support for a governor whose influence might have dwindled among the people. Again, the implication is that the crowd would not have made such a powerful impression if they had appeared in their ordinary different dresses. I am suggesting that there is an assumption that *aso ebi* has a driving force, an intimidating impact conveyed through its colorful uniformity, an imposing presence that frightens the opposition. It could have been these hidden qualities that have contributed to its growing deployment by political groups, and others, in Nigeria.

It seems that any group, be it political or social, that does not adopt *aso ebi* during its functions is seen as a deviation from the norm. To illustrate this, before the official commissioning of the newly constructed electricity project in the Olorunsogo Abule-eko area of Lagos State by the governor, some of the local inhabitants had engaged the local organizing committee in a dispute over their decision to sew *aso ebi* only for a limited number of individuals seen as their cohorts. Threatening to boycott and thwart the impending commissioning by the governor, these inhabitants chanted a slogan: *Ti o baa ni aso ebi, o gbodo wa*, meaning "No *aso ebi*, no attendance." The chairman of the Ikorodu local government went ahead and purchased *ankara* materials and made *aso ebi*, which he distributed to these people a few days before the arrival of the governor. It was observed that two sets of *aso ebi* uniforms were visibly present during the commissioning (Awusa 2011). Femi Awusa, a member of the organizing committee, said he never knew that *aso ebi* could become such a big issue in this event.

Observing this scenario, perhaps one can interrogate the *aso ebi* construction of solidarity in terms of Herbert Blumer's (1953) notions of social movements and their adoption of esprit de corps—feelings of devotion and enthusiasm for a group that are shared by its members. In Blumer's definition, esprit de corps might be conceived as the coordination of feelings on behalf of a group or movement. In itself, it is the understanding that people have of belonging together and of being recognized with one another in a mutual endeavor. In developing feelings of intimacy and closeness, people have the sense of sharing a common experience and of forming a select group.

Considering the above PDP scenario, I would argue that in the case of *aso ebi* this intimacy is only temporary and short-lived as long as the uniform is still worn on the bodies of members and at the venue of the event. In other words, it is assumed that there is a false sense of intimacy that inhabits members, one that is predicated upon a contingent need to expand fake friendship, albeit temporarily, for that occasion. Blumer, however, insists that esprit de corps creates the "in-group-out-group relation" to reinforce the new conception of collectivity that the individual has formed as a result of the movement and of his participation in it (1953, 205). One can as well, in line with Blumer, say that *aso ebi*'s esprit de corps creates the "in-group-out-group relation" as long as the "in-groups" have reached a compromise to don the uniform and not based on any other criterion. However, one can still argue that *aso ebi*'s esprit de corps is not totally constructed; rather there are constant and systematic re-modifications that make it difficult to grasp the "real" essence of comradeship professed by the friends.

That *aso ebi*'s gift economy and esprit de corps are not totally constructed might recall Claude Lévi-Strauss's criticisms of Mauss's "phenomenological" approach to gift giving. This approach makes a complete break with native experience and the native theory of that experience. It suggests that it is the exchange as a constructed object that "constitutes the primary phenomenon, and not the individual operations into which social life breaks down" (Lévi-Strauss, cited in Bourdieu 1977, 5). Pierre Bourdieu equally argues that "phenomenological" analysis and objectivist analysis bring to light two antagonistic principles of gift exchange: the gift as experience, or, meant to be experienced, and the gift as seen from outside. Bourdieu argues that the temporal structure of gift exchange, which objectivism ignores, ensures a deeper understanding of the truths that define the gift. Bourdieu's thesis attempts to distinguish between the act of gift giving, swapping, and lending. This he does by suggesting that the "operation of gift exchange presupposes (individual and collective) mis-recognition of the reality of the objective 'mechanism' of the exchange, a reality which an immediate response brutally exposes" (5).

Bourdieu's theory of misrecognition of the gift as symbolic capital might have argued against my *aso ebi* rules and techniques of regulating the social body. Bourdieu calls for urgent recognition of the fact that brutally materialist reduction is liable to make one forget the advantage that lies in abiding by the rules of gift. He goes on to argue that perfect conformity to the rules of gift brings both primary and secondary benefits. These include the prestige and respect that almost invariably reward an action that is apparently motivated by nothing other than pure, disinterested respect for the rule of gift. It seems that there is a disinterested respect for the rule of conformity in *aso ebi* played out through buying *aso ebi* and receiving a gift.

However, especially important are Blumer's notions on esprit de corps, morale, and ideology. They all emphasize not only that a friendship network is constituted of its structures or opportunities but also that the internal mechanisms are the clues that bind a group together. Such internal mechanisms can be recalled when esprit de corps is, for example, invoked in individuals dressed in military uniforms. In terms of *aso ebi* uniforms, sometimes there seems to be no prior internal mechanism binding friends together as some "friends" are being conscripted for the purpose of wearing the uniform for a particular event. Some friends do not like *aso ebi* as a form of solidarity but sometimes are compelled by fear of social exclusion to buy it and participate in it. To outsiders (those not wearing *aso ebi*), therefore, the esprit de corps seems to be visibly alive and existing in a "real" sense, but to insiders (those wearing *aso ebi*) it is only a fulfillment of a call to temporary social duty. Esprit de corps calls for the studies of how emotions are constituted in the friendship networks. Typical methods for researchers to do this, according to Fernando Santos-Granero (2007), should be in excursions, parties, cultural happenings, services, and emotional speeches.

David Snow and his colleagues identify two main attributes of solidarity embodied in esprit de corps: a corpus of associates that can be classified as a collectivity and a spirit that is enmeshed in feelings of identification with that group. They remark that solidarity requires the "identification of" and "identification with": the identification of a collective entity and a partici-pant's identification with a body of affiliated actors (2004, 80).

Placed alongside people's use of *aso ebi* as a form of solidarity, it shows that solidarity is perceived as "identification of" membership only through uniform and that the second concept of the individual's "identification with" the group through feelings of comradeship is not always manifest. According to Snow and his colleagues, this "identification with" relates to "an under-standing of solidarity as a collective consciousness which gives rise to social cohesion and depends upon an awareness of and identification with a collec-tivity" (2004, 80). Emile Durkheim refers to a collective consciousness—a set of "collective perceptions"—that precedes and transcends the individual and that drives humans to behave in certain ways (Durkheim, cited in Ver-hezen 2005). This definition seems to clarify the fact that by transcending the individual, a collective consciousness institutes regimented comportment, grants reciprocity, and enables individuals to relate in terms of shared mor-als and goals and not through matters around the physical body as seen in *aso ebi*. However, a related line of scholarship that favors *aso ebi* suggests that "because the physical body is the vehicle for experiencing reality, it is an essential component of personal and social identities" (Goffman 1963; Doug-las 1973).

Nevertheless, since collectivities do not literally have a distinct, homoge-nous, bodily form, collective identity depends upon the "identification of" a body associated with a group. For some groups the "identification of" a body of players requires projection of a figure of a concrete physical entity (Snow et al. 2004, 87). Military organizations, for example, convey such a notion by wearing uniforms and marching in formation as a homogenous mass. Other groups, such as social movements, use other methods to mark membership boundaries, relying on decals, T-shirts, bumper stickers, and other "tie signs" (Goffman 1963).

CONCLUSION

In foregrounding the creeping sense of egotism and/or commercialization that bedevil *aso ebi* practice, especially in the changing circumstances of the moral economy of intimacy, it is obvious that fabric embodies the concept of a "thing" bestowed with monetary value that is capable of disintegrating relationships. The popularity and contested meanings of *aso ebi* uniforms in Nigeria both confirm and qualify Phyllis Martin's powerful statement that "clothing matters and dress is political" (1995, 165). *Aso ebi* uniforms are tangible but malleable archives of social reality that enable their wearers to imagine, if not create, new identities and realities. They are indeed "social skins" that influence how members interact with themselves (T. Turner 1993). Solidarity and oneness are slogans that people who wear *aso ebi* usually hold at the back of their minds. This chapter might have suggested that solidarity and oneness may be something close to a utopia if seen in the manner in which they are deployed by groups who wear *aso ebi*. Again the meanings of friendship are also questioned, and it could be understood at least that *aso ebi* friendship is constructed flexibly on the shallow surfaces of uniformed dresses. This suggests, in line with Jennifer Craik, that "the enforcement of appropriate rules and manner of conduct codified in uniforms is more important than the elements of uniforms themselves" (2005, 7). In *aso ebi*, outside this construction, friendship is presented as something that is exclusionary.

This chapter suggests that gifts as they are offered in *aso ebi* are also mute gestures of reciprocal transactions. Gifts and *aso ebi* are two aspects of an inevitable responsibility that confronts particular individuals who plan for social events in Nigeria. The one goes with the other such that any failure to adorn oneself in *aso ebi* attracts no gifts. Both recognize the significance of processes of fetishization that mask the reality of *aso ebi* as both a thing and a process that comprises explicit social relations. This chapter has suggested that commodification has become the bane of late capitalist sociality, and it seems *aso ebi* has given in to this form of existence. It suggests that life could be a commodity traded on a shallow surface of material adornment. Perhaps this idea might, in a remote sense, remind us of what the French philosopher Henri Lefebvre calls "a false world" (1991, 35) in his nihilistic articulation of the effects of capitalism's visuality upon humankind. If this "false world" is worth interrogating, then this chapter has posed a critical question. Here, the body is presented as a political entity upon which varying signs of sartorial contests are played out through the phenomenon of *aso ebi*.

CHAPTER 5

Framing the Mutual Life of
Aso Ebi *in Lagos*

Copies, Copying, and Fashion Magazines

By the 1980s, *aso ebi* was at the center of a web of relations driving the beauty economy in the city of Lagos. From what were known as "fashion magazines" to tailors, from *aso ebi* fashion websites to popular photographers and individual *aso ebi* performers, a network of consumerism was created to feed fashion thereby rendering the city of Lagos visible. Most Lagosians had meticulously studied the prerequisite for visibility and successful assimilation into the fashion cultures, and the declining economy, of the postcolonial city. Perhaps in formulating plans for economic survival in the city, Lagosians simultaneously devoted time to improvising means of social survival. *Aso ebi* became crucial to understanding the city's sartorial culture through what was known as the *Owambe* party. As an important site of *aso ebi* performativity, the *Owambe* party became a critical terrain for negotiating elegance, social belonging, material, and symbolic power. In addition to the emergence of cheaper and faster methods of printing, this *aso ebi* gave birth to fashion magazines in Lagos.

In the light of the above, I argue in this chapter that through *Owambe* parties, *aso ebi* came to exist as a condition of Lagos cosmopolitanism. In other words, to become a cosmopolite one must ultimately indulge in endless *Owambe* parties where different *aso ebi* styles are exhibited. Within this system a reciprocal transaction exists among the photographers, the fashion magazines, individuals, vendors, and tailors in urban Lagos. The bigger network entails the introduction of more cosmopolitan elements into *aso ebi*, thus foreshadowing a broader sociocultural turn toward "modern" fashionability. Finally, while the language of *aso ebi*, both in its socializing message and its dress codes, is framed around notions of uniformity, the practice of *copying* enables individuals to transcend the burdens imposed by *aso ebi* uniformity.

ASO EBI AS A CONDITION OF LAGOS COSMOPOLITANISM

Many authors have acknowledged the historical and geographic contexts that give rise to certain types of cosmopolitanism.[1] These contexts are underlined by a common verdict that "no single conceptualisation is adequate" in understanding cosmopolitanism (Vertovec and Cohen 2002, 3). I recognize these numerous texts, and while I do not wish to engage them individually, I acknowledge the multiplicity of ways in which it is possible to speak to difference.[2] Through this I chart a specific description of what I call *Lagos cosmopolitanism*. While there is nothing new about cosmopolitanism in Africa,[3] in Lagos the conditions created by urbanization and visual and social transformation produced a new kind of cosmopolitanism that is evidently disseminated through the new technological capital as seen in the Nigerian home video industry known as Nollywood, and in cell phones, the internet, and print media, among other things. However, in the ensuing postcolonial urbanism witnessed in Lagos since the event of independence in 1960, sartorial elegance and the desire for visibility became forces of the modern city. By the 1980s neoliberal reforms had almost occasioned a need for status consolidation in the city of Lagos, a need that was coterminous with the quest for public visibility. This scenario was played out in what was known as *Owambe* parties.

The practice of *Owambe* parties, in addition to a combination of the above visual elements and the instabilities in the textile economy within the commercial city of Lagos, provided an unstable space for the material expressions of cultural ideals, individual excellence, and the collective tradition embodied in Lagos cosmopolitanism. *Aso ebi* is, however, an essential part of this cosmopolitanism. Cyprian Ekwensi, one of Nigeria's foremost novelists, notes the importance of *aso ebi* in this type of cosmopolitanism in Lagos. He suggests that women in Lagos are attracted by the "glitter of the fast life of the city and that most have been restricted too severely by the provincial mores of home." He narrates the desires of his fictional character Aina for Lagos thus:

It was a way of life she liked. The glamorous surroundings, the taxis, the quick drinks. This was one reason why she had come to the city from her home sixty miles away: to ride in taxis, eat in fashionable hotels, to wear the aso-ebi, that dress that was so often and so ruinously prescribed like a uniform for mourning. (1963, 72)

Ekwensi seems to capture *aso ebi* as part of the distinctive, and attractive, features of Lagos life. Again, it is assumed that Aina's desire for *aso ebi* could only be realized through her connection with the city of Lagos. What is interesting is how the quotidian practices of Lagos evoke spectacles of desires from the province and how *aso ebi* features prominently in these spectacles.

Owambe is a term associated with the ubiquitous revelries in Lagos. And these revelries are constantly invoked on every modest occasion such as "your first job, your first car, college graduations or your house opening" (David 2009). Reminiscing on her past experiences in Nigeria after fifty years of independence, Rukky Ladoja captures the spirit of *Owambe* thus:

The word is a Yoruba one that roughly translates as "always attending." These parties are predominantly defined by the large number of guests—ten of whom you'll know and seven hundred that came in off the street. Other key factors are the quantity and quality of the food, a musician or band, endless hours of dancing and mass uniformity of *aso ebi* fabric. (2010, 34)

Ladoja goes further to identify the circuit that revolves around *Owambe*, which includes the "exorbitant amount spent by partygoers on a weekly basis sewing new styles of *aso ebi* for every event they attend; the event planner; headgear specialists and party photographers." She aptly crafts the Nigerian photographers, "Nigerazzi," a term she borrowed from "paparazzi," and remarks that "they have created a niche market for themselves by making photos available for sale, mere moments after high-spirited shots are taken." Ladoja seems to have provided a succinct account of this section in her summary. Her last words, "uniformity of fabric," capture this concept. This supports my further argument that *Owambe* is synonymous with *aso ebi* and photography. From the number of guests Ladoja quotes (inclusive of seven hundred anonymous guests), one expects that the number of *aso ebi* wearers would have soared at every *Owambe* party. And these are the numbers that the photographers struggle to cover.

The increasing demand for this type of social gathering on the streets of

Lagos became more pronounced during the late 1980s when the then military government encouraged a culture of corruption and profligate spending. By the late 1980s, Nigeria had already slid down the economic ladder, and the standard of living had declined in such a way that many young people leaving school cared less about securing government jobs. Indeed, the minimum wage was so low that the civil service attracted minimal applications from university graduates and others. What happened instead was a propensity to be lured into criminality.

The massive corruption that was encouraged by the military government of Ibrahim Babangida occasioned a system of fraud known as *419* (named after a section of the Nigerian criminal code known as 419). Ill-gotten wealth was openly displayed on the streets of Lagos, which was notorious for such spending because of its location as the center of commerce. The embargo on the importation of cars was lifted and more "posh" cars found their way into Nigeria. Weekly celebrations of ill-gotten wealth by the cabals close to the corrupt military regime were carried out on the streets of Lagos. Most of the cabals were uneducated, and because of the stupendous amount of wealth they controlled, young people were discouraged from enrolling in schools; instead they were lured into the fraud of 419. The weekly *Owambe* party came with *aso ebi*, which, again, was another open space of generosity, since there was always a provision of free food for poor, uninvited guests. Bunmi Darling recollects the 1980s when her mother enjoyed *aso ebi* in typical Lagos *Owambe* parties where whole streets were disrupted throughout the night until dawn. She recollects that the streets and roads were sometimes blocked for two days at a stretch and provided an avenue for women to exhibit fashionable *aso ebi*. In recent times these street parties have been replaced by event halls (Darling 2011).

Apparently, in the *Owambe* party the realization of cultivated beauty, the erasure of any questionable demeanor, and the negotiation of symbolic power became indexes of public approbation. *Aso ebi*, no doubt, was at the heart of these struggles. What is surprising is the seriousness with which *Owambe* was pursued by Lagosians then and how it fed into the lawless system of the military era. This is where one needs to analytically extract some of the factors that contributed to the entrenchment and fashioning of *aso ebi* in urban Lagos. It is clear that *aso ebi* was not ensconced by the corrupt practice of the system; rather it was nurtured by the system.

Johnson Omoregbe remarks that under the leadership of Ibrahim Babangida, Lagos in the 1990s was a haven of the open display of ill-gotten wealth:

"Many fraudsters who were aided by some government officials sought public relevance through open parties known as *Owambe* organized on the streets of Lagos. During these periods most streets on the Lagos mainland were blockaded on weekends during *Owambe* parties" (Omoregbe 2010). The reason for this, according to Omoregbe, was that people wanted to show themselves—especially their *aso ebi* clothes, friends, and what they possessed—through these parties. Referring to his street on number 14 Akerele Street in Mushin, Lagos, Omorogbe recalls:

> This street was always blockaded during that period, and I had to park my car on the other street most Fridays because they usually blockaded ours around six pm every Friday till the next morning, and sometimes till Sunday. During this period, individuals take laws into their hands, and this attitude was encouraged by the military system, which had no regard for the rule of law. Even though it was wrong to block these public roads, you discover that these people were aided by the police, whom they bribed to look away.

What is significant from Omoregbe's description of Lagos in this period is a system that thwarted the normality and formalities of Western modernity and represents what Tejumola Olaniyan calls the "postcolonial incredible" (Olaniyan 2004; Adesokan 1996). Quite indicative of the lawlessness of the military era in Nigeria, "postcolonial incredible" admits the unimaginable, authorizes the disorderly, embraces the defiant, and thus engenders the crisis that would bedevil the postcolonial more generally. By 1999, however, Nigeria had become a democratic nation, and the democratic institutions in Lagos State aspired to a recuperation of infrastructural and social sanity that previously had eluded the city. In this regard, the Lagos state government prohibited the blockading of public roads for *Owambe* in 1999 during the administration of Bola Ahmed Tinubu. However, the full implementation of this law was not effective until 2007 when the incumbent governor, Raji Fashola (who incidentally is an attorney), took over (*Lagos State Ministry of Information Year Book* 1999). According to Shedrack Okoro, "By 2007, when Governor Fashola outlawed *Owambe* in the streets, most photographers like me followed the celebrants to designated party centers across Lagos" (Okoro 2010). As noted by Ladoja earlier, it is in response to these ubiquitous celebrations that one could find the growing number of photographers like Shedrack who hung around the streets to meet the demands.

The importance of the *Owambe* party in the promotion of the *aso ebi*

fashion in urban Lagos is further underscored by Peter Marris, who emphasizes the importance of family parties in the city of Lagos. These parties have
created a space where "the foregathering of relatives and friends has become
more important than the rituals that mark the phases of life" (2004, 31). Marris observes how funeral parties serve as spaces of *aso ebi* display and how
such situations evoke visual impact in some public spaces in Lagos. Marris
is specific in emphasizing only funerals, which suggests that other parties,
such as wedding parties, birthday parties, housewarming parties, chieftaincy
parties, and child-naming parties, also make an important visual impact. It
is crucial to note that this practice has also penetrated the diasporas, and
Nigerians all over the world seek every trivial moment to invoke the euphoric
and nostalgic reminiscences of a typical Lagos *Owambe* party of the 1980s
and 1990s. Nigerians in the diaspora now forge a common cultural identity
by invoking *aso ebi* at every *Owambe*, which happens at the slightest opportunity. Reporting on a typical *Owambe* party in faraway Baltimore, Maryland,
Imnakoya (2005) writes:

> At 10 o'clock on a Sunday night, the Nigerian music was thumping and the
> party, on the outskirts of Baltimore, was still churning. The remnants of a
> feast—goat meat, plantains, fried fish, moin-moin and jollof rice—littered
> rows of tables. Some of the hundreds of Nigerians, who had gathered to hon-
> or a friend, still swirled in circles on the dance floor in colorful, embroidered
> African outfits ("*aso ebi*") with head ties that regally swept up toward the ceil-
> ing. A cloud of paper money, which Nigerians traditionally throw to express
> appreciation while dancing, fluttered and twisted to the floor.

If a typical *Owambe* party is an occasion to exhibit affluence and ebullient
jocularity, it is equally an occasion to display fashionable *aso ebi* dresses. The
spectacular display has often been misinterpreted by non-Nigerian observers as reckless overindulgence and wasteful consumption, especially with
its concomitant high spending and spraying of money in *Owambe* parties.
"Diva Elegante" attended an *Owambe* party in London where *aso ebi* had kin-
dled nostalgia and yearning for home. Even while he was trying to make his
way out of the party, he got caught "in yet another web of *aso ebi* invitation
for another wedding party coming up next weekend" (2009). These parties
are potential opportunities for people to appear in any of the omnipresent
fashion magazines in Lagos. And with the expectation of "one's dress style
being viewed in public spaces through these magazines, one is considered

important and fashionable and almost a celebrity" (Nwike 2010). Some people, therefore, see these occasions as a space for competitive aso ebi fashion display.

It is clear that large gatherings with money-spraying barons and spectacular *aso ebi* crowds became possible channels for class legitimation and social belonging. Expressions of urban modernity became largely determined by public ceremonial displays and large networks of friends mainly dressed in *aso ebi*. By the year 2008, new forms of statuses and wealth had occasioned the desire by a few Lagosians to develop new kinds of artisanal services that would launch *aso ebi* practice into a more cosmopolitan modernizing project. These service providers, popularly referred to as "event organizers," engaged in the tailoring, distribution, and delivery of *aso ebi* to prospective clients.[4] They also created websites through which they disseminated *aso ebi* dress styles. Some examples of these websites include *BellaNaija, Aso ebi Planner*, and the *Aso ebi Gallery*. Babalola Olusoga, the founder of *Aso ebi Planner*, said that in 2009 they organized "*Aso ebi* Bridal Exhibitions," "which recorded a great turnout of fabric merchants, bridal houses, event planners, make-up artists, caterers, et cetera." The second show, organized in 2010, was at "Silverbird Galleria in Lagos and lasted for five days." Olusoga claims to have risen "from planning *aso ebi* to organizing an international fashion show which brings together international photographers, fashion designers, tailors, dignitaries, cultural icons, artistes, fun-seeking Lagosians, and everyone who believes in the unity of family which *aso ebi* symbolizes." He said the third show was held between February 7 and 11, 2011, and encapsulated a "bridal exhibition, fashion show, and royalty pageant and was well attended by renowned indigenous fashion designers, supermodels, fabric merchants, cloth weavers, wedding planners, event managers and many more who assisted families in creating that sense of love that is uniquely *aso ebi*." The show presented to the public a formidable "line-up of fabric merchants and bridal vendors displaying award-winning designs, services, and fabrics, also introducing vendors from the UK, USA, and other African countries" (Olusoga 2011).

Another organization, known as *Aso ebi Gallery*, is located at 3A Block G, Frank Komodo Street, Abraham Adesanya Estate, Ajah, Lagos State. The owner, Mrs. Habiba Sani Adapoyi, describes the organization as "an event management, planning and marketing outfit for both corporate and personal events." She said they "take the stress of people's occasion through packaging *aso ebi* and souvenirs and delivering them wherever they want." Their work also includes "selecting and distributing *aso ebi* to guests" by managing the dialogue between the textile suppliers and guests. According to her, all the customers have to do is "to relax." She said they have "well trained and experienced photographers and camera crew who are professionals and well versed with the new photographic technologies" (Adepoyi, 2011). Adapoyi is a tailor who has devoted over six years to promoting *aso ebi* as a cosmopolitan fashion style. She combines elements of Western-style dress and local fashion ideas to adapt *aso ebi* into an entirely new context of high fashion. According to her, "We create miniskirts *aso ebi*, trousers, and head scarves," and in this way she has shown that *aso ebi* is no longer encumbered by "tradition."

The activities of *Aso ebi Planner* and *Aso ebi Gallery* already corroborate the tensions that define fashion categories. Such tensions could be seen in discourses about a fashion system that is neither truly "African" nor entirely "Western."[5] *Aso ebi* is adapted into miniskirts and other cosmopolitan fashion styles, and the fashion shows seem to have localized versions of metropolitan fashion shows seen in cities such as Paris, London, and Milan. One can therefore view *aso ebi* in Lagos within this juxtaposition or intersection of multiple social and economic relations that absorb cosmopolitan influences.

By 2015 AsoEbiBella.com created its website for the exhibition of various hip styles of *aso ebi* dresses. The unique attribute AsoEbiBella.com brought into *aso ebi* is that it allows other designers to upload their photographs to the site, thereby advertising their styles. According to the site, "AsoEbiBella.com is a platform to share your best styles with the world. You can find the best style and colour combination inspiration right here for men, women and kids too! Welcome and happy sharing." With this approach, the site seems to bring democratization into the fashion discourse of *aso ebi*. This is a technological intervention that enables anyone with a computer and an internet connection not only to partake in the production, consumption, and circulation of fashion ideas and images of *aso ebi* dresses but also to fashion their personal world in the competitive sartorial spaces of the city.

Lagos has served as a city of fashion, providing ideas for various trends that people in the hinterland and others in the West African subregion emulate. The landscape of *aso ebi* practice is thus interceded by the dynamics of a visual matrix of local and global elements. Many individuals around the world have depended on these *aso ebi* fashion sites in their rise to becoming fashion icons and fashion authorities. This digital phase of democratization is linked, as *New York Times* fashion writer Eric Wilson notes, to the earlier phase of cheap chic: blogs that are "in a sense democratizing the coverage of style, much as designers and retailers—with lower priced fast-fashion collections—have democratized fashion itself" (2009, 14). Some of the democratized elements of fashion are represented by the *Aso ebi Planner* and *Aso ebi Gallery* enterprises, both of which have taken *aso ebi* practice from the enclosed spaces of conservative tradition and launched it into indeterminate spaces of urban practice. *Aso ebi Fashion Show* serves as a metaphorical exemplification of the archetypal *aso ebi* practice itself, which is performed for the audiences of wedding ceremonies, child-dedication parties, street parties, and political rallies, among others. If fashion needs a stage, then Lagos is the stage for *aso ebi* fashion (Mustafa 2006, 195).

No doubt, in the enterprise of global image commodities and cultural hegemonies, Lagos's visual culture assumes a central place. It is impossible to navigate the street for five minutes without confronting sights such as public Nollywood viewing centers where the plebeians converge, photography studios, tailoring shops, artists' shops, and a public ceremonial event besieged by amateur and professional photographers looking for prospective clients. The exceptionalism of Lagos lies in its unprecedented social ceremonials that promise diverse display opportunities of elegance and fashion, performed for multiple gazes, including that of the camera. *Aso ebi Fashion Show* therefore may have contributed in shaping avant-garde sensibilities. Again, while making *aso ebi* "hip" in Lagos, this show might also have contributed to the intensification of photographic representation of various styles of *aso ebi* dress designs in Lagos fashion magazines.

If the cosmopolitan city is a cluster and an aggregate of invisibility and, as Jonathan Raban (1998) puts it, a "province of anonymity," then one can argue that being seen is a proclivity that redefines the veil of anonymity around an individual's persona.[6] Furthermore, if new ways of consuming are linked to new ways of seeing, then new ways of consuming *aso ebi* practice may be linked to new ways of seeing social events in Lagos where *aso ebi* is worn, including *Owambe* parties, *Aso ebi Fashion Show*, and their entangled circuits.[7] From what has been described above, it is possible to suggest that *aso ebi* is a condition of Lagos cosmopolitanism. One can assert that the city may provide reasons why the practice of *aso ebi* continues to gain currency in contemporary Nigeria. While Lagos itself seems to offer its own reasons for some of these changing dynamics,[8] I locate a central facilitator of these dynamics in Lagos in the "fashion magazines" where most of the *aso ebi* photographs are reproduced.

FASHION MAGAZINES AND THE PRINT MEDIA

By the year 2000, *aso ebi* had come to dominate the pages of most fashion magazines in Nigeria. However, tracing the history of fashion magazines in Nigeria can shed light on why *aso ebi* has dominated these pages and has flowered through this process.

In Nigeria, the "event" or "fashion" magazine is a common term used to refer to some homespun, soft-sell publications that are produced by individuals who masquerade as publishers. Some of these magazines operate on the banal level but occasionally publish a few good-quality photographs. Sometimes their texts are marred by grammatical errors. They also defy certain ethical conventions and are composed of photos of people (especially women) dressed in mainly "traditional" costumes. Some of the publishers are barely educated people who care less about the quality of their publication than the financial benefits they will accrue. In Lagos alone, there are more than five hundred magazines of this type, and making a detailed inventory of their names seems to be a futile endeavor. The format is either eight inches by ten inches or twelve inches by fifteen inches, with glossy colored photos of women, mostly dressed in *aso ebi* uniforms; the magazines are priced between one and two dollars or more.

While one of the earliest print cultures in Nigeria started in Lagos with the *Lagos Times*, which was first published in 1880, an active print media flourished by 1920 through the publication of the *Lagos Daily News*, which ran until 1936. The *West African Pilot* began in 1937 as a nationalist project for the campaign against colonial rule. By the 1960s, Nigerians had cultivated the habit of publishing photographs of their events and ceremonies in the newspapers. By then, although there was virtually no advanced printing technology—and cameras were still not available as they are today to engender the kind of radical proliferation of publications now seen in Lagos—one could occasionally spot in the daily newspapers a few photographs of people who had celebrated one ceremony or the other. For example, on Tuesday, August 10, 1965, the *Daily Times* of Nigeria reported, beneath a family photograph, "Mr. Godwin Anih of No. 40 Babani Street, Ajegunle, Apapa Lagos and his wife celebrated the naming ceremony of their newly born baby. Their child received the name Juliana Nwakaego Anih. Picture shows Mr. and Mrs. Godwin Anih and little Juliana Anih on her mum's arms." Similar reports, in fact, followed a weekly routine in the *Daily Times*, and certain individuals looked forward to them.

This was probably the only way most photographs of private celebrations came into the public view, and it was a significant achievement for those whose photos were published. One of the reasons for this, I suggest, could be that since newspaper viewership was one of the indications of a "bourgeois" pastime during the early nationalist period, for one's photograph to appear in the few newspapers was regarded as a remarkable feat and a sign of modernity. Modernity was often tied to elitist belonging and lifestyle, and appearing in the newspapers formed an important part of this. Olatunde Bayo Lawuyi remarks that by the 1950s and 1960s, almost all newspapers in Nigeria advertised the elite, especially through their social events and obituaries (1991, 251). This period witnessed the establishment of many government newspapers, such as the *Nigerian Outlook* (1960), *Morning Post* and *Sunday Post* (1961), *Daily Sketch* (1964), and *New Nigerian* (1966). It was an era that also saw the introduction of radio and television into the community. Those who dominated the media advertisements were government officials and politicians canvassing for electoral support or inveigling people to demonstrate their backing for ethno-regional interests and development. It was clear that:

> not only does the ruling elite make the news, it is the news as endless verbatim reports of politicians' speeches, accounts of elite weddings and birthday parties, and the pages and pages of expensive obituaries testify. And if the poor are invisible, the very poor are a downright nuisance—some regimes have treated them literally as rubbish. (Barber 1987, 261)

In the 1970s through the 1980s, newspapers, radio, and television were largely controlled and sustained by the government and their cronies. However, by the 1970s oil boom era, emerging upper- and middle-class individuals joined this category.

Between 1973 and 1977 there were a few magazines that published photographs promoting fashion. These include *Drum, Spear, Trust, Lagos Life,* and *New Breed.* In *Spear,* for example, a regular column known as "Traditional African Life" allowed some *aso ebi* photos to appear in its pages. These photos were seen among photographs of wedded couples and birthday parties. *Drum* (1977) had two pages known as "Photo Page" and "People in Pictures," *Lagos Life* (1974) had "Lagos Pictorial," *Trust* (1973) had "People in Pictures" and "Fashion Page." During the early period of the Structural Adjustment Programme in Nigeria, in the mid-1980s, there was intense activity in the print media in Lagos. In 1983, during the height of the military dictatorship of Major General Muhammadu Buhari, the *Guardian*, an elite newspaper, emerged with a column that published stylish photographs of women. By the 1990s there were glossy magazines such as *Society, Metro, Channelle*, and *Chic*, targeted at the emerging female elites. Others include *Black Orpheus, TSM* (The Sunday Magazine), *Quality, She, New Spear, Eko, Classique*, and *Climax*, all of which appealed to a more general public (Denzer 2002, 95). *Everywoman*, another popular magazine, appeared but went under shortly afterward. The weekly magazine *Poise* eventually emerged as one of the most successful of all. With a detailed publication of women in various styles of *aso ebi* dresses and other stylish designs, *Poise* replaced the popular monthly *Woman's World*, published by the *Daily Times* group from 1964 to 1990, the longest-running women's magazine in Nigeria (95).

These increasing activities in women's print media might have echoed new efforts toward global women's empowerment initiated in the 1970s. However, by 1994 economic turmoil occasioned by myriad national crises in Nigeria forced most of the magazines to fold. Undoubtedly, these magazines constituted the foundations of a popular orientation in fashionable clothing during the period between the mid-1980s to the early 1990s. What was apparent in the 1980s was a growing tendency by most newspapers to publish dress styles and other activities of fashionable women and the elite class. While this practice, as noted earlier, may have been informed by the deepening global interest in women's issues, its intensification under the economic crisis of the IMF Structural Adjustment Programme in Nigeria in 1986 is paradoxical. However, while the SAP impoverished the poor and demobilized the middle class and the rich, the struggle for economic and class reinvention by the distraught middle class may have found justification in public visibility. Again, with the profligate corruption engendered by the military, which cast an ambiguous veil around the image of those connected with the ruling cabal, positive image laundering became inevitable through the print media. For example, the politicians, the wealthy, the celebrities, traditional rulers, high government officials, policy makers, generals, and influential leaders in every field sought public acceptance of their already questionable image (especially their dubious connection with the military cabal) through the print media. Their interest traversed fashion such that successful fashion designers and publishers of these print media emerged as the iconic champions of Lagos's vibrant popular culture under the SAP. Furthermore, many local tailors and dressmakers benefited from the government ban on foreign clothing.[9] For these tailors, the challenge was to meet the increasing demand for weekly *aso ebi* uniforms, a demand that at that time was almost unparalleled.

In the 1980s, *Woman's World* featured a "Designer of the Month" page, and its successor, *Poise*, regularly celebrated the achievements of designers. Although most newspapers ran a weekly fashion page, some of them also had other popular features devoted to style and women achievers: "Women in Business" and "Elegance Is" in the *Sunday Vanguard*, "Style" in the *Guardian*, and "Meet a Designer" in the *Nigerian Tribune*. These developments mark the precursors of the later emergence of the magazines I discuss here. And one could also reason that the ubiquity of such magazines in the later part of the twentieth century might have been occasioned by late capitalist production. The logical connection of late capitalist production with *aso ebi* is further underscored by the fact that by the year 2000, the importation of cheaper textile materials used for *aso ebi* coincided with the emergence of cheaper and less cumbersome means of printing technology. This enabled the so-called publishers to engage in the production of these magazines. By the year 2000 most newspapers still maintained fashion columns. However, most significant was *ThisDay* newspaper, which developed a new colorful series known as *ThisDay Style Magazine* that would eventually emerge as a potpourri of elite high visibility in both fashion and lifestyle. The magazine was also launched online, and its formulation of Nigeria's fad is scripted by a hegemonic discourse of personal achievement colored with bourgeoisie fashion. In presenting women and men as the fashion icons of the week on their front cover, *ThisDay Style Magazine* interweaves everyday visibility and lived experience into an imagined sartorial agency. The complexity of this agency reveals a system that was constantly being produced, sustained, and disseminated by acts of seeing and being seen in Lagos social circles.

By the mid-2000s most of these magazines had become fully reduced to mere photo catalogues of new styles in *aso ebi* uniforms. The reason for this is the discovery that "many people in Lagos want their shows to appear in one magazine or the other, [which] makes this tendency more pronounced among the publishers" (A. Williams 2009). Not only that, but it was also observed that "for you to sell these magazines, there must be unique designs of 'traditional' dresses in it, and these designs could only be seen among those wearing *aso ebi* in weddings and other social activities" (A. Williams 2009).

Further reasons could be that "people believe that once your wedding or party appears in the magazine, that you are rich or a celebrity" (Ujam 2010). Through magazine viewership, therefore, one can assume that notions of wealth and celebrity prototypes might have entered into the visual economy of the city as a fashionable, socially prestigious indulgence. While the magazines could be described as products of the fraught dialogue between

cosmopolitan modernism and postcolonial crisis, they also seem to promise a fashionable utopia and an imagination capable of sustaining the city's
power of magnetism. In fashioning *aso ebi*, therefore, one encounters a vivid
intersection of multiple socioeconomic relations, crystallizing into a mutual
engagement based on the circulation of the fashion magazines. The quest for
unique *aso ebi* fashion is fired and sustained by this mutual dialogue, a spirit
of coexistence and trans-economic relations among different players in urban
Lagos. As I discuss this mutual dialogue, I suggest that perhaps they may have
constituted part of the aesthetic and visual seductions of the modern city.

FRAMING MUTUALITY IN *ASO EBI*

By the year 2008, the above-mentioned magazines had succeeded in establishing a certain visual repertoire of "traditional" attire that was emulated by
the general public. However, such emulation was effectively consolidated in
a mutual operation existing between photographers, fashion magazines, vendors, textile merchants, tailors, and their customers. Perhaps this mutual deal
serves as a suitable index to articulate the city of Lagos as a melting pot of
cultures and transactions.

A. The Photographers and the Photographed

Images in fashion magazines have become a model from which people design
themselves.[10] Many authors have studied the different ways in which images
have traveled across space and time and are thus incorporated into peoples'
daily lives in Nigeria and Africa.[11] However, the question for Lagos might be,
How do these images get into the fashion magazines? The activities of popular photographers provide a ready answer. And it seems that, indeed, popular
photography is a practice that is fundamental to the survival and expansion of
fashion magazines in Nigeria. In Lagos, popular photographers travel to different venues of weddings or other events, searching for individuals dressed
in unique *aso ebi* dresses to photograph. For example, I followed the photographer Shedrack Okoro (who claims to be an employee of *Treasure Life*
magazine) to a wedding ceremony in the Lekki Peninsula of Lagos. I watched
Shedrack as he approached one of the *aso ebi* girls and introduced himself as
a photographer of *Treasure Life*. Not caring for a detailed explanation from
Shedrack, the *aso ebi* girl, whose name I later found is Nnenna Nwike, posed
for the camera while Shedrack took a snapshot that would eventually appear
in the next edition of *Treasure Life* (figs. 14 and 15). Afterward Shedrack

Figure 14. Shedrack Okoro taking a side view of Nnenna Nwike's *aso ebi* style. Lagos, April 5, 2010. Photo: Okechukwu Nwafor.

showed me his photos that were published in *Treasure Life* and confirmed that many of them were taken at weddings with women in *aso ebi* uniforms. According to Shedrack, "I like the *aso ebi* thing because it has allowed me to still remain an employee of *Treasure Life* magazine" (Okoro 2010).

My interrogation showed that an ethical dialogue between the photographer and the photographed is virtually nonexistent. Both have silently conceded to a mutual understanding that Shedrack elucidated further: "We don't charge them any money, but they appear on the fashion magazines free of charge." And when I questioned what those who were photographed stand to gain, Shedrack said, "They are happy to be seen in the magazines." Thus with the expectation of one's dress style being viewed in the public space, "one is considered important and fashionable and almost a celebrity" (Nwike 2010). My interview with Nnenna Nwike, a student and a friend of one of the wedded women, and who with more than thirty other women appeared in some of the fashion magazines, confirmed that they were comfortable with their photos appearing in these magazines. For example, in figure 17, through Shedrack, I contacted about five women who appeared in red *aso ebi*, and their statements were in tandem with Nkemakonam Udenta's (2011) statement:

Figure 15. Shedrack Okoro taking a back view of Nnenna Nwike's *aso ebi* style. Lagos, April 5, 2010. Photo: Okechukwu Nwafor.

When I saw myself in the magazine, I was very happy, and after two days some of my friends started calling me on phone telling me that they saw me. There are many people dressed in *aso ebi* that very day, but the photographers select those whose dresses are unique. So for me it is good, and I love *aso ebi* because without it I might not have appeared in the magazine.

Nkemakonam, second from the top left in figure 17, is also a fashion designer who has built a network of friends through her tailoring outfit. Most people whose parties she attends are her clients, who invite her to wear the *aso ebi* for them. Some people, therefore, see these occasions as a space for competitive *aso ebi* fashion display. The nature of these public displays again speaks to the mode at which visual economy operates in the city.

Figure 16. Peter Iriah.
Lagos, November 2010.
Photo: Okechukwu
Nwafor.

Figure 17. *Poise* fashion magazine. Lagos, August 2010. Photo: Peter Iriah.

Figure 18. Front view of woman in *aso ebi*. Lagos, August 2010. Photo: Peter Iriah.

Again Peter Iriah of *Poise* fashion magazine (fig. 16), whom I contacted in Lagos through a phone number placed in *Poise* (fig. 17), told me that most of his photos are *aso ebi* women taken at wedding receptions where the subjects pose with the expectation that their photos will be seen in public through *Poise* (2011). Peter showed me some of the photos he took that were supposed to be published in the next edition of *Poise* at the time of conducting this research (figs. 18, 19, 20).

Photographers encourage the intensification of *aso ebi* practices through their engagement with people at the venue of the events. This has also led to an invention of various performativities around *aso ebi*. On November 30,

Figure 19. Back view of
woman in *aso ebi*. Lagos,
August 2010. Photo:
Peter Iriah.

2009, I attended a wedding party in the Sonya area of Lagos. The venue of
the wedding was a vast expanse of empty land that approximated the size of a
football field located along the Apapa–Oshodi Expressway in Lagos. The wedding ceremony was between Uju and Tony, Tony being the younger brother
of the owner of Capital Oil Limited in Lagos, who actually owns the space of
the wedding ceremony. My reason for attending this party was, among many
others, to understand how fashion magazine photographers operate in such
a society gathering where dressing is always taken seriously. A total of more
than ten photographers were present at this wedding. Some of the photogra-

Figure 20. Front view of woman in *aso ebi*. Lagos, August 2010. Photo: Peter Iriah.

phers wore uniformed black T-shirts with the word "Crew" inscribed on the back, and most of them searched for guests who were dressed in a unique style. There were many guests dressed in different forms of *aso ebi* uniform. Benson Uchendu was among those who wore the T-shirt with the "Crew" inscription. He told me that "Crew" means photographers from a fashion magazine known as "*Poise* fashion magazine." Uchendu said his target was to deliver fifty good pictures of women in *aso ebi* uniforms to the publisher of *Poise* . In the bid to meet this target, Uchendu photographed everyone in attendance, including those who did not demand photos. When I asked him whether people felt embarrassed when he photographed them against their wishes, he confirmed that most often people want to be photographed, believing that they will appear in the fashion magazines (Uchendu 2009).

From this, one can suggest that the mutuality surrounding *aso ebi* fashioning is framed around goals such as Benson Uchendu's: "to deliver fifty good pictures of women in *aso ebi* uniforms to the publisher of *Poise* fashion magazine." The question is, What could have driven Uchendu toward taking fifty photos of "only" women in *aso ebi* if the fashion magazines were not there? This question gives one ample room to interrogate this concept of mutuality, which I suggest sustains the fashioning of *aso ebi*.

B. Fashion Magazines

Shedrack, Peter, and Benson took their photographs to the publishers of *Treasure Life* and *Poise* fashion magazines, respectively, who paid them off. Because *aso ebi* has become the central component of fashion in parties and social events, the publishers advise the photographers to target those aspiring to hold these parties or events. Again, the magazines emphasize these parties in their captions. For example, the caption on page 30 of *Today's Fashion* says, "Want your party covered? Call Femi on 08055273211, Sunday on 08029119773, Shola on 08062336685" (fig. 21), and on page 18 of *Style Royale*: "Your event needs coverage? Call Udo: 0806738663, Emma, 08028979482" (fig. 22). This is also observed by *Top Style* magazine (fig. 23): "*Top Style* was at the wedding celebration of Oby and Ebere Nnanyelugo; Ifeoma and Dubem Aroh recently. See the full story in pictures. Do you have a special event or celebration coming up this season? Call our team of professional photo journalists on 08036565474 today, and see your event featured in full colour in our next edition." While captions like these serve as useful sources for viewing the marketing tactics of photographers, they also offer a perspective perhaps more representative of the general Lagos fashion magazine scene. Much effort is geared toward the promotion of sartorial elegance.

This brings me to the use of the term "photojournalism," which underscores the level of understanding of the publishers regarding the meanings of the photograph. I suggest that their understanding of photography is devoid of any substantiality. There is a limit to creative possibilities when the term "photojournalist" is deployed. This is because the publishers perceive the photographers as mere suppliers of "raw materials." This goes to confirm my submission that there is a surface effect to the overall transaction. If the publishers believe that they have a mandate to supply the public with a journal-

Figure 21. *Today's Fashion* 2, no. 6 (2009): 7.

your Events need to be covered? Call
Udo : 08066738663, Segun : 08022880359, Emma : 08028979482

Figure 22. *Style Royale*, No. 7 (2009): 8.

istic account of the latest fashion styles, then their deployment of the term "photojournalism" may be justified. It is possible to interpret this statement as part of a growing business pursuit by the editors who wish to expand the marketability of their magazines. But, ultimately, emphasizing "people's event appearing in full colour" might show that these editors also understand the increasing potential that photography possesses in adding "colour" to an event. The magazines' reliance on photographers affirms the mutual transactions existing between the magazines and other actors. It is also uncovered in the manner in which the statement "your events need to be covered" is crafted on top of photos of ladies dressed in *aso ebi* in figure 22, and one might suggest that the covering of one's event is not far from covering one's *aso ebi* styles in the events. The captions are based on the assumption that Nigerians' penchant for events and celebrations and their demands for the services of the photographer are perhaps expediently linked together.

In line with the perceptions of such magazines that there is already a public acceptance of an overt visual showmanship as well as sartorial glamour and display, the publisher of *Trade Fashion and Events* magazine, Akin Wil-

Figure 23. *Top Style* 1, no. 2 (2007).

liams, remarked that most people want to see themselves in public places and that this practice has commercialized photography (Williams 2009). Many publishers have resorted to this type of publication because they have seen that through pictures in these magazines people have become increasingly interested in being seen in fashionable dresses in society magazines: "People call us on [the] phone and ask us to come and cover their events, and they demand the photographs to be published in even two editions. We sell our magazines and sometimes charge these people for covering their events" (A. Williams 2009).

Through a creative combination of textual and photographic information, the publishers offer a luminous framework through which the viewers might negotiate a more complex relationship between clothing, identity, image, and desire. For example, in featuring Mrs. Oniru's fiftieth-birthday party in Lagos, *Ovation* magazine seemed to use its caption to emphasize the dresses of people they showed in their magazine. The caption that reads: "what society people wore at Mrs Oniru's 50th birthday party" (fig. 24) draws the attention of the viewers to the dresses of Mrs, Oniru's friends in their solidarity *aso ebi* uniforms. What one must observe in figure 24 is that the use of *aso ebi* is restricted to only the head scarves and shawls. This is a creative method of using *aso ebi* that does not in any way downplay its importance. It is often common to see women on weekends in Lagos attending occasions dressed in matching head scarves but no other *aso ebi*. It is possible that this restriction could be a means of ensuring greater freedom in individual creativity around *aso ebi* dress designs on the rest of the body.

The captioning in figure 24 contrasts with that of, say, Chief Akindele's family (fig. 25), which *Ovation* did not deem necessary to caption in such a way. From this it can be assumed that the publisher believes that the viewer's interest lies in the more fashionable clothes worn by Mrs. Oniru's friends rather than those of Chief Akindele's family. In other words, it seems that photography and dress sloganeering overlap in the messages the magazines wish to convey. Furthermore, it seems that this slogan has more potential to attract buyers than any other birthday message. Photography is used to present a world that is both enviable and nostalgic and to attract the viewer into the desirable lived experiences of others.

Unlike photos of women, photos of men are less frequent in magazines, and they are usually not seen in *aso ebi*. Masculinity can hardly afford such visualization and subsequent objectification. Women's affinity to photography and *aso ebi* seems to contrast sharply with the uneasiness shown toward the medium by many males.

Figure 24. *Ovation*, no. 60 (2003): 80.

Figure 24b. Detail. *Ovation*, no. 60 (2003): 80.

Figure 25. *Ovation*, no. 60 (2003): 26.

What would happen if the women were not celebrating in their different *aso ebi* uniforms? Would the fashion magazines still exist? The continuous reference by the magazines to people's events indicates an interdependence that ensures greater expansion, consumption, and creativity in *aso ebi*.

C. The Vendors and Customers

The mutuality that exists in *aso ebi* continues through the vendors and their customers who stand to benefit from the photographic endeavors of Shedrack, Peter, and Uchendu and the efforts of the publishers of the magazines. This is seen among the vendors' stands in Lagos. For example, Johnson Uzoeche (fig. 26), a vendor whom I met along Tejuosho Road in Yaba, Lagos, told me that many women come to buy the fashion magazines from him. Some buy them because their *aso ebi* photos appear in them while others intend to use them as a fashion catalog for their "traditional" dresses. He confirmed that his greatest sales as a vendor come from the so-called fashion magazines (Uzoeche 2010). Chiagozie, whom I met in Uzoeche's shop buying the magazine, remarked that a copy of the fashion "magazine allows her to get the best designs for her tailor, and that gives her an opportunity to be voguish." Chiagozie was flipping through a copy of *ThisDay Style Magazine*, and

Figure 26. Johnson Uzoeche, Tejuosho Road. Yaba, Lagos, March 2010. Photo: Okechukwu Nwafor.

she showed me a page that read, "The Aso ebi: Family Pride or Commercial Gimmick?" (fig. 27). She said one of the *aso ebi* ladies inserted in the middle of the article is her friend and that she bought the magazine for that reason. Ayo Obese, another vendor in Lagos, remarked that among all the people coming to his newsstand, "many would prefer to view the *aso ebi* images in the fashion magazines, and they prefer to buy those magazines that contain more photos with unique designs, which they intend to copy" (Obese 2010). In other words, one could conclude that the consumption of these magazines is anchored on a tendency to copy *aso ebi* dress designs.

D. Customers and Textile Merchants

From the vendor the magazines continue their journey. Uche Okoye took some fashion magazines to Ifeyinwa Oguchi's textile shop in Balogun market, from where she hoped to copy colors of her *aso ebi* dresses for her forthcoming marriage ceremony (fig. 28). She showed Ifeyinwa the magazine, pointing to the color of a particular *aso ebi* dress she wanted, and Ifeyinwa helped her to locate it. However, Ifeyinwa remarked:

style&living

lifestyle isabella e.c. akinseye

The Aso Ebi
Family Pride or Commercial Gimmick?

Aso ebi translated to English means 'family cloth'. It is usually worn at major ceremonies such as weddings and burials as a uniform or identification that you belong to a certain family. Now Aso Ebi is worn by nearly every Tom, Dick and Harry whenever there is a cause for celebration and in Nigeria we know how to celebrate, one of the reasons why we were ranked by Transparency International as the happiest people. We have parties for everything; birthday, naming ceremony, weddings (all religions and cultures included), graduation, any form of achievement, shop launching and house warming just to mention a few. Having fun is not bad but the key is moderation.

A typical example is a child's birthday, there are usually two stages; the early part of the day is dedicated to the child, so there is kiddy related entertainment, candy floss and the likes. Then there is the night party, that is the real groove where you see all the adults coming out to bubble in their 9 inch killer heels with matching designer bags and you said it aso ebi. Yes people can buy aso ebi for a one year old's birthday party.

These are hard times. Whatever happened to people calling colours just like it is on the invitation card and ending it there? But no! Aso ebi is for the select not just family but anyone that can afford to buy it. Now you can only buy the particular lace or damask or ankarra from the designated person who, trust me, is making a kill. I have heard of stories where people fund their wedding by selling aso ebi. Personally sourcing for the aso ebi usually proves a futile exercise; imagine spending your Saturday morning combing through Balogun market, your chances of finding it is slim but you are most likely going to find something close to it which is just as bad as wearing your own outfit. Most of the time, you are cajoled, coerced, coaxed and even blackmailed into buying from the source as credit is offered ironically even during the credit crunch.

But it does not end there; in fact the competition is just beginning to sew the most innovative, creative and drop-dead-in-your track outfit. Just have a look at any of these weekly fashion soft sell papers. Sewing does not come cheap either, there is always this tailor or seamstress or designer that is well known and hence comes with a ridiculously inflated price. If it was me, I would give the road side tailor but how many people have faith like that. They are thinking that their aso ebi worth more than all their shares put together, would be ruined and all that dosh down the drain. So they go with the

* Grace Ihonvbere & Mabel Amadi looking divine in lovely lace aso ebi and dripping in diamonds!

The 'aso ebi' has its advantage, you automatically become the cynosure of all eyes depending on how daring your couture is and the bling to accessorise it.

tried and tested and make all preparations to be set for the D-Day, some even go as far as making the outfit smaller as an incentive to lose weight.

I got a call from a mutual friend of a friend I met at University that is tying the nuptial bow in a few months.

It went something like this...
MF-*How are you?*
Me-*Fine, Wassup?*
MF-*I have some bad news for you.*
Me-*I'm not on the train right?*
MF-*Yes one of the groomsmen just pulled out and everyone else on the train is family apart from me...but don't worry you can still get involved. I'm short of hands in Lagos and there'll be lots to do. You are buying the aso ebi right?*
Me-*For which one traditional and white wedding? I don't know o depends on how much it is.*

The conversation went on briefly with her giving me the dates, promising to get back to me on how much the aso ebi would cost and informing me that as soon as another groom man comes aboard, I would be back on the train.

I am wondering what I really stand to gain by buying the aso ebi. For one, if I am going to be busy helping out that means I would be seen, but to be identified as one of the helpers or should I say hostesses, the aso ebi would come in handy. But in the light of the present situation, I really need to weigh the pros and cons before making my decision.

The aso ebi has its advantage, you automatically become the cynosure of all eyes depending on how daring your couture is and the bling to accessorise it but really the celebrant should be the centre of attention. Then of course you are entitled to the special goody bag or souvenirs. Your aso ebi is like a V.I.P ticket throughout the day and indeed you are treated like family. Unfortunately, that is where it all ends except of course you still owe. Then begins the calls, texts, emails...in short anything for them to get their money even after the wedding is long gone and concluded.

So, I think I would rather be indebted to my bride-to-be friend by not buying aso ebi and make it up with a nice thoughtful present than be in debt...at least not for aso ebi maybe for more meaningful things like a house or a nice car at least I can use it long after her wedding to bring her a personalised yearbook about the good ol days-no husbands, no kids and all that freedom. Thereby in my own little way preserving the sanctity of aso ebi to be strictly an expression of family pride and not a commercial gimmick.

Figure 27. *ThisDay Style* 14, no. 5145 (2009): 69.

Figure 28. Taking the fashion magazines to Ifeyinwa Oguchi's textile shop to copy color. Lagos, November 29, 2010. Photo: Okechukwu Nwafor.

> Sometimes when I don't have the particular color they want, I go to my colleagues to search for it, but some of these women just see a particular *aso ebi* color and a particular material in these magazines and feel that they can get it in the market. But the truth is that these materials are what we call "stock materials." They come once and disappear. When you explain to these women, some of them would not understand. Some who understand would just request for something close to that, while some would insist on getting that particular one they saw in the magazine. (Oguchi 2010)

This affirms the multiple roles that *aso ebi* dresses in magazines play, especially in relation to fashioning *aso ebi*. The *aso ebi* photos in the magazines therefore determine the trajectory of visuality around dress and styles.

E. The Tailors

The circuitous itinerary of these magazines does not terminate at the textile merchant's shop. They continue to the tailor's workshop, where they serve both utilitarian and aesthetic purposes between the tailors and customers, respectively. This is a remarkable interdependence. However, while some customers take the magazines to the tailors to copy from, the tailors personally acquire and stock numerous magazines for other customers who may not have any particular design in mind. However, it is important to note that before the 1990s, the major source of clothing designs for these tailors derived from foreign style catalogs, published by the major international dress pattern companies, such as *Elle, Simplicity, Butterick,* and *Vogue* (Denzer 2002, 98). But by the mid-1990s, devaluation of the Nigerian currency kept the cost of these magazines out of the reach of most tailors, and they started looking inward for local fashion ideas. As in the 1990s, popular sources of design include some Lagos magazines such as *Ikebe Super* and *Super Story,* which feature between ten and twelve designs per week. Other magazines include *Fashion Focus* and *Dessence Fashion Catalogue,* which feature between forty and sixty drawings or photographs per month. My fieldwork in Lagos in early 2013 revealed that more than three hundred types of such magazines presently flood the Lagos popular newsstands.

Felix Ofeimun, a tailor along Tejuosho Road in Yaba (fig. 29), Lagos, showed me two magazines: one from where he copied and the other where his tailored dress appeared. He pointed at the second magazine and said, "I made this *aso ebi* clothing this girl is putting on, and she appeared here because the design of the dress is good, and the photographers took her and published her in the magazine" (Ofeimun 2010). Ifeoma Nwokoye, owner of Ifez Fashion Center, a tailoring outfit on No. 4 Ademola Street, Surulere, Lagos, also told me how she shows her clients fashion magazines from which they chose designs (Nwokoye 2010).

F. Others

After I met Adaobi Onwuchekwa in the Balogun textile market in November 2010, she told me how images of *aso ebi* dress designs circulate between her and her friend in the United States. In November 2010, Onwuchekwa said she scanned some copies of photos of women dressed in *aso ebi* that she culled from *Elite* magazine and sent them through email to her cousin living in Dallas, Texas, who would soon come back for a traditional wedding ceremony in Nigeria in December. Her cousin asked her to send her many copies of different *aso ebi* styles from many fashion magazines from where she could choose the color and design for her *aso ebi* in her forthcoming wedding. The interesting thing is that Onwuchekwa was one of the women who would wear her cousin's *aso ebi,* and she had to send copies to her cousin to approve before she could buy the clothes in large quantity in readiness for other people to

Figure 29. Felix Ofeimun. Tejuosho, Lagos. April 6, 2010. Photo: Okechukwu Nwafor.

purchase from her. The arrangement, according to Onwuchekwa, was that her cousin would send money from the United States, and she would begin the initial preparation by co-opting friends who would wear the *aso ebi*. By the time her cousin came back from the US, the whole *aso ebi* arrangement would be done. Chiamaka Udenwa notes, "When my friend who live[s] in Abuja did her traditional marriage in November 2009, she sent me a color and design of the *aso ebi* she wanted me to wear through her handset. Because we were staying far apart from each other, I had to buy the design in Lagos and sew it before the wedding. The wedding took place in the village, so I just came back with my *aso ebi* to the wedding" (Udenwa 2010). Such statements are also a clear picture of circulation and the importance of new electronic technology and media in the dissemination of such *aso ebi* designs.

COPYING AND *COPIES*: TRANSCENDING THE BURDENS OF *ASO EBI* UNIFORMITY

It is interesting that while copying has historically framed transactions in the African textile economy starting in the eighteenth century, it has also shaped the dealings among the photographers, magazine producer and vendors, tailors and textile merchants. Hillel Schwartz (1996) argues that on the one hand, copying makes us what we are. While cultures cohere in the faithful transmission of rituals and rules of conduct, Schwartz argues, copying gives meaning to the original rather than the other way around. For example, through a constant awareness and copying of variously inflected visual matrices in the city of Lagos, tailors invent the language of originality. One can therefore argue that there is an absence of originality in an interwoven network of inspiration and ideas constantly evoking the new. The mutual dialogue I have described above foregrounds the *copying* concept. In one instance, this began with the photographer who copied the image of the "original" *aso ebi* dress of Nnenna Nwike. While the critique of originality might also problematize the "originality" of Nwike's *aso ebi* dress, this photographer extends the language of copying by making copies of the photos available for the magazines to reproduce. Shedrack Okoro actually informed me that he sells multiple copies of his photos to different magazines. Shedrack's action is validated by Rosalind Kraus (1984), who writes:

> By exposing the multiplicity, the facticity, the repetition and stereotype at the heart of every aesthetic gesture, photography deconstructs the possibility of differentiating between the original and the copy, the first idea and its slavish imitators. The practice of the multiple, whether one speaks of the hundreds of prints pulled from the same negative or the hundreds of fundamentally indistinguishable photographs that could be made. . . . It has been taken to undermine the very distinction between original and copy. (49–68)

An essay published by Walter Benjamin in 1936 would add that the nature of photography is to destabilize the very notion of authenticity in the original through "copy" (Benjamin 1968, 217–51). Schwartz attempts to make sense of our fascination with replicas, duplicates, and twins. He charts the repercussions of such entanglements with copies and fakes of all kinds, whose presence alternately sustains us and disrupts notions of authenticity, identity, and originality.

Copy, as Terence Cave has indicated, "is both imitation and plenitude: it is the one and the many, through replication and profusion." (cited in Groom 2003, 10). We inhabit a world of copies where coordination from a fixed point of originality is unachievable: it is within an exuberant world of copies that we arrive at our experience of originality (Schwartz 1996). Copies proliferate, spreading from their point of origin, and in this process things fall into the realm of mutability and illusion (Malkan 2005). If, in this instance, Nnenna Nwike in *aso ebi* becomes the point of origin and the original, which Shedrack copies with his camera, then the realm of mutability is seen in the unending reproductions that Nnenna's images suffer in the hands of the fashion magazines. In this instance, and in recognition of Kraus's statement, one can argue that while the reproductions in the magazines might have little relationship to real-life performances, they nonetheless blur the distinction between original images and copies while in circulation. They have been uprooted from their origins (the real wedding and other social events) and inserted into another context of endless appropriation and consumption, yet individuals appropriating them never contest their originality. At the level of social engagement, individuals await the emergence of new styles of *aso ebi* dress designs from the copies in the magazines. Through this reproducibility, new visual languages are invented that produce the rich repertoire of *aso ebi* fashion.

While copies may be dismissed as banality, I argue that they have achieved some levels of success in their efforts to assist individual women in fashioning elements of singularity in design stylistics. The desire for uniqueness, to stand out in the uniformed collective of *aso ebi*, is visibly noticeable in each individual woman. While the colors of the *aso ebi* dresses may be the same, the design styles often vary. The ubiquity of these styles has enhanced viewership among the urban populace who are incited by the photos to seek individuality of design. In this way, copies appear to resolve the dilemma of group representation, group dressing, and group image embodied in *aso ebi* uniformity. This is achieved in the magazines through multiple isolation of individual women from their groups through the fragmentation of spaces. What this suggests is that copies may have intensified the rate of circulation of the dress styles. In their effort to advertise the uniqueness of each individual's *aso ebi* style, the magazines conceive individual dresses outside the collectivity imposed by the *aso ebi* groups. These magazines, I suggest, project enticements among viewers and at the same time give those who are photographed a sense of sartorial individualism and elusive sense of independence.

At the same time, this sense of individualism heightens the popularity and uniqueness of *aso ebi* beyond its rejection by some sections of the public as banal uniformity. For example, Chioma Okoye notes that since she started watching the ubiquitous fashion magazines, she no longer attends any party in Lagos looking casual (unless the dress code is specifically given as casual), "because it is almost a norm for most people to put on *aso ebi*, and these parties are perfect spaces to show off one's expensive and unique *aso ebi* dresses, jeweleries, bag, and shoes" (Okoye 2010). From this statement, one could assume that in the city there is a sense in which these magazines have redefined some public spaces as spaces of fashion display. What happens now is—in line with Okoye's remarks—a situation in which most people, especially women, who have accepted the uniformity imposed by the *aso ebi* tradition invoke exceptionalism in their designs in order to stand out among the humdrum color uniformity of *aso ebi* wearers. Fashion competition has become a popular phenomenon, enacted around an aspiration toward design singularity and sartorial agency and performed within the aesthetics of individual tailoring. In other words, there is a transcending of *aso ebi*'s imposition of equality through uniformed dress color. A competition of creative expertise thus exists that has a multiplier effect on the tailoring business of Lagos. The tailors put considerable skill into garment production from the multiple copies of various designs available in the magazines.

CONCLUSION

This chapter has shown that *aso ebi* was at the heart of the social contestations, aspirations, and power that came with *Owambe*. A visual culture has emerged in Lagos in which *aso ebi* images help produce the fabric of everyday life. This is perhaps in line with Douglas Kellner's statement that "in our social interactions, mass-produced images guide our presentation of the self in everyday life, our ways of relating to others, and the creation of our social values and goals" (1995, 18). While shaping collective views about fashion in general, and sartorial behavior around *aso ebi* fashioning, the fashion magazine images may have provided the materials out of which people forge their various subjectivities. The chapter has offered insight into the importance of circulation of visual images in the conversation that takes place between *aso ebi* wearers, photographers, vendors, and the fashion magazines. New forms of *aso ebi* dress designs are no doubt a development that has been spread by, among many other factors, the emergence of fashion magazines and their photographers in Lagos. From this chapter it is evident that Lagosians, especially women, have become conscious of their *aso ebi* dress designs each time they attend social events.

Aso ebi, now a practice on the leading edge of a crucial socioeconomic exchange in the city, invokes what I call "Lagos cosmopolitanism," obviously a reflection of the historical conditions that enact the crisis of the postcolonial city as seen in the *Owambe* party. Such cosmopolitanism also manifests in the incorporation of both local and foreign elements in the process of fashioning *aso ebi.*, We find the intersection of local and foreign elements in new forms of modern capital seen in *Aso ebi Planner* and *Aso ebi Gallery*, through which various spectacular fashion shows in urban Lagos are enacted. These spectacular fashion shows help the *aso ebi* performers to articulate new styles of fashions.

Through a process of mutuality around the circulation of *aso ebi* images there is a redefinition of the borders of the city's visual economy: the magazines depend on photographers who take photographs of *aso ebi* in weddings and other events to market their magazines; the *aso ebi* wearers depend on the magazines for new and unique designs; the tailors depend on the magazines for unique designs of *aso ebi* to satisfy their clients, and the photographers depend on the *aso ebi* wearers to keep their jobs. Indeed, the fashion magazines have enabled *aso ebi* to dominate the visual culture of Nigerians' everyday lives primarily because the outfits, originally made for special events and parties, eventually regress into the everyday dresses of most Nigerians. This has become a way to distinguish these *aso ebi* outfits from the very expensive work of high-end fashion designers in Lagos.

While the acts of copying dress designs and wearing those copies help individuals to overcome the uniformity imposed by *aso ebi*, the emergence of fashion magazines lends itself to the plurality of images in the city, fills the void of obscurity, and helps the individuals to invent new forms of *aso ebi* fashion, on which their individuality also depends.

CHAPTER 6

Surfacist Aesthetics and the Digital Turn

By the year 2000, digital cameras and devices had become ubiquitous in Lagos. An increasing visual agency was beginning to manifest among city dwellers through such devices as camera phones. Similarly, there was an explosion of other, cheaper digital devices and technologies among professional and amateur photographers. What distinguished professional photographers in the city was their ability to exhibit expertise with this new digital photographic media. Most photographers made use of digital cameras and bought digital printers for quick passport photographs across the side streets. Others equipped their workplaces with computers and learned the new digital technology of Photoshop. Social events were again integrated into this new digital wave. Photographers attended weddings, took photographs, rushed to digital laboratories, printed the photographs, and delivered them back to the owners in swift moments.

The intersections of sartorial practices with this new digital movement cannot be overemphasized. Instant picture-taking and the act of dressing up for occasions have become intertwined. The central element of most social events often revolves not around food or any other item, but around *aso ebi* fashion.[1] The importance attached to *aso ebi* also influences its relationship with the digital medium. A politics of exclusion seen in the physical practice of *aso ebi* has been extended into the digital realm. Photographers manipulate the *surfaces* of their *aso ebi* photographs on the request of the customers for the purposes of exclusion or inclusion of certain elements and props. Glamour is not only fashionably impressed on the physical bodies through *aso ebi* and other textile paraphernalia; it is also symbolically inscribed on the fabricated bodies through digital Photoshop.

In recognition of these digital shifts, in this chapter I use *aso ebi* to show that textiles have taken a preeminent position in the discourse of identity and its intersections with photography in contemporary Nigerian society.[2] Here, *aso ebi* clothes, serving as textiles, allow Nigerians to redefine their relationship to a certain urban fashionability that is disseminated by Western sartorial styles and photographic genres. As a result, *aso ebi* serves as a vehicle to address the substantiality of the surface in photography as initially proposed by Christopher Pinney (2003) in relation to Indian practices. In this chapter, by looking at *aso ebi* photographs—those I personally took at weddings in Lagos and those taken by Kingsley Chuks—I take Pinney's notion of *surfacism* into a broader set of cultural issues in Lagos. The approach to this chapter, which draws on ethnography, art-historical models of visual studies, and literary theory, is my attempt to explore how combined methods of analysis can raise research questions beyond conventional theories of visual analysis.

THE VISUAL ECONOMY OF SURFACISM

In Animasaun Digital Studio in Lagos, the role of the computer operators is to ask each customer if they would want a special surface treatment in the photos. Along with this service comes a higher monetary negotiation. A special surface treatment requires the computer operator to use Photoshop to enhance the beauty of the photo through surface effects so as to make the faces or backgrounds glow and shine. In employing the Photoshop digital software to alter bodily accoutrements in photography, it is assumed that there is a visual language that is being invented with the development of the new electronic capital such that the embellishment of the human figure attracts more money. This could be seen as an effort to render the physiological effect of this form of photography to bring out the optical impact of shine. Photographers such as Kingsley Chuks in Lagos and computer operators in Animasaun Digital Studio play with the surface quality of photographs and in the process fashion a visual language that is tied to the new capital of computer and digital technology.

Krista Thompson has described surfacism as "a concentration on the materiality or visual texture of objects within or of the picture plane" (2009, 485). Surfacism draws attention to highly structured and elaborately refined objects as well as their highly sophisticated manner of representation. Over the years, artists and photographers have accentuated the tangible materiality of objects using surfacism. In the visual economy of European art, John Berger argues that two historical events in the sixteenth century gave impetus to the development of surface aesthetics—namely, the discovery of the art of oil painting and the rise of new moral economies around wealth and capital (1972, 84). He remarks that oil paint enabled artists such as Hans Holbein the Younger to develop tangible impressions and a sense of illusionism, texture, luster, and solidity in what he portrayed. Through the medium of oil painting, Holbein peopled his entire picture plane with objects, scrupulously detailing the surfaces in such a way as to convey "a sense of touch" (82). In Holbein's painting *The Ambassadors* (1533), two statesmen, Jean de Dinteville and Georges de Selve, are adorned in exquisitely and highly embroidered garments in the court of Britain's King Henry VIII. Their elegance, majesty, and pose serve to direct the eyes around the surface area of the painting, which is inhabited by a collection of material possessions, including objects symbolic of the sciences and arts. In the work, with the exception of the merchants' skin, almost all other surfaces, including the textile paraphernalia and the aesthetically structured instruments, convincingly announce the visual intensity of their surface details. Berger relates this new tactile rendering of the material world in oil paint to the "new power of capital" and "new attitudes to property and exchange" (88). In art-historical terms, this painting is reminiscent of a visual antecedent of the fashioning of power and prestige through material possessions. From its earliest inception in European art, Berger argues, surfacism gave visual form to a way of seeing that was confined to the market economy, new forms of self-fashioning, and the optical effects achievable specifically through oil painting.

Although Berger traces the origins of surfacism to the sixteenth century, some art historians connect surfacist practices with aesthetic pursuits that flowered in Europe in the seventeenth and eighteenth centuries. Svetlana Alpers, for example, notes that Dutch painters of the seventeenth century were overly preoccupied with the surface characteristics of things and often treated their works naturalistically, like a mirror or a map (1983, xxv). Similarly, Christine Buci-Glucksmann also remarks that artists of the Baroque period embellished the surfaces and surroundings of their paintings with a superabundance of decorative details. She asserts that surfacist aesthetics disfigure the visual image by showing its dependence on the materiality of the painting medium, which acts as a mirror image (Buci-Glucksmann, in Jay 1988, 17). For Buci-Glucksmann, Baroque surface aesthetics were visibly manifested on normalized models of visuality in such a way that their means of construction, especially through the medium of the mirror image, were made visible.

It is important to look at surfacism within a broader historical perspective of colonial and postcolonial visual culture. George Lau notes that the intensive modification of exterior surfaces in the Recuay culture of ancient Peru was a strategic field for negotiating status and identity. The style's principal media (pots, buildings, sculptures, textiles) formed part of political programs, both modest and grandiose, of chiefs and their close relations (2010). Citing James J. Gibson, Lau notes that "at the interface between mediums and substances, surfaces are where the action is"(262).

Lau's surfaces invoke resemblances between objects, different media, and materials in which he argues that surfaces can be more than inert bearers of images. They can have their own agentive qualities. In a much broader expansion of these agentive qualities of surfaces, many authors have explored the sensorial properties of surfaces such as color, brilliance, sharpness, and size, and suggest how these qualities can embody and engineer cultural patterns in extraordinary, unpredictable ways.[3] As will be shown in subsequent discussions, the surfaces of Chuks's photographic works, their colors, their tactile materiality and flatness of the shapes engineer the local cultural forms of *aso ebi* visuality.

Elucidating the historical conditions under which surface aesthetics figured in the past may offer insight into their production in the visual economy of postcolonial photography. Christopher Pinney (2003) observes that surfacism has characterized much popular small-town Indian photographic practice. Again one could argue that surfacism can be seen in the use of backdrops and the creation of photographic mise-en-scène by West African studio photographers in the twentieth century. In this manner, surfacism becomes an engagement with the superficial accoutrements of the image rather than a "narrativized indexical depth" (204).[4] Pinney's subsequent arguments on photographic surfacism identify the surface not as a layered phenomenon but rather as a practice that negates the chronotopic parameters of earlier European photographic exposures. These earlier photographic exposures include those linked to early European travel and the much-discussed "ethnography" in colonial states. Pinney has argued that the implication of colonial depth practices implies a surface that was constantly rendered invisible. In this manner it is assumed that photography is a spatiotemporal phenomenon that must follow a narrative sequence rather than an object that is bounded by a flat pictorial space. Such photographs being an index of peregrination and ethnography are opposed by the reworked photographs in Animasaun Digital Studio in Lagos, which are taken in a time-bound space but are transformed into "achronotopic" spaces through the digital medium. Unlike Berger's sixteenth-century paintings, the naturalism and realism in the picture plane of these photographs are replaced with a flat pictorial surface that does not convey a specific sense of time and space.

FROM ANALOG TO DIGITAL

When I visited Shegun Adekoya in his studio on Segan Street, Egbeda, Alimosho, Lagos, he told me that he bought a digital camera in 2003 and a computer and small digital printer in 2005. According to Adekoya, "I use my printer to print only passport photographs, but I go to [a] commercial digital printing laboratory to print bigger sizes of digital photos" (Adekoya 2010). In Adekoya's studio there were no studio props or other paraphernalia to show that photos were being taken in the studio. Instead he informed me that most of his photographs were taken at "events":

> You see, many of the customers stopped coming to the studio, so you discover that most of the photographs I work on were taken outside, especially in weddings and other functions. I edit them with Photoshop and make them beautiful so that the customers will like them. The problem is that many photographers rework their photos, and people normally look more beautiful in the reworked photos, so it makes them believe that you are a good photographer, and they think they actually look like that, not knowing that we rework the photos with Photoshop.

He made use of Photoshop software in working over the surfaces of the photos, recontextualizing some of them in a way that gives them the impression of a studio setting before taking them to the digital studio for printing. It is obvious that "the shift to the digital has shown that photographs are simply raw materials for an endless series of digressions" (Burnett 2004, 28).

There were about ten more digital printing studios in the Egbeda area of Lagos alone, and there were always about one thousand photographers that patronized a particular studio in a day. In Animasaun Digital Studio, for example, there were about ten computer operators aside from the chief computer technician. Each operator attended to one particular photographer at a time. Each photographer directed the operator accordingly in terms of digital manipulation of surface qualities of their photographs. Physical back-drops similar to those used by such early photographers as Seydou Keita and Malick Sidibé in Mali, and J. D'Okhai Ojeikere in Nigeria[5]—who worked with analog cameras—have been replaced by nonmaterial backdrops of the digital computers. Technology thus shifts the manipulation of the physical, tangible photographic mise-en-scène to manipulation of the intangible digital sur-faces. This practice is what is obtainable in the city of Lagos, and indeed other Nigerian cities, on an almost daily basis. However, weekends mark the height of this practice, because this is when many social events happen. On week-ends, more individuals come out of their respective homes in the morning only to return in the evening with scores of beautifully designed photographs bearing a background that never existed in their imagination. These digital backgrounds and beautifully manipulated clothes and bodies are the selling powers of the photographs. Perhaps one may offer some possible reasons for this new idiosyncrasy. Didier Gondola has suggested that "the social and eco-nomic chaos that characterizes the African city grafts itself onto the bodies of youths" (1999, 31).

From this perspective, getting shiny, digitally reconstructed bodies con-summates the city dwellers' entry into the world of perfection. It provides them with a symbolic satisfaction of abundance and prosperity, thus allow-ing them to reproduce a body that was an alternative metaphor for a chaotic social world. Most of the weekend social celebrants in Lagos bedeck them-selves in dainty *aso ebi* dresses. In posing for the camera amid the chaos of city life, the body is regenerated, it finds its redemption, it lives and shines in the cult of digital manipulation.

Nigerian society is one in which excess in all its ramifications is the hall-mark of wealthy livelihoods. It is a society where the idea of class values and social statuses is always enacted by visible emblems of affluence in social gatherings: monies exchanging hands and textile materials being displayed. When one views figure 30, for example, and how the photographer Mbadi-mma Chinemelum inserts his clients into a sea of excessive textile overflow, one understands that any lack in the individual's persona is believed to be ultimately transcended in the emerging photos. Mbadimma confirms that his clients prefer photos with excessive textile decoration, "especially one in which both the clothes and bodies have been 'beautified' with Photoshop" (Chinemelum 2013). He said his clients are always happy to see themselves with "beautiful skin and shiny dresses." Beautiful skin and shiny dresses therefore serve as the transformative surface process required to engender a new being, a consummation of the technological invention, of the digital software, required to arrive at the new self.

It is crucial to highlight an important dimension to the rise of *aso ebi* fashion in contemporary Nigerian social settings, as it helps to clarify the surface discourse in this chapter. Over the years, *aso ebi* has devolved into superficiality. The rise of digital photography and the invention of digital software such as Photoshop and CorelDRAW in the year 2000 coincided with the importation of cheaper textile materials used for *aso ebi* fashion. Both the digital software and *aso ebi* fashion, I argue, are practices that are embedded in surface treatments and the reconstruction of reality. When the deep human relationship that *aso ebi* professes dies, digital photography and profuse textile decoration help to resurrect them. Damaged by strange ambiguities of unstable social relations, *aso ebi* is constantly reinvented in the dreamlike screens of the digital photographer, where estranged lives are painstakingly united by software.[6] Any unseen distance, difference, or exclusion is literally reconciled by the intimacy invented by digital photography, in which the bodies now unite in the seeming uniformity of textile materials.

DIGITAL "SNAPPING" AS GROUP CURATING

At 10:00 a.m. on June 15, 2010, I went to All Souls Anglican Church in Lekki, Lagos, which was the venue for the wedding between Longfellow and Nkechi. I had been invited by a friend who happened to be among the *aso ebi* women attending the wedding. I had already made my intentions clear to this friend of mine that I was coming with a camera to photograph the occasion. When I reached the venue, none of the guests had arrived. I was seated outside the church premises with a few photographers who had come along uninvited to do "photography business" (as is the norm at most public functions in Lagos).[7] At about noon the couple arrived, escorted by a group of *aso ebi* women including Chinyere, who had invited me. As soon as they alighted from the car, Chinyere summoned her *aso ebi* friends, and they positioned themselves in a group and invited me to snap them. After the first snapshot, they all swarmed around me—already aware that I work with a digital camera—to view the pictures from the screen of my camera. One of the women, Uju, complained how her head was positioned in the photo and insisted that I delete the photo and snap another one. Not wanting the rest of her friends

Figure 30. Photo: Mbadimma Chinemelum. Lagos, 2013.

to repeat the same act, I decided to take several shots and then select from the best. After this round of snapping, Obioma complained about her eyes in one of the photos—that she was looking away from the camera, unlike her friends, who were gazing at the camera—and demanded that I delete it. In fact, she asked me to print from one of the numerous photos I had taken where she thought she looked beautiful. As I watched some other friends of the celebrant snapping photos of each other, the same process that I underwent with the *aso ebi* women was being enacted. Some friends snapped while others swarmed around them to see what the photos looked like.

My photographic experience here is informed by the constant intervention of those who were photographed because of the digital camera I was using. There was an interactive forum between me and the *aso ebi* women. Such interactions reenact, enhance, and alter body gestures and poses during photographing. The sense of aesthetic in the occasion is heightened by viewing the image through the screen of my digital camera. And the competitiveness invoked around glamour is such that when all the women saw themselves on my camera screen, some believed they were less beautiful and wanted the photo to be deleted and the whole process repeated. In this manner, deleting becomes the forte of the digital mode as opposed to the analog camera. Daniel Rubinstein and Katrina Sluis argue that the camera's delete button constructs the logic of a photographic rectitude and infallibility (2009, 13). During the process of my snapping, the screen of my digital camera served only as an arena for the instantaneous invention of personal beauty within group expressions of glamour. The screen became a tangible surface that offered immediate creative "insight" about images that were already visually accessible. This is where the surface becomes an index of group glamour and romanticization. In Pinney's understanding, the surface entails "the dialogical spaces of face-to-face encounter" (Pinney and Peterson 2003, 208). Unlike the studio, where the face-to-face encounter is between the photographer and the photographed, in the digital mode during social events the face-to-face encounter is transferred to the digital screen, where it becomes a process of engagement between the photographer, the referents, and the digital screen.

Again, those photographed are not interested in the space-time conjunction of the image; rather the focus is on the surface of the image itself and how it can be a site for possible reconstruction. In the group digital photo sessions in which I participated as photographer (unlike the analog world, where the photographer retains independence), photos are not just passively allowed to inhabit the camera but are acted upon on the spot, actively created, posed for, and reconstructed. The photos are revised to form or illustrate surface narratives, revisualized, and set into animated dialogue with people. In this instance, one could see that the first journey of the photo's creative process begins on the screen of the digital camera. Instant viewing on my screen is akin to the immediacy of vision that the analog camera cannot afford.

Rubinstein and Sluis observe that "during the first years of the 'digital revolution,' digital technology was largely inserted into the framework of existing traditional photographic practice" (2009, 11). Globally, the 1990s were characterized by a radical change from analog technology (darkroom tradition, chemical processing, and film) to digital technology of image treatment. Two remarkable achievements of the screen and the delete button were the lessening of the time in taking a picture and the time from taking it to view it on the screen. This introduced some flexibility into picture taking and allowed a new scope for perfection of the process. "Immediacy," a term employed in film theory, also applies to the way in which digital cameras provide an instant vision of events. Joseph G. Kickasola remarks that "immediacy" represents a modest term that is phenomenologically true for all of us; it is a term with a refreshingly consuming, sensational quality capable of provoking our sense of the indexical, without engaging that faculty in its fullness (Kickasola n.d.).

Digital photography could actually make a bid for a true apotheosis of art because of its capacity for intense and participatory meaning-making. In digital snapshots, agency is offered on the screen of the camera, which is the immediate arena of engagement for the subject to discuss the layers of meaning contained within the photograph. It is therefore experiential in such a way that offers the photographed an opportunity to "curate" the photographic process. An important feature of this mode (as against the analog camera) is that it no longer affords photographers a dominant voice in the curation of the photographic process, nor does it offer them room to impress a singular, personal narrative upon group displays. Rather, by looking through the screen of the camera and commenting, photographing becomes an active process of group participation and interaction. During my photography session, the fact that Obioma wanted to position her face in the same manner that her friends had reflects Geoffrey Batchen's view that "as a collective activity of picture-making, snapshots show the struggles of particular individuals to conform to the social expectations, and visual tropes, of their sex and class" (2008, 133). In this *aso ebi* photo I took, everyone simultaneously desired to adhere to the popular notions of "looking beautiful in the photo." Could digital snapshots be described as odes to conformist uniformity in the manner in which Obioma and her fellow *aso ebi* friends wished to conform to the conventional practice of being "photogenic"? That Obioma and her *aso ebi* friends wanted to look beautiful and insisted on deleting the supposed "ugly" photos perhaps shows that there is a sense of conformism prevailing in perceptions of how one must look in a photo.

ALTERED SURFACES: WHAT IS A SNAPSHOT?

Kingsley Chuks took me to his studio, where he had reworked some of the photos he took at the wedding. Most photos he took were of people in *aso ebi* uniform since in present-day Lagos (and as seen in previous chapters) a great percentage of guests who attend parties dress in *aso ebi*. However, the celebrants requested that he treat the photos very well before making an album for them, and informed the celebrants that he would alter the photos to create variety. He started by changing the backgrounds in some of them. Certain ladies in *aso ebi* were given a different background that utterly changed the photos, making it difficult for one to identify the original context under which the photographs were taken. More than six of the photos were given backgrounds with the use of Photoshop (figs. 33, 34, 36, 38, and 40). The original photos retained the original background. Viewing Chuks's photos allowed me to arrive at the conclusion that he—as well as many other photographers in Lagos—is an "artist-photographer" in the eyes of his clients. Indeed, Chuks might well have attained a certain level of renown in his professional generation. That does not mean he is validated by any cultural institutions such as galleries and museums in the celebratory manner that formally qualifies a practitioner as an artist-photographer. But what he does with Photoshop allowed me to discover new areas of engagement with contemporary postcolonial photography, especially photographers who are not validated within the ideological, institutional precincts of art orthodoxy.

This attitude about photography did not exist in 1960s Nigeria when, according to Pa J. D'Okhai Ojeikere, "most weddings usually had one commissioned photographer hired most of the times by the bridegroom" (2010). Pa Ojeikere, who owns a photo studio along Ogubanwo Street in the Ketu area of Lagos, achieved international acclaim through a book written about him by Andre Magnin. Ojeikere told me how he had covered weddings in the 1950s and 1960s and showed me some photos of the weddings he covered. "I used to be the only photographer in most weddings I covered," he said. These days there are usually innumerable photographers during most social activities. Figure 31 shows a group photograph of a wedding that Pa Ojeikere covered in 1969; he said the total number of photos he took that day was not more than thirty. In this group photograph, Pa Ojeikere notes that all the different *aso ebi* groups had converged together such that one may observe multiple dress styles and uniforms. In recent weddings in Lagos, almost everybody has a camera—either hand cameras, camera phones, or automatic analog cameras. A question then arises: Could this photographic ubiquity aptly fit into what Geoffrey Batchen describes as the "boring pictures" and "snapshots" category? This constitutes another area of scholarly engagement.

There is a growing recognition among photography theorists of essentialist postulations of a history of photography that is ideologically tied to categorization. These theorists have also worked to open up this historical canon to embrace further sundry classifications such as the snapshot.[8] For example, James Elkins has unveiled the inherent divisions and tensions of disciplinary boundaries—in "high art" and vernacular practices—among art history scholars. In recent times, through the efforts of these theorists there is an increasing validation of the historical premise of snapshot aesthetics, but this is based only on the self-referential investigation of snapshot aesthetics' influence upon "fine art" (Elkins 2007).

Snapshots have come to be part of the "ethnographic turn" that tended to displace art history with visual culture. Snapshots have been described as the most "ubiquitous and familiar of photographic genres" capable of provoking a desire for alternative histories of photography. But because snapshots are the most numerous and popular of photographic forms, they represent an interpretive problem that is absolutely central to any substantial scholarship devoted to the history of photography (Batchen 2008, 121).

However, the argument I advance here is an identification, or perhaps an incarnation, of "art-photography" within the precincts of popular photography. Kingsley Chuks might have taken his photography beyond snapshots, considering the creative processes surrounding their snapping and eventual production through the special attention given to the surfaces. Unlike other photographs where the snapping is done on the spur of the moment, without much work, most *aso ebi* photographs that Chuks took underwent painstaking, imaginative processes during snapping and their final production, a practice resembling art-photographic conventions.

The fact that Chuks's clients appreciate his creative input—demanding that he reworks the surfaces—shows that there is an elevation of the snapshots and the vernacular, everyday genre of photography to the level of aesthetic objects. Indeed, the argument one may need to advance here is that Chuks's photographs may no longer be seen as banal pieces of visual consumption, because they satisfy popular demands and inhabit private spaces. Chuks's effort is rather a deviation from the normative and institutionalizing assumptions of postcolonial photographic practice. He has highlighted the importance of the surface located on the image and the various invented contexts it undergoes in the digital studios of the photographer. His effort also shows that the very materiality of the digital object is not the mechanical and the physical.

In a vivid description of Seydou Keita's photographs, Kobena Mercer (1995) observes that "with various props, accessories and backdrops, the photographer stylizes the pictorial space, and through lighting, depth of field, and framing, the camera work heightens the mise-en-scène of the subject, whose poses, gestures and expressions thus reveal a self not as he or she actually is, but 'just a little more than what we really are'" (cited in Pinney and Peterson

Figure 31. Group wedding photograph. Lagos, 1969. Photo: J. D'Okhai Ojeikere.

Figure 32. *Aso ebi* women. Lagos, 1969. Photo: Kingsley Chuks.

Figure 33. *Aso ebi* women against a Photoshopped plain background. Lagos, 1969. Photo: Kingsley Chuks.

Figure 34. *Aso ebi* women against a Photoshopped textile background. Lagos, 1969. Photo: Kingsley Chuks.

Figure 35. *Aso ebi* woman in red. Lagos, 1969. Photo: Kingsley Chuks.

2003). This comment recognizes the fact that the pictorial space is located in the real studio of the photographer, where real clothes and backgrounds and props are used to reveal a substitute self. In the present context of my discussion regarding Kingsley Chuks's *aso ebi* photographs, the pictorial space is most often located in the digital studio of the computer, which allows him room to perform all the decorative activities on the surface of the photograph. The pictorial surface of the photograph becomes more surreal than real. The surface is shifted from the factual, concrete exploitation of the physical body and space in the studio of the photographer to the manipulation of the non-

Figure 36. *Aso ebi* woman against a Photoshopped textile background. Lagos, 1969. Photo: Kingsley Chuks.

physical body and spaces of the computer. In other words, by de-linking the physical sites of wedding ceremonies, Chuks's photographs emphasize a new kind of geography, privileging immobility and stasis over what Stephen Groening (2008) calls "place-loyalty."[9]

Thus, on these surfaces, the context and location of the digital object are manipulated, allowing for relationships and juxtapositions that were previously not possible. Chuks has shown that the nature of digital photography, therefore, is not presence and history but translation and modification. Separated from the presupposition of truth, Chuks's digital image is no longer bound by the conventions of truth. It is free to be as expressive as a painting. The photos live up to what Pinney describes as "refusal of the realist chronotopes" (Pinney and Peterson 2003, 218) by stripping away all the "organiz-

Figure 37. Family members of the bride in *aso ebi*. Lagos, 2009. Photo: Kingsley Chuks.

ing principles of Cartesian perspectivalism or the surface arts of describing"
(Thompson 2009, 498; see figs. 32, 35, 37 and 39). I suggest that Chuks's delib-
erate obliteration of the Cartesian perspectivalism amounts to what Deborah
Poole describes as "hiding what lays hidden underneath the untidy surface
details" (2005, 164). It could also mean excluding from view what Elizabeth
Edwards (1997) calls "visual excess" of context and the "off frame." Thinking
through Edwards's phrases further suggests that this "visual excess" begets
the surface details that threaten to undermine the very subjects Chuks aims
to pronounce. This creative subversion functions as an erasive medium and
closely reflects what historical oil paintings did with the pictorial surface of
the image. Norman Bryson has argued that "historical oil paintings first erase
the surface of the picture plane: visibility of the surface would threaten the
coherence of the fundamental technique through which Western represen-
tational image classically works the trace, of ground-figure-relations" (1983,
111–17). By placing figures against a monochrome bright gray background
(fig. 33), Chuks literally pulls the ground from the representation, highlighting the organizing structure, the erasive illusion, of Photoshop editing.

In figures 34, 36, 38 and 40, Chuks's employment of such textile-like back-

Figure 38. Family members of the bride in *aso ebi* against a Photoshopped textile background. Lagos, 2009. Photo: Kingsley Chuks.

grounds extends into a broader engagement with the history of postcolonial photography, which foregrounds the historic relation between photography and textile commodities in the African context. An interesting metaphor to tinker around with, especially in the visual loudness of textiles in West Africa, is what Krista Thompson calls "the visual scream of the commodity" (2009, 499) in which the fascination with the visual appeal of textile resonates across both fashion and photography. The attraction that textiles possess as a form of personal adornment and visual representation may be seen as a means of articulating visual subjectivity in Africa outside of Western economies of vision: it is no longer anti-fashion to appear in public photographs dressed in "traditional" textile materials. Chuks's digital treatment of the pictorial space in the *aso ebi* photos is in keeping with surfacist aethetics' revelatory potential. It brings into focus alternative ways of seeing that dominant forms of postcolonial photographic representation conceal from view, by foregrounding the creeping consciousness of digital technology in Africa.

Considering the nature and stylistics of Chuks's surfaces (often through textiles), one may need to invoke George F. Lau's argument that the role of surfaces extends to "covers for the human body and forms that are likened

Figure 39. Family members of the bride in *aso ebi*. Lagos, 2009. Photo: Kingsley Chuks.

to the human body, personal ornaments, attires and their essential role for personal and collective identity" (2010, 263). From this, one can identify a striking homology in Chuks's attempt to (re)construct the surface of the photographic spaces using textiles, through which he fashions both personal and collective visual identities, and the fact that the same textiles are employed to fashion *aso ebi* bodies in the figures. For Lau, there are parallels that suggest cognate expressions of a cross-media style based on enriching surfaces—by perceiving and rendering design through background space. The background space constitutes the arena where time and space experience a dramatic reconfiguration. And for this reason there is a need to reflect on Mikhail Bakhtin's concept of chronotope in relation to time and space.

Bakhtin describes the chronotope as a site within a narrative where time and space "thicken" and merge, each assuming the qualities of the other (1981, 202). He goes to great lengths to categorize these various chronotopes, such as "the chronotope of the road," "the chronotope of the drawing room or salon," "the chronotope of the idyll," and so on. To this list I would add the "chrono-

Figure 40. Family members of the bride in *aso ebi* against a textile background with lady in blue from figure 39 Photoshopped out. Lagos, 2009. Photo: Kingsley Chuks.

tope of the photograph" as the surface where the magical emanation of the image comes into confluence with the surreal pictorial space. This surface becomes the site where time and space are made to undergo achronotopic transformation such that the image and its referent are on equal terms.

The notion of real time has changed since digital languages have been present in our everyday lives. Time is no longer perceived as the passing of a continuous action, confronted with the logic of the analogical pointers of a watch or the time-space fixer of the analog camera. In the information-flow society in which we live, the notion of time is now digital, of discontinuous and ubiquitous character (omnipresent). The notion of displacement and of intervals (as it was) is gone, and time acquires a different dimension, which is arbitrary, intensive, and diverted from traditional parameters. The spatiotemporal changes introduced by Chuks are in line with Lev Manovich's observation that "the digital object presents a new functioning of space and time, info-subjectivity, new dynamics of cultural production and consumption"

(2001, 45–48). In this regard, time in Chuks's photos is never existent in the pictures. Time has been blotted out (figs. 32, 35, 37, and 39) and replaced by a surface that is only timeless (figs. 33, 34, 36, 38, and 40). The spatiotemporal relations in the image have been frozen into a digital reconstruction and is only possible on the surface of the photos.

As could be seen in Chuks's photographs, the extant perception of space-time in photography is becoming connected to the constant manipulations propitiated by the digital mode. Chuks reminds us that through Photoshop editing, we live within a logic of an indefinitely present time that constantly subverts our relation with the past and the future, with memory and forgetfulness. In this sense, new circumstances of temporal apprehension are established through digitality that stretches and subverts the logic of realist times.

Surfaces have been theorized as extensions of body and mind that are intended to be layered and networked (Gell 1998; Knappett 2006). I would add that some surfaces are meant to relate to other, similar surfaces. Such a proposal helps to explain Chuks's widespread distribution of surfaces across the figure-space boundary. Close examination of Chuks's creative resources reveals a subversion of the rigid determinism of spatiotemporal surfaces into a process that incorporates the fictional processing mechanism of the digital system. Contrary to Bakhtin's view, time and space are no longer equal and interdependent. One can exist without the other. These photos could be read in terms of "achronotopic" surfaces that do not allow the viewer to interpret construction through space and time simultaneously, such that there is no revelation of any layeredness and interdependency. A logical argument here is that in Chuks's digital system, the viewer can no longer be immersed in the photograph; neither can they pierce their ways through any wedding context. In figures 32, 35, 37, and 39 the discarding of formal photographic structures of linear-perspective and decisive moments during the events photographed (figs. 33, 34, 36, 38, and 40) foregrounds a tendency to dislodge the spatiotemporal flow in favor of a creative enterprise in the Photoshop medium.

My further inquiries about the people Chuks photographed and the circumstances surrounding the digital photographs yielded some interesting results. The women in figure 32, according to Chuks, are members of the Egbeda Social Club who asked him to remove them from the occasion (Chuks 2010). So the assumption here is that there is a quest for detachment or, put differently, a desire to be removed from an occasion by the clients. The discovery made here is that most people whom Chuks photographed do not care whether their space is invaded by intruders during the actual process of photographing. Chuks told me that some *aso ebi* groups he photographed did not ask intruders to stay away from the photo, knowing fully well that these individuals would eventually go away during editing. He said that some of his clients demanded that those who did not appear in *aso ebi* be Photoshopped out of the group. In some of the chapters in this book, I have addressed the issue of exclusion in *aso ebi*. In some wedding parties, those who did not appear in *aso ebi* uniform were denied food and wedding gifts. Now a similar exclusion is being imported into photography. According to Chuks

> Those who did not dress in *aso ebi* sometimes did not fit into the group photograph. For example, during the photo session in some weddings, when a call is made for a group photograph of friends of the bride, everybody comes out dressed in *aso ebi*. You would notice that the group would not be happy to allow anyone not dressed in similar *aso ebi* as them to join the photograph because the person, according to them, will spoil the photo. (Chuks 2010)

This statement may be understood if one looks at figure 38, for instance. Everyone appears in *aso ebi*, and one would imagine that anyone who dresses differently wanting to join the group would be vehemently rejected. To demonstrate this further, the people in the background in figure 37 have been removed. It is assumed, therefore, that in figure 38, the couple demanded this exclusion. It thus can be established that the art of surfacism achieved through Photoshop editing plays many roles: first, it lives up to the aesthetic expectations of clients; second, it excludes undesirable elements; and finally, it invents the studio space. And again it could be argued that in some instances the art of surfacism is informed by a sense of exclusivity: a need to ward off invaders.

CONCLUSION

In this chapter, I have suggested that *aso ebi* may have informed the revolution seen in digital Photoshop editing among Lagos photographers. The urge to appear in fashionable *aso ebi* dresses has influenced the surface reconstruction of most wedding photographs. I have shown that the proliferation of photographers in social events in Nigeria is a trend that came with the new technological capital of digital cameras and the digital photo lab. Photography now offers a creative platform to alter surface qualities of many photos taken at weddings and other social events, thus removing them from the time and space of such events to an invented time and space. It is assumed here that what obtains in recent times in popular photography in Lagos, and in certain postcolonial photographic practices, is a mobile studio where the props and studio spaces have been replaced by the digital technology of Photoshop studio spaces. The Photoshop software has aided certain *aso ebi* groups to possess their own spaces and exclude those who do not appear in the same uniform as theirs.

Conclusion

In this book, I set out to investigate the meanings of *aso ebi* in urban Lagos, its historical trajectory, and its visual constructions. I pursued questions as to why and how *aso ebi* is intensifying and the nature of this intensification. Overall it has been ascertained that *aso ebi* has journeyed through a maze of social, visual, cultural, and political paths, practically arriving at an indeterminate space that reveals a new culture of solidarity and fashion. It has become obvious that what is called *aso ebi* is a practice that is defined by the politics of everyday life, along with the impact of commercial culture and visual traffic in the city of Lagos.

I took a leap into the colonial history of Lagos through which what I hope a nuanced interpretation of colonial sartorial practices has emerged. While *aso ebi* was believed to have been historically located within Yoruba family networks, this study has unequivocally established its proliferation through church missionaries of early twentieth-century Yorubaland. Through the missionaries, *aso ebi* experienced further intensification among church organizations, Yoruba age grades, and eventually hometown organizations. Through these networks I charted a genealogy of *aso ebi* to suggest how this genealogy reinvented its meanings in line with the changing realities of urban cosmopolitanism.

The choice of Lagos city for this study derived from an understanding that *aso ebi* has virtually become a city affair. This is not to dispute the fact that *aso ebi* is a ubiquitous phenomenon in Nigeria but rather to show that as the fashion center of Nigeria, Lagos possesses some unsurpassable scale and force in the constitution of novelty and glamour. Victor Lewis might well have supported this assertion in his contention that "in Lagos the *Aso ebi* event is the fashion show that disseminates new ideas and new ways to look at fashion and sartorial presentation" (Lewis 2009). Again, my assertion is supported by the emergence of complex efforts aimed at promoting *aso ebi* culture and dress styles. Through this axis, I unveiled why certain individuals in the city have historically attached importance to *aso ebi*. What emerged is an attempt by various individuals toward commercializing *aso ebi*. In this way *aso ebi* became a practice that spoke the language of hybridity and brico-lage through modern fashion, thus ushering in a new tradition of solidarity and visual culture. This redefinition is also momentous when some scholars, in the course of twentieth-century Nigeria, identifed a shift away from the emulation of "foreign culture" to a reaffirmation of the "indigenous cultural heritage," with dress as a significant element of such a shift (Wass 1979). While I may have traced the trajectory of this shift through *aso ebi*, the redefini-tion of *aso ebi* from core "traditional" elements to "high" fashion serves as an important space to articulate the meanings of "indigenous cultural heritage."

It has become obvious that the discussion of *aso ebi* became enmeshed in a history of traditional dress that has prevailed at social events in Lagos, starting from at least the first half of the twentieth century, which is prior to the period I have studied here. Christopher Steiner points out that "by the late 1920s imported textiles had become so tightly woven into the fabric of Afri-can life," such that what is known as "traditional dress" in Nigeria today has a long history of European capitalist mediation (1985, 105). This history dates to the fifteenth century. However, because *aso ebi* dress is often regarded as "tra-ditional dress," one question that I addressed in this book is the issue of how traditional *aso ebi* actually has, which, as I argued, mapped authenticity as a contentious issue into the analyses of "traditional dress." This idea has also been elucidated in Leslie Rabine's work on the Senegalese textile industry and is akin to my tracking of Chinese mercantile networks in Lagos. In Dakar, Senegal, Rabine (2002) observed how Indonesian batiks were imitated in the Dutch, French, and British textile factories and aimed at African markets. Designers in Indian-owned British companies also copied these Indonesian motifs and targeted African markets. While the same designers invent pat-terns to be sold as distinctively African, Rabine concluded that "what is 'Afri-can' about the fabric is not a particular image of authenticity imprinted on the cloth, rather it is mobile social history and an open geography that produce the cloth" (138). While my conclusions support Rabine's submission, it should be noted that there is a constitution of postcolonial agency that is occasioned by the quest to embrace the imagined notions of "traditional dress." Again, this postcolonial agency is ostensibly promoted by the vicissitudes seen in the textile economy. I therefore assert that late global capitalism has redefined the contours of sartorial practices in *aso ebi* in postcolonial Lagos. In discussing consumer taste, I have given some attention to textiles as critical commodities within an ensuing economic network between Nigeria and the rest of world spanning many centuries.

I arrived at the conclusion that *aso ebi* is being fed by the underlying visual and consumerist hype that underpin the late capitalist system as it unfolds in the cosmopolitan city of Lagos. The tenor of the argument that resonates across the chapters suggests that human life under *aso ebi* has become largely defined by the economics, and materiality, of mundane living under late capitalism. These economics are reflected in chapter 2 through the textile economy, in chapter 3 through notions of wealth and large followership, in chapter 4 through commercialization of *aso ebi* friendship, in chapter 5 through further commercialization in fashion magazines and photography, and in chapter 6 through computer software. In the process, individuals who practice *aso ebi* seem to have lost the sense of a "precolonial humanism" (for want of a better phrase) with which *aso ebi* was originally identified: there are no longer free *aso ebi* gifts. Instead what obtains is a fetishization of various forms of commodity culture ranging from the textile economy, personality cults through mass followership, the negotiation of symbolic power through mass-produced images in the magazines, exchange value in human relationships through gifts, and a form of exclusion achieved through the surface effects of digital photo editing. It seems that for *aso ebi* there is no escape from the endless crisis of what Hudita Nura Mustafa calls "postcolonial ruin." Instead, it has become an essential part of what I call "Lagos cosmopolitanism."

This study became necessary at a period of Nigeria's journey through unconscious nationalism and a time of ambivalent discourse around the postcolonial. Since 1960, after Nigeria's independence, most political parties have switched to the use of *aso ebi* during their national conventions. Sometimes these conventions are fraught with a feud that exposes an insider/outsider politics of *aso ebi*. It is obvious that *aso ebi* can be used to create a boycott among political opponents just as it can be used to rally supporters among politicians and individuals in the larger society. That *aso ebi* is a product of a fraught dialogue between defective colonial bequests (seen especially from the example of the Christian missionaries) and postcolonial devastation is undeniable. This is exemplified by the unresolved economic crisis through the SAP, endemic corruption, and social inequality and insecurity, all of which have been fructified by the military and political maladministration of Nigeria. The failure of the nation-state could not but portend a dangerous struggle by her citizenry to regain the psyche of putative lost or dying statuses. Individuals must therefore reinvent themselves through whatever means available. *Aso ebi* became one of these means. It fed into the lawlessness of the military (*Owambe* under the military readily comes to mind), ate into the putrefaction of degenerate politicians, nurtured the lost glory of the dwindling middle class, and glided through the emptiness of the social systems (see chapter 5).

While clothing and fashionable consumption take their place within the context of mass leisure as it is interpreted by Peter Bailey and cited in Christopher Breward (1995), I have portrayed clothing not just as a simple utilitarian, everyday object but also as something that defines a person's status in society.[1] Defining this status in the context of Lagos is prefigured in, among many other manifestations, a common association of the crowd dressed in *aso ebi* with a celebrant's prestige and wealth. This is a politics of numbers that is also expressed in the image of the "big man" who must attract large numbers of people so "that he may have a large crowd dressed in *aso ebi* clothes following him when he goes in the streets," a demonstration of his public acceptance (Bascom 1951, 8). Again, the ubiquity of *aso ebi* practice also resides in the ready availability of cheap textile materials known as *ankara*.

Particular points I raised have made it possible to come to terms with the issue of how "our own visions of the city are acquired and represented" and how what I call "fashionable images" may have influenced the city dwellers' understanding of culture and the meanings of "tradition" (Sharpe and Wallock 1987, 2) The choice of *aso ebi* in Lagos, therefore, has shown that traditions are "invented" and that this process of invention is as a result of the changes in the visual and political economies of *aso ebi*.[2] In Nigeria, photographs of *aso ebi* dresses in what are known as "fashion magazines" have become a norm, such that viewing a social event in such magazines without *aso ebi* now seems unlikely. In this sense, it is obvious that some individuals who attend social functions feel the constant surveillance of their public selves by photographers attached to these fashion magazines, bearing in mind the publicity images they might create in the pages of the magazines. I have studied the role of photography and these magazines in the construction of *aso ebi* dress culture in social gatherings of Lagos. My study has shown that through a tripartite conjoining of photography, fashion magazines, and their websites, as well as Lagos tailors, group glamour and sartorial workmanship are commercialized through *aso ebi*.

I have argued that the fashionable image has become democratized through acts of copying, and copies of, photographs of *aso ebi*. It has become clear in the course of writing this book that many people would like their social events and their attendant *aso ebi* dress styles to appear in these fashion magazines and online fashion websites. Popular photographers who copy these images from social events have also played a key role between the people, the tailors, and other agents of style dissemination.

Judith Perani and Norma Wolff have remarked that in Lagos and other large cities in Nigeria, each weekend is marked by lavish celebrations and ceremonies, to which people are expected to wear their most fashionable ensembles (1999, 179). In fact, Perani and Wolff note that people see these occasions as opportunities to exhibit the newest-trend clothes or launch new cloth patterns. However, it is instructive that Perani and Wolff locate the exhibition of fashionable dressing within social gatherings in Nigeria but do not discuss the nature of these fashionable dresses, although they mention *aso ebi* in passing. I have expanded on this hint: in the end it becomes clear that each weekend in Lagos does not just come with fashionable ensembles, as remarked by Perani and Wolf, but that the key element of these fashionable ensembles was the *aso ebi* uniform. Inherent in these uniforms, however, are altercations that no outsider may have imagined among the supposedly harmonious *aso ebi* groups. I have attempted to elucidate these altercations and the supposed causes and consequences they have on *aso ebi*.

Such consequences suggest that *aso ebi* is fraught with internecine discord that engenders a constant invention and reinvention of meanings in the practice. Through a nuanced interpretation of the meanings of wealth in urban Lagos, the social borders of *aso ebi* practice are constantly reshaped. When notions of family solidarity, political camaraderie, friendship, gifts, and love are invoked by *aso ebi* users, life becomes entangled within ambivalent, equivocal, internal politics. First, the gift that one would ordinarily assume to be a gift becomes a negotiation colored with reciprocity, with a stringent fine of social exclusion if breached. Second, a strong attachment to the artifact of material adornment defines the intimacy of love to which *aso ebi* makes claim. Third, in its bid for financial recouping, *aso ebi* friendship expands, beckons to strangers, and threatens the essential ingredients that bind "real" friendship together.

Interviews conducted around Lagos show that many people who engage in *aso ebi* do so not because of their avowed commitment, altruism, or professed friendship to their *aso ebi* group but because it has become a convention and social obligation. Any deviance to this sartorial commitment has attracted exclusion. Therefore, for some people, participation in *aso ebi* is a practice that comes with indifference, subtle compulsion, and indisposition, all of which are subsumed under the rhetoric of friendship and solidarity. There is always a visible fear of exclusion. By definition, such exclusions, it was discovered, typically do not extend to the boycott of friends or family members but simply those (whether friends or strangers) who fail to appear in *aso ebi*. In other words, there may not be any real family membership or friendship in *aso ebi*, and one can only become a friend if one appears in *aso ebi*.

A recurring thematic thrust in this book has been the issue of dress style, sartorial presentation, and group fashioning in *aso ebi* and how it depicts the nature of friendship, group affiliations, and conviviality in Lagos society.[3] Here I have narrated the story of the textile economy as a metaphor for under-standing the social, economic, and aesthetic sensibilities of individuals and groups in Lagos.[4] I have attempted to develop further the idea of the anthro-pologist William Bascom, who, in 1951, studied about 354 photographic sam-ples of a locally manufactured cloth in Nigeria known as aṣọ òkè. He linked the popularity of these textiles to their use as *aso ebi* by some social clubs in Lagos (Horn and Gurel 1968, 182). The question that was missing in Bascom's research was how these clubs popularized the textile fabrics, especially for use as *aso ebi*. However, what I have tried to show is the way *aso ebi* was pop-ularized from the 1960s through spotlighting the rich in the newspapers and magazines, from which it became obvious that *aso ebi* clothing constitutes a public image. This, I suggest, may have given rise to the emergence of fashion magazines in Lagos through which *aso ebi* dress styles were circulated.

I suppose the question one might have is, Why did I write this book? While *aso ebi* evidently lacks a scholarly investigation in book form, I have attempted an exposition of *aso ebi* as a signifier of cultural identification and urban nationalism. I have shown how *aso ebi* created debates and discourses around the notions of solidarity and belonging in Nigeria. This book is a study of how, through *aso ebi*, Nigerians built, imagined, and (re)interpreted social groups and networks. Thus, in addition to contributing to literature on visual cultural practices in Africa, especially in Nigeria, the book contributes to social and cultural history that focuses on dress to ascertain the nature of changing urban practices in Nigeria. Looking at the practice of photography in relation to *aso ebi*, the work is a visual history that focuses on *aso ebi* to discuss how, at different epochs, Lagosians as actors were attentive to dress in their participation in social activities, which in turn served active economic needs at some points. The historical works, contemporary analysis, and "participant observation" methods I have focused on help to explain how men and women in Lagos have shown agency in their actions and reactions to local and global events.

I have accentuated the plight of Lagos as an African city in dire need of visual cultural analysis and fashion studies. That Lagos provides a microscopic lens into the labyrinths of an African urban world has further justified a book of this nature. In recognition of the fact that new forms of urban cultural and mercantile networks have reinvented a web of histories and styles in most African cities, it became interesting that this study exposed Lagos as a city of fashion and a "modernizing exemplar" of urban identities in Nigeria (Enwezor 2002 19; Ofeimun 2005, 118).

The book has shed light on the role played by fashion consumption in the development of cosmopolitan sensibilities and cultural identities in Lagos. This is evident through the politics inherent in the historiography of clothing and the practice of everyday life in urban Lagos. I have reviewed materials drawn from a range of critical and conceptual paradigms through which I forged a fresh analysis of theoretical, historical, and contemporary consumption habits in *aso ebi* among Lagos residents. Again, given the fact that "there is still little done on the visual culture experience in Africa," especially Nigeria, this project became imperative (Oguibe 2001, 9). This, no doubt, helped to "accumulate a body of knowledge on the history of clothing and visual cultural practices in Africa" (9). In this vein, not only have I attempted to present a history of photography in Nigeria through a specific, contextualized reading of postcolonial photography, but I have also underscored the urgent need to transcend the abiding literatures on the analog medium in postcolonial photography. I beckon scholars to view postcolonial African photography through the prism of the digital age. Doing so will help in forging a preliminary base for its theorization.

Finally, all the chapters in this book are united by their common concern with *aso ebi*. It is my argument that *aso ebi* in the twenty-first century is a hybrid cultural phenomenon that is acted upon by many factors. A central facilitator of these factors is the commercialization that has become the bane of late capitalism. I argue that photography and other visual manifestations in urban Lagos form part of these commercial cultures. This, among many other factors, is crucial to understanding the evolving meaning of *aso ebi* culture in urban Lagos.

NOTES

INTRODUCTION

1. Ankara is the batik-inspired, colorful cotton cloths printed industrially. The name *ankara* must have been made especially popular when the Turks and China began making cheaper versions and imitations of the wax prints for massive African consumption. While this history of Ankara is debatable, John Picton (1995) suggests that the term is a corrupt version of Accra, the Ghanaian capital city, believed to be the transit route for foreign wax-print fabric into the Nigerian markets. This position seems to be endorsed by Oyelola (2007), See also Motunrayo, Oyedele and Babatunde, (2013, 167).

2. Plain white or loom-patterned cotton cloths with strips of blue and red yarns were already popular in Yorubaland at this time and constituted an important elite paraphernalia. Little or no references were made to the colors and local names of the textiles produced and traded along the Bight of Benin by West African weavers in the period spanning the tenth to seventeenth centuries. Lack of visual evidence on those cloths again complicates attempts to determine their types and uses in various capacities. Both the vertical loom and the treadle loom strip cloths have been suggested as the two woven styles brought from Oyo and Ijebu-Ode during the eighteenth century that became popular in the Allada market. These cloths were prevalent in production and consumption within the entire sociocultural life of the Yoruba people, including, perhaps, the family uniformed fabric. It was most likely that *ashigbo*, which was a kind of cotton cloth woven in Yorubaland, then constituted the main uniformed cloth for burial events. See Kriger (2005).

3. Archaeological evidence suggesting when cotton production was thought to have flourished in West Africa dates to the tenth century. Fragments of cotton textiles dating between the eleventh and eighteenth centuries, retrieved in some burial caves across the Bandiagra Cliffs and other West African regions, showed evidence of the treadle loom, which was very popular in Yorubaland even till the present period. This proves the trans-Saharan trade network in textile across the Nile Valley through the Sahara to the West of Africa, with characteristics that suggest Yoruba origins. More researches have noted that spinning cotton in West Africa was done entirely by hand using a small

spindle made of a shaft of wood or reed with a certain kind of ceramic whorl used to achieve a balance during the spinning process. See Kriger (2005, 87–116); Kriger (2007, 76–77, 70–72); Bolland (1991); and BL, Sierra Leone (1796, 136r–156r).

4. This comparison of the rise of the Western city to that of Lagos is in keeping with my model to investigate how the modernity of Lagos emerged from peculiar historical processes some of which are strongly tied to material culture. For example, the rise of aso ebi enables me to track the economic changes of Lagos, as well as the city's distinguishing elements, from other rural communities in Nigeria. In comparison, one can find an example of the transition from a rural to an urban community in the mill towns of England in Ash and Wright (1988).

5. Eugenie Lemoine-Lucciono has also remarked that "clothing draws the body so that it can be culturally seen and articulates it as a meaningful form"; cited in Wilson and de la Haye (1999, 2).

6. See, for example, Victoria Rovine's interesting description of fashion in her book *African Fashion, Global Style: Histories, Innovations and Ideas You Can Wear* (2014, 15–18).

7. For more on similar crises of *aso ebi* in colonial Lagos, see Keyes (1993, 374–76).

8. For similar remarks on *aso ebi*, see also Bascom (1951, 8).

9. See, for example, Malinowski (1920, 97–105).

10. Compare with Taussig (1980); and Ugwu-Oju (1997).

11. For comprehensive discussions on the nature and history of gift giving, see, for example, Verhezen (2005); Douglas (1990); Cheal (1988); Roberts, Richards, and Bengtson (1991); Komter (2005); Malinowski (1997); and Malinowski (1978).

12. Victoria L. Rovine (2014) deals with similar modes of urban stylistic dissemination in Africa. Other books that explore the multidimensional aspects of African sartorial modernity include Mokake (2010); Gott (2010, 69–70, 45–48); Rabine (2002); Maiwada and Renne (2007, 25–58); and Grabski (2010).

13. Other literature that addresses similar intersection of fashion and visual culture includes Grabski (2009), which tracks the interface between fashion production and the visual experience associated with urban life in Dakar, Senegal. Grabski's analysis underscores the imbrications of fashion in Dakar and the city's conceptual and visual landscape, the street and the mass media, and finally dialogues within and beyond Africa. She concludes that not only do fashion makers select visual and conceptual elements from the urban ocular field, but rather by creating new propositions for visual consumption, fashion makers also constitute visual experience in Dakar (215–28). See also Mustafa (2001, 47–53); Scheld (2007, 232–52); Barber (2000); and Denzer (2002, 93–114).

14. See, for example, Lipovetsky (1994); Entwistle (2000); and Buckley and Fawcett (2002).

15. The varying contextual reach and social embeddedness encapsulated in the dressed body have been explored in many texts. For example, Karen Tranberg Hansen (2003) explores the philosophical import of dress as a "thing" that undergoes a "social death" within the ephemeral materiality of complex social relations. For more on this

social embeddedness and the dressed body, see Rovine (2004); Eicher (2001); Renne (2010); Trowell (1960); DeNegri (1962, 4–12); Gardi (1970); Heathcote (1972, 12–19); Plankensteiner and Adediran (2010); Gardi (2009); and Eicher and Ross (2010).

16. Our understanding of such analyses—to be specific, about the scope of this book, which is clothing practices—can be enriched through studies on the global textile trade, See, for example, Crill (2006); Berg (2003, 228–44); Steiner (1985); Johnson (1974b, 178–87); and Akinrinade and Ogen (2008, 159–70).

17. The most relevant of these are, but not limited to, Comaroff and Comaroff (1997); Martin (1994); Tarlo (1996); Cohn (1996, 106–62); Kennedy (1990, 118–40); Bhatia (2003, 327–44); Rabine (1997, 145–68); and Tulloch (1998, 359–82).

18. Little of the only literature that dealt with uniforms did so within the ambits of a colonial official dress and the Boy Scout movement; see, for example, Parsons (2006, 361–83); and Callaway (1992, 232–47).

19. Doris Essah's "Fashioning the Nation: Hairdressing, Professionalism, and the Performance of Gender in Ghana, 1900–2006" (2008) elaborately maps the political genealogies of fashion in nationalist discourse and foregrounds the nature of performativity that attends the everyday in Africa through fashion. See also Barnes and Eicher (1993); and Eicher (1995).

20. See also Roach and Eicher (1965).

CHAPTER 1

1. Oba Kosoko (1845–1851) was a powerful and recalcitrant *oba* who became the *oba* of Lagos in 1845 after plotting a coup against Oba Akitoye, his uncle, in 1845. His reign was warlike and marked by incessant battles with his deposed uncle, who went to exile in Dahomey. Kosoko believed he suffered injustice for not being appointed as *oba* in the first place in 1841 when his uncle Oba Akitoye was appointed. He therefore plotted Akitoye's overthrow. During Oba Kosoko's reign, the British came to him to sign a treaty to stop slavery, but Oba Kosoko rejected the offer. In response to his stubbornness and his refusal to sign the treaty, the British naval army bombarded Lagos in 1851 and conquered the city, sent Oba Kosoko to exile, and reinstalled Oba Akitoye as *oba* of Lagos in 1851.

2. Titilola Euba observes that modes of dressing in Yoruba follow a hierarchical order that has often established seniority with prestige and expensive outfits (2002,140).

3. Captain John Adams's remarks on the country extending from Cape Palmas to the River Congo, pp. 96 and 101.

4. Gollmer 1845 CA 2/043.

5. The Yoruba Creoles were the descendants of African American and Jamaican immigrants.

6. See, for example *Anglo African*, June 6, 1863, 6; September 5; October 31, 3; and November 21, 1863, March 25, 1865, 3; *Lagos Weekly Record*, January 23, 1892, May 14, 1892, 3; May 28, 1892, 2. June 4, 1892, 3, among many others.

7. For more on the sartorial altercations between missionaries and "the natives," see, for example, Ruther (2001, 108); Lester (1998, 44–54); Meyer (1998, 311–37); Hendrickson (1996, 213–44, 435); and Tcherkezoff (2003, 72).

8. *Lagos Observer*, May 7, 1887, 2.

9. Ibid. See also Echeruo (1977).

10. Belo Babatunde Salami, "The Educated Muslims Dress," *Times of Nigeria*, November 1, 1920, 4.

11. Ibid., 2.

12. *Times of Nigeria*, May 3, 1920, 4.

13. *Lagos Observer*, April 2 and 16, 1887, 4.

14. For more on this, see *Lagos Observer*, January 18, 1883.

15. See *Nigerian Pioneer*, July 14, 1922, 12; *Nigerian Pioneer*, Friday, April 30, 1920.

16. Oloko-Dana, "Dress Well to Look Well," *Nigerian Pioneer*, July 28, 1922.

17. *Lagos Record*, August 6, 1887, 6.

18. Rev. Mojola Agbebi, "The Spiritual Needs of the Africans," *Lagos Standard*, July 31, 1895, 8.

19. "Outward Adornment," *Lagos Standard*, March 11, 1896.

20. For a selection of work on this theme, see, for example, Craik (1994); Tarlo (1996); Idiens and Ponting (1980); Femenias (2005, 184–230); Roces (2007); Hay (1989); Hay (2004); Odhiambo (1992, 15); Hay (1996, 251); and Pallinder (1990, 13). To buttress further the politics of colonial encounter with dress, Adegboyega Edun, according to P. F. de Moraes Farias and Karin Barber, had changed his name from Jacob Henryson Samuel and wore only Yoruba dress when in England and remained in European suits while in Nigeria. The article, interestingly, includes a wonderful photograph of the *alake* of Abeokuta, in full ethnic dress, next to the governor of Lagos colony, Sir William MacGregor (who was the governor of Lagos colony from 1899 to 1904), also in full ethnic dress, with kilt, sporran, and tam o'shanter. However, Edun's and indeed other self-avowed interests in indigenous culture and rejection of Western ways should not be taken as a given; rather they should again be inserted into a more political context. Emphasizing this further, Craig McLuckie (1993) cautions of the problem of taking the likes of Pallinder's research at face value and remarked that "Edun's interest in the Yoruba Language and his adoption of it as a language of instruction in the Methodist Boys' High School can be construed as a cynical ploy to attract new students to regain a lost government grant because of low enrolment. Again that he spoke only English to his own children seems to underscore this point." See Farias and Barber (1990); McLuckie (1993, 15–225). This is an encapsulation of the nature of politics that existed between the colonialists and the locals over struggle for dress. Also see Chauduri (1976, 161–62); Wickramasinghe (2003); Cordwell and Schwartz (1979); Martin (1995); Martin (1994, 401-426; Ross (1998); Niessen, Leshkowich, and Jones (2003); Norris (2003); Mustafa (1998); Zorn (2004); and Lise (2003, 215–42), among many others.

21. Jean and John Comaroff, while investigating the nature of modernity in Southern Africa, locate clothing and dress at the center of the "long conversation" between

Africans and Europeans. They argue that colonialism in nineteenth-century Southern Africa was aided by Western clothes. The British missionaries enforced what the Comaroffs call "conquest by consumption" by persuading the Bachuana (Bachuana is an older variant orthography of the Tswana ethnic group in Botswana) to adopt Western commodities (1997; see esp. p. 222). Phyllis Martin observes that in order to impose a psychology of discipline, humility, and servitude, the missionaries dressed their converts in simple clothes, while shorts and rude tunics were the near-universal clothing of unskilled laborers (1994, 410). Karen Tranberg Hansen notes that in Zambia, secondhand clothing "played pivotal roles in the political economy of the West's expansion and in the triangular North Atlantic slave trade" (2000, 24, 52). Again Leslie Rabine remarks that "the Kikuyu in Kenya, find that their own indigenous dress was forbidden to them as English missionaries had them adopt European clothing." Rabine suggests that fashion became a means for the Kikuyu, known for their early and fierce struggles against colonialism, to express their anticolonial feelings (2002, 75).

22. For more on robe giving, see R. Ross (2008, 101); and Renne (2004, 133).

23. See Hansen (n.d.).

24. The emergence of *aso ebi* as a form of uniform needs to be interrogated not just from the point of view of Yoruba cultural life but also in terms of a colonial legacy of uniformed dressing. This is necessary because an imposition of a colonial uniformed code of dressing upon the subjects as a form of domination and rule could be helpful in understanding why the subjects have transformed uniform into high fashion in the postcolonial context. Although such a direct link has not been substantiated in the literature so far, the evidence is overwhelming in the possible emergence of *aso ebi* in late-nineteenth and early twentieth-century Lagos. One of the major articles that touched on uniforms in this context is Renne (2004, 130).

25. The first European missionaries to work in Nigeria were Wesleyan missionaries who visited Badagry and Abeokuta in 1841 and members of the Church Missionary Society (CMS) who landed at Badagry in 1842 and reached Abeokuta in 1846. In 1846 the Presbyterians began work at Calabar, and two years later a Baptist mission was started at Victoria, which is now included in the Republic of Cameroon. See Burns (1978, 269); see also Atanda (1980).

26. The new morality preached by these religions repudiated the scanty dressing habit of the locals and advocated and encouraged the wearing of clothes and the full covering of the body, especially when in public or at religious ceremonies. This desire for proper dressing inspired the idea of uniformed dressing among the colonial administrators and the missionaries. See Onyewuenyi (1990, 160).

27. For this photograph, see Akinwumi (1981, 188).

28. John Nunley (1987) traces the use of *aso ebi* among members of Ode-lay Society in Freetown, Sierra Leone, during the mid-twentieth century. Ode-lay, according to Nunley, emerged from the Yoruba-based hunting, *Gelede* and *Egungun*, traditions. Most activities of *Gelede* and *Egungun* are retained by the Ode-lay to this date. According to Nunley, the most important contribution of the Ode-lay Society was their street

parades, which were held in the morning before weddings of members and upon the return of member/hunters from the bush. Their use of *aso ebi* in these parades must have occasioned the preponderant deployment of the same type of uniforms as in the wider societies in Sierra Leone. The interesting aspect about Nunley's book is that it not only traces Sierra Leonean "*ashobi*" (a corrupted version of *aso ebi*) to Yoruba masking traditions but also charts the link between Ode-lay costumes with urban life and the textile economy in Freetown. See . Nunley (1987, 61). See also Drewal and Drewal (1984, 134–36).

29. W. H. Clarke, cited in Onyewuenyi (1990, 159).

30. Onyewuenyi (1990, 159).

31. Lagos, Annual Reports of the Colony of Southern Nigeria for the Year 1889.

32. Ibid.

33. Lagos, Annual Reports of the Colony of Southern Nigeria for the Year 1909; Talbot, P 1926; Murray, K.C and Hunt-Cooke, A. 1936.

34. Keyes's study (1993) was a major breakthrough in an attempt to track the history of *aso ebi* in Lagos. She notes how the general Lagos society was outraged and embarrassed by "this new fashion that women called aso-ebi." She observes that "officials, colonial administrators, husbands, fiancés, and the press all rallied against it," claiming that it "was irreligious, immoral, indecent." It was a situation that was impelling Lagos into a bankrupt society where women were indebted to textile merchants and their husbands relapsed into financial crises. Keyes was emphatic that *aso ebi* was originated by "respectable, educated, Christian women of high social standing in highly fashionable churches." See Keyes (1993, 325–29).

35. Egbẹ́ Kila was a friendly Yoruba society that reigned in 1919 and was well known for its spectacular show of conspicuous consumption and display of wealth. See Watson (2003).

36. *West Africa*, September 18, 1920.

37. *Nigerian Pioneer*, March 11, 1921.

38. *Lagos Weekly Record*, September 17, 1919.

39. *Lagos Standard*, February 24, 1915, 4.

40. *Nigerian Chronicle*, April 10, 1914, 6.

41. The name "*aso ebi*" derives from an *oriki* name for a fabric used in traditional funeral rituals. See Akinwumi (1990); and Lamb and Holmes (1980).

42. Akinwumi had remarked elsewhere that the "*aso ebi* custom started in the 1920s with [a] few bereaved members who were using the uniform handwoven fabrics for easy recognition in church congregation." See Akinwumi (1990, 131, 172). See also Ajisafe (1931).

43. For this subversive connotation, Keyes has described *aso ebi* as "imported cloth, baptized with a ritual name, made into local garments and worn for important Christian events in churches which specifically banned local dress" (1993, 327).

44. The next port the British gained was Akassa, the base of the Royal Niger Company. The promulgation of the Niger Coast Protectorate in 1890 brought all the other

ports on the Nigerian seaboard under British control. The headquarters of the protectorate was at Old Calabar, and vice consulates were established at Old Opobo, Bonny, New Calabar, Brass, Forcados, and Benin River. See Ogundana (1972, 110–21, esp. 115); and Hilling (1969, 365–378, esp. 370).

45. *Daily Times*, April 25, 1966, 8. See the photograph on page 8.

46. See the photograph in Byfield (2004, 36–43). Other organizations similar to the AWU in Lagos were the Lagos Women's League (LWL, founded 1901), the Women's Part (WP, founded 1944), and the Lagos Women's Market Association (LWMA). G. O. Olusanya (1992) observes that Madam Alimotu Pelewura, leader of the LWMA, gained the support of both the LWL and WP in a campaign protesting the imposition of price control measures during the Second World War. The LWL was led by Charlotte Obasa, which promoted health education, more employment opportunities for educated girls, better conditions for female nurses and government workers, more girls' schools, and a better standard of living for Africans in general; see Olusanya (1992, 55, 72).

47. Mrs. Funmilayo Ransome-Kuti belonged to a new generation of the intelligentsia that emerged in early twentieth-century Nigeria. Mother of the late Afro Beat legend Fela Onikulapo-Kuti, she channeled her energies toward the insipient call for nationalism and independence in the fourth decade of the twentieth century. A strong advocate of the attainment of Western education as a criterion for liberation of the Nigerian nation from the colonialists, she was educated at the Abeokuta Grammar School and the Wincham Hall School for Girls in England. Together with her husband, Rev. I. O. Ransome-Kuti, she was founding member of the National Council of Nigeria and the Cameroons (NCNC), the leading nationalist organization in the 1940s. Judith Byfield observes that "as a well travelled part of the new intelligentsia that emerged in early twentieth century Lagos, she was equally comfortable in Yoruba attire." See Byfield (2004, 36–43).

48. Lillian Trager (2001, 3) remarks that "the hometown (*ilu*) is the place where kinship connections, usually the place where one's father's lineage is from. Beyond a place of origin, it provides a source of social identity and a web of social connections."

49. It is evident from the *oba*'s wardrobe that the idea of "cultural authenticity" is no longer defined by what is African or Western. Joanne Eicher and Tonye Erekosima propounded the theory of "cultural authentication" as a useful approach toward understanding the process of change in dress. They argue that cultural authentication presupposes not only an act of borrowing but also an act of making a borrowed artifact culturally relevant to the borrower. Subsequent chapters might suggest that cultural authentication in *aso ebi* emerges when foreign textiles are made to assume new social role and meaning in the practice. See Eicher and Erekosima (1995).

50. H. Laurens van der Laan (1983) also remarks that in the 1920s some Indian companies began to buy real textiles in India for shipment to West Africa. The business flourished such that in 1929, through European networks, Indian and West African trade were combined to form one organization, thus linking Madras textiles with Lagos, Freetown, and some other major cities in West Africa. Van der Laan argues that if Indian

firms had not pioneered the direct textile trade link between Asia and West Africa in the 1920s, Europe might never have combined the Indian and West African trade. See van der Laan (1983, 287–97).

CHAPTER 2

1. See, for example, Appadurai (1986, 32–33); and Breward (1995).

2. Economic independence was not envisaged in the textile industry even before 1960. For example, Kaduna Textile Ltd. was established in 1957 with Britain playing a key role. At the company's demise, another textile company was established in 1964. This Kaduna-based company, originally United Nigerian Textiles Ltd., now United Nigerian Textiles (UNT) Plc, was started by Cha Chi Ming—the former director of the Cha Groupa Hong Kong–based Chinese company—in 1964. The UNT Plc mill in Kaduna is producing plain baft cotton cloth that is sent to Lagos to be printed in its Nichemtex Industries Ltd. plant (in Ikorodu), some of which is sold as fashionable *ankara* in Da Viva textile shops in Lagos. For a comprehensive text on the rise and fall of the Kaduna textile industry, see Maiwada and Renne (2013). See also Abimbola (2010).

3. The history of lace as a fashion fabric in Nigeria is well explored in the exhibition titled "Austrian Lace—Nigerian Fashion" held in the Museum of Ethnology, Vienna, Austria, in October 2009. The exhibition encapsulates the genealogy of the lace fashion in Nigeria. It shows how lace metamorphosed from a fabric used throughout Nigeria as a contour cloth for underwear, curtains, and blouses in the Niger Delta and Eastern Nigeria into Yoruba high fashion. Interestingly, before the 1960s lace was considered a low-class fabric. Its momentous incursion into the realm of sartorial opulence and class in the 1960s is rather paradoxical. Its ubiquitous use in the 1970s suggests a response to the high import trade that came with the oil boom era. A quick resort to foreign goods in the 1970s corresponded with the high import in lace as well. Lace played an important role in the *aso ebi* practice, especially with its combination with aṣọ òkè. Refer to J'D'Okhai Ojeikere's photos (2000) for a combination of lace and aṣọ òkè. *Ankara* is another name given to African wax prints and roller-print patterned textiles. These wax prints were first handmade in Indonesia before the nineteenth century and were eventually mass-produced by the Dutch in the nineteenth century. In the 1990s there was an adoption of *ankara* as the name for these wax prints. "*george*" is the square cotton Madras "handkerchief" of about a yard long in stripes and checks made in South India in the eighteenth and nineteenth centuries for the West African market; and the squares are traded by both Adeni Jews and West African women. Madras was of two categories: "Real Madras" and "Imitation Madras." However "Real Madras" was very popular in Lagos during the early twentieth century as a prestige cloth, particularly among the Igbos and the Niger Deltans. During the fifteenth century, ship captains had conveyed cloths to West Africa along the Cape route, but after the opening of the Suez Canal in 1869, a second route became available. By the 1890s Madras cloth was exported to London and auctioned at the Cotton Exchange. Indian producers sold Madras to British

trading firms with branches in West Africa. In the nineteenth century, European textile manufacturers, on recognizing the increasing market prospects of the Madras, began to produce similar Indian Madras on power looms. Some of the patterns produced by some European manufacturers in Germany and elsewhere were eventually known as "Imitation Madras." In the late twentieth century *george* or Madras was sold mainly in London side-street shops and targeted at West African clientele. This is very similar to the imitation of the Java wax prints by the European textile producers as shown in this book. For more on *george*, see Evenson (1994); Evenson (2007); Eicher and Erekosima (1987); Eicher, Erekosima, Anderson, and Peek (2002); Lutz (2003); Lutz and Eicher (1996); and van der Laan (1983, 287–97).

4. Most literature could not identify the actual date of origin of aṣọ òkè, but P.S.O. Aremu has traced the history to the precolonial period before the introduction of any form of modern weaving technology in Nigeria. See Aremu (1982).

5. See, for example, Aremu (1982, 3, 6); Asakitikpi (2007, 101–115); and Oyelola (1980, 132).

6. The introduction of foreign yarns has undermined local textile production that uses handspun fiber techniques. This is because foreign yarns are easy to manipulate and more effective. From 1990 to date, only a few weavers of aṣọ òkè produced *etu* and *sanyan* types of aṣọ òkè using traditional handspun yarn. For instance, *alaari* types of aṣọ òkè are no longer manufactured in Iseyin, the celebrated home of aṣọ òkè, because many who processed the vegetable dyes have taken to different vocations. This has also impacted the aesthetic, social, and economic life of the aṣọ òkè. See B. Ojo (2006, 11); See also Perani and Wolff (1999, 179).

7. Note my deliberately chosen italics from this statement, which was used by Susan Bordo and cited in Hansen (2004a, 167).

8. John Picton has noted that when the Dutch ceded their West African territories to the British in 1872, many of the mercenary soldiers recruited on the Gold Coast to assist in the establishment of their East Indian colonies returned to settle in West African territories such as Elmina and other ports through which slaves were taken, including Lagos. These freed slaves were thought to have brought with them a taste of textiles from Java, Indonesia. See Picton (1988); and Sylvanus (2007, 207).

9. It was thought that large imports of cheaper printed cotton cloth from England in the late 1800s caused the decline in the export of locally woven fabric from Nigeria. This decline also created stiff competition for the indigenous textile industries. European commercially printed cloths are multicolored with elaborate designs. They are also lighter in weight and less burdensome in terms of sewing, wearing, and maintenance. Given these qualities, imported textile materials, such as damasks, velvets, lace, satins, and silks, gained currency as highly desirable for clothing, while locally made textiles were abandoned, although some authors have contested this seeming fact. See Renne (1992); Renne (1995; and Nielsen (1979).

10. Marion Johnson (1974b) notes that it was part of the colonial strategy to cripple indigenous industries in order to establish Western capitalist interest in Africa. Quoting

Lord Lugard (then high commissioner of the Protectorate of Northern Nigeria), Marion observes that, "reduced to its crudest expression, the desire of the importing merchant [of British goods to Nigeria] would no doubt be to see native industries other than the production of raw material for export, crushed, in order that they may be superseded by imported manufactures." Judith Perani and Norma Wolff observe that in the event of British colonial control over areas of West Africa, the cotton mills of England sought to increase their export market while increasing importation of cotton from Nigeria. In 1889 the governor of Lagos, Alfred Moloney, suggested using Manchester cottons instead of indigenous cloth and hiring fresh weavers to work in cotton production, noting that their wages would allow them to buy reasonably priced cloth imported from England. See Perani and Wolff (1999, 179).

11. Quoted in Allyn Gaestel, "Versage: Contemporary Nigerian Knock-Off Designer Street Wear" (August 25, 2017), Heinrich Böll Stiftung, https://ng.boell.org/2017/08/25/versage-contemporary-nigerian-knock-designer-street-wear, visited October 12, 2018.

12. Note the article that discusses the ban on imported clothing by the Obasanjo regime. See Ezekiel, Bryson, Omonubi, and Otiono (1985, 13).

13. Misty Bastian (1996) noted that, among many other forms of clothing, the preferred form of female attire during 1987–1988 in Eastern Nigeria was the wrapper and blouse combination. Her study of dress styles in Eastern Nigeria shows that southeastern Nigerian women wore a combination of the wrapper and blouse using matching fabrics or contrasting ones. Sometimes the wrapper involved two pieces made of *george* (an expensive, embroidered and/or painted cloth from South India). See Bastian (1996), 104–106.

14. Akinrinade and Ogen (2008, 159–70).

15. The introduction of the Structural Adjustment Programme, by the International Monetary Fund (IMF) and the World Bank, coupled with Nigeria's defective economic policies and the upheavals that came with late global capital, caused the once vibrant textile industry in Nigeria to suffer an unprecedented decline. There was a shift toward the consumption of locally made clothes. In fact, the harsh realities of the SAP compelled a good number of professional women to switch their career to local cloth production. See Akinrinade and Ogen (2008, 166); Onimode (2000, 100–155); and Denzer (2002, 93–114, 97).

16. Hollandais is one of the brand names for the wax-print textile mass-produced by the popular Dutch textile manufacturer Vlisco for West African clientele. Hollandais was very popular among Igbo women in the 1980s when it was a mark of wealth. In an interview with Maria Nneka Nwafor (2011), the retired schoolteacher said, "In the 1980s among Igbo women, the measure of a good, loving and wealthy husband was the number of Hollandais in his wife's wardrobe and which she was able to flank in various public events."

17. Elisha Renne has also exposed the relationship between the Nigerian politicians and *agbada* in her work. A strong resonance between the Nigerian politicians during the shift from military dictatorship to civilian rule enacts a fruitful link between politics,

power, and *agbada* dress. See Renne (2004). Misty L. Bastian, on the other hand, connects the rise of *agbada* to the 1970s oil boom in Nigeria when "Hausa style," or *agbada* (a Yoruba term), was deployed by Nigerian politicians who jettisoned the Western-styled suit and embraced *agbada* as an expression of national unification after the end of the Nigeria-Biafra civil war in 1970. See Bastian (1996, 97–132).

18. In a sociological study carried out on the use of aṣọ òkè among the youths in Lagos in 2009, A. O. Olutayo and O. Akanle (2009) showed that aṣọ òkè was no longer popular. Instead their findings showed that it has been replaced by *ankara* imported from China and other places. Although their study records low usage among the youths in Lagos, it is equally observed that even among the elderly population aṣọ òkè does not command much patronage. See also Agbadudu and Ogunrin (2006).

19. For more on the Nigeria-China textile relations, see Renne (2015); Renne and Maiwada (2020)

20. In interviews I had with more than twenty textile merchants in Oshodi textile market they confirmed that majority of their textile fabrics come from China. Some of them said they purchase from merchants who import from China in Balogun market, Lagos.

CHAPTER 3

1. The oil boom era in Nigeria was the period between 1971 to 1977 when there was an embargo on Arab oil supply to the United States. Nigeria's oil became the most sought after and highly priced by the United States. That was a period when the economy abandoned its initial agricultural sector, and oil thus constituted about 90 percent of Nigeria's foreign exchange.

2. Many authors have examined how the visual symbolism of color, and its manifestation, in fashionable dress has helped to shape cultural and social processes in the society. The authors offer a critical and historical investigation of how color has been a component part of fashion essential to discourses of identity, social and economic demarcation as well as colonial expansion. (Faiers and Bulgarella 2016).

3. In her study of the personal *oriki* of nineteenth-century "big men" in the small town of Okuku, in the present Oyo State of Nigeria, Karin Barber shows how, in the Yoruba socioeconomic worldview, the concept of buying clothes amplifies an individual's visibility and grandeur. Although Barber's popular culture was located in the nineteenth century, she also warns of the problem of assigning any unitary "belief system" to any single historical period. *Oriki* is an inspirational literary chant of the Yoruba. It is usually declamatory and takes the form of poetry and praise songs. Some of the settings in which this happens is at traditional wedding ceremonies, chieftaincy coronations, and masquerading arenas. In the case of traditional wedding ceremonies, some women chant praise poetry to inspire the bride, and the bride bursts into emotional expressions of joy often exhibited through tears of joy. For the purpose of inspiration, the Yoruba people employ the use of praise poetry, songs, and sacred invocations, as well as inspir-

ing names. Even as the name shows, *oriki* is a name or a praise poetry that "opens up" or "expands" a person's head. The etymology of the Yoruba word for inspiration reflects the belief of the people in Ori—that is, the head. See Barber (1995, 210–11).

4. Compare Mariane Ferme's reference to uniformed dress, which is *aso ebi*, in her book, *The Underneath of Things* (2001, 171).

5. Furthermore, viewing people as significant markers of wealth—and in order to understand Miers and Kopytoff's concept of wealth-in-people more clearly—there is a little deviation of this model from some individual entrepreneurs in early Yoruba land. For example, in advice to Daniel Conrad Taiwo's son, who just took up the mantle of the family's leadership after his father's death, the *Lagos Weekly Record*, among other things, advised Taiwo's son to guard against "the hoarding of the wealth of Croesus—which for the Native can never serve any useful purpose," and instead advised him "to spend his money on the crowd in order," just like his father, to make his influence felt from Ilorin to Bida and Egbado-land, a means of expanding his followership. This short newspaper clip indicates that Taiwo's influence stretched beyond Lagos because of his proclivity to spend on the people. His wealth attracted support from far and wide. It is instructive to observe how loyalty and support were interpreted as wealth by this newspaper. It is also remarkable to observe that such loyalty was attracted in nineteenth-century Lagos by the rich through investment on the crowd. A look at how the rich in present-day Lagos attracted the crowd would enable a contextual juxtaposition. See *Lagos Weekly Record*, June 23, 1906; see also *Lagos Observer*, Thursday August 6, 1885; and *Lagos Weekly Record*, June 23, 1906

6. Aṣọ òkè, usually considered as prestige cloth by the Yorubas, is usually worn by Yoruba men and women throughout southwestern Nigeria, which basically includes contemporary Ekiti, Oyo, Ogun, Ondo, Osun, and Lagos states. Yoruba stocks in parts of Kwara, Kogi, and Edo states also wear this type of cloth. Common fashion styles often used for aṣọ òkè are *buba* and *iro* (blouse and wrapper), *gele* (head-tie), *agbada* (large gown), and *buba and sokoto* (top and trousers). See chapter 2 for a complete analysis of aṣọ òkè.

7. Outside aṣọ òkè there are similar instances in certain African countries where cloth is used to depict class and status. For example, in Asante, Ghana, specific textiles are imbued with a certain cultural valence that marks the wearers as possessors of enormous wealth. There is a purchasing supremacy that distinguishes the Asante aristocracy from ordinary citizens. The similarity *kente* has with *aso ebi* might become clearer from the fact that in the words of Thomas Edward Bowdish, (1966, 35) "The chiefs and their cohorts wore Ashantee cloths of extravagant price from the costly foreign silks which had been unravelled to weave them in all the varieties of colour as well as patterns." Perhaps the old notions of "king" in Asante society approximates the concept of "big man" in contemporary Nigeria but in such a way that, in the discourse of class hierarchy, one can designate the king as "the biggest man." For the mere fact that kings hold such positions, they were not expected to wear the same cloth as the commoners. Kingship apparel is contrived to emphasize the immense physical gait as well as the influential

characterization that inhere in "bigness." The amplification of a sense of bigness in leadership dress requires frequent wrapping and a costume of immense physical magnitude. This not only serves as a consolidation of the aggrandized image of a "big man" but is also emblematic of strength and wealth, becoming a visual metaphor of a leader's power. A good example, according to Judith Perani and Norma H. Wolff, was offered by the *oba* of Benin in Nigeria at the annual Ugie-Erha ceremony to commemorate the *oba*'s father and the *oba*'s reception of Britain's queen in a 1956 visit to Nigeria. The *oba* wore a coral-bead costume including crown, collars, tunic, and slippers. A Benin chief once explained that "when the king is wearing this heavy beaded costume, he does not shake or blink but stays still and unmoving." Emphasizing this fact further, Kwame Arhin (1983) notes that the social position of the higher orders was established by their wealth, of which clothing was a marker. In Mawri society in Niger, padding the body with ample, expensive, and multiple layers of cloths indicates an inner fascination for upscale sartorial and social prominence. Likewise, in the "traditional" Kalabari society of Nigeria, dress was used to demonstrate social and political achievements. See Adjaye (1997, 31) and Perani and Wolff (1999, 91).

8. From the 1940s through the 1950s, a growing body of scholarship on the African class system emerged with a few linking nationalist assertions with the rise of African "middle class" while others, inspired by a growing model of class formation in the Western world, attempted to understand a similar trend in the African continent. See, for example, Kilson (1958, 368–87). During the Twenty-Ninth Session of the International Institute of Differing Civilizations, held in London in September 1955, there was a unanimous conclusion that African nationalist movements were primarily driven by an emerging middle class. See *Development of a Middle Class in Tropical and Sub-Tropical Countries.* (1956, 453). See also Hodgkin (1961, 27–29), and the comprehensive survey of class in Wallerstein (1967, 497–518). Some other studies have also explored class in relation to the formation of political parties in Nigeria; see, for example, Sklar (1963, 480–81); and Sklar (1979, 531–52). For more on class division in Africa, see Awolowo (1947, 312). While categories of class in 1945 were based largely on educational differences, those of the 1960s were founded on economic divisions. This was a fundamental innovation. There is also a huge literature on social stratification in Nigeria. The references cited here are but a small part of the literature; see, for example, Lloyd (1953, 327–34); Lloyd, Mabogunje. and Awe (1967, 129–50); Smythe and Smythe (1960); Sklar (1963); Dudley (1964); and Williams, (1970, 258). For the class formation in colonial Lagos, see Mann (1981, 201–28).

9. On February 16, 2011, Pius Adesanmi, a Nigerian academic, delivered a keynote lecture at the African Textiles Exhibition of Carleton University's Arts Gallery, in Canada. The title of the lecture was "*Aso ebi* on My Mind." In this lecture, which centered on the practice of *aso ebi*, Adesanmi explored, among other things, the genealogy of the crowd in both the Western and African social contexts. European intellectuals, according to Adesanmi, going all the way back to the legacy of Nietzsche, despised crowds and the masses as polluters of culture. He notes that *aso ebi* is a befitting space to articulate

the concept of the crowd as owners of "culture" both "high" and "low" in the African context. The crowd, as could be seen in Yoruba *aso ebi*, Adesanmi argues, is a perception of the African masses as custodians of culture. See Adesanmi (2011).

CHAPTER 4

1. An idea of this moral economy could be seen from this discussion in "*Aso Ebi* Madness, a Personal Encounter," published on Saturday, March 9, 2009, at http://www.bellanaija.com/2009/03/28/aso-ebi-madness-a-personal-encounter/

2. In 1946, Hubert Ogunde published a play titled *Human Parasites*, which was a major attack on the *aso ebi* craze. The play condemned *aso ebi* as a "social evil." Ebun Clark, reviewing Ogunde's play, described *aso ebi* as follows: "'When someone wants to celebrate a marriage or a funeral obsequies [*sic*] she chooses a piece of cloth to wear on the occasion and approaches relatives and friends to buy the same stuff to wear with her as uniform on the day. The number of people to wear the uniform will depend on her popularity and social connections. (. . .) The custom has lent itself to much abuse in that the occasions for celebrating marriages or funerals occur so often that one may be asked by friends to buy 'Aso Ebi' more than 10 times a year." It is interesting to note that this number has escalated in recent times. See *Daily Service*, February 5, 1944; cited in Clark (1975, 6–7).

3. See Akinwumi (1990, 174). Similar rejections by some churches have also appeared in recent times. For example, an article titled "RCCG Outlaws Aso Ebi, Ungodly Wedding Engagement," in the *Nigerian Tribune* of August 13, 2017, reports that the compulsory uniform outfit, popularly known as "aṣọ ebi," has been outlawed in the Redeemed Christian Church of God (RCCG). Wife of the general overseer of the church and Mother-in-Israel, Pastor Folu Adeboye, stated that "compelling members of the church to participate in aṣọ *ebi* during special programmes in local assemblies was ungodly." The news that some members of the church without financial power to buy such uniforms were excluded from the programs for which the uniforms were sewn was seriously repudiated by the church leadership. She noted that *aso ebi*, which should ordinarily be for the family, must not be elevated to the point of making it overshadow the spiritual life of the congregants. She warned that such an un-Christian act of keeping church members out of programs because of *aso ebi* must never be heard of again among the women in the church, adding that those caught would be severely sanctioned. She stated that the concept of appearing in compulsory uniformed attire for an occasion started with the world and should not be allowed to take a firm space in the church.

4. Aso ebi was banned under a colonial order of October 21, 1946 titled "Women's Undesirable Practices." A few weeks after *aso ebi* was banned, drummers protested that the ban should be revoked because it was causing hardship for them, as they no longer accompanied women *aso ebi* groups to events. Due to the ban, women *aso ebi* groups kept low profiles devoid of the spectacular drumming sessions. The drummers argued that despite the ban, "young women are indulged in the habit of equipping themselves with costly dresses for dancing about the town in groups: and to the best of our knowl-

edge and belief, these dresses are bought in [the] majority of cases by young men." See Salawu Atanda and others' petition of December 12, 1946; NAI Ije Prof 3366/2; see also "Aṣọ *ebi* Was Banned by the Ijebu" (1946). In an interesting poem in the journal *Nigeria* titled "Aso-ebi," T. C. Nwosu (1965, 221) had this to say:

> I have seen madness dissolve madness
> And craze beget yet another craze
> And fashion turn the scales of praise
> And clothes give a false look of freshness
> And yards of aso-ebi threaten the sky
> Settling friends and parting them
> Leaving many homes high and dry
> The steersman knocked off the helm.

5. See Young Men of Ijebu-Ode Comprising of Various Age-Groups Petition of October 7, 1946, to Oba Alaiyeluwa; and Gbelegbuwa II, Awujale of Ijebuland, Letter of October 16, 1946, to Resident, Ijebu Province.

6. These tensions rightly confirm Jennifer Craik's point that "enforcement of uniform practice is central to the social life of the uniform." She also notes that "enforcement involves both rewards and punishment for transgression." See Craik (2005, 4); and Familusi (2010, 2).

7. See chapter 1 of this study for an analysis of Yoruba hometown associations in the context of *aso ebi*.

8. See, for example, Trager (2001, 239); Little (1972, 275–88); Aldous (1962, 6–12); Little, (1962, 197–211); Cornwall (2007, 27–46); and Denzer (1994, 1–39), among others.

9. See Janus (1915) "Lagosians on Dits," *Lagos Standard*, February 24, 1915, p. 4. Again in 1946, one Mr. Salau Shonibare complained that *aso ebi* costs "£10 Ten Pounds per a head . . . and others are costing more than that" for each funeral, a worrying situation that, according to Shonibare, amounts to "life demolished." It is interesting to observe an increment in *aso ebi* cost during this period from ten shillings in 1915 to ten pounds in 1946. See Mr. Salau Shonibare, letter of November 18, 1946, to His Worship the Resident, Ijebu-Ode, NAI Ije Prof 3366/13–14.

10. For example, Ifeyinwa Umunna (2010) remarked that "most people who cherish *aso ebi* these days would recruit any stranger—whether friend or not—because they want to sell the fabric materials they bought at an exorbitant price and make more money, and that they are not interested in whether you are their friends or enemies." Again, Ronke Akerele (2010) noted, "One of my friends had once offered an *aso ebi* of her friend's friend to me to buy. I told her that I don't even know the celebrant and they still wanted me to be part of the *aso ebi* ladies. Moreover, I hate the idea of selling a cheap fabric to people at an exorbitant price. So I rejected it."

11. Some of the early texts that deal with friendship in this regard include Suttles (1989, 95–135); and Wolf (1977, 167–77).

12. For a deeper understanding of this kind of reciprocity, see Verhezen (2005). See more in Komter (2005, 124); Emerson (1902, 302–6); and Blau (1964). For more on the economy of gifts, see Strathern (1988); Godelier (1999); and Raheja (1988); see also Douglas (1990, vii–xviii); Cheal (1988, 40); and Roberts, Richards, and Bengtson (1991, 11–46).

13. See Malinowski (1997, 15–17); see also Malinowski (1978). Malinowski's study reveals the significance of ceremonial gift exchange among the Trobriand Islanders. He found that among the islanders the economy of gift exchange played important roles in strengthening social networks, intensifying interpersonal communication, and enunciating reverence for the transcendental forces of "sacred" objects.

14. See Bell and Coleman(1999, 4). Montaigne's position that friendship flourishes among equal persons is refuted by Yahudi Cohen, Eric Wolf, and Eliot Deutsch, all of whom contend that friendships can also be established between people of unequal social, economic, or ethnic backgrounds, provided they are characterized by balanced exchange and exclude any kind of dominance of one party over the other. See Cohen (1961, 173); Deutsch (1994, 15–27, 20); Wolf (1977).

15. For some historical texts on this subject, see Deutsch (1994); Guichard et al. (2003, 7–17); Suttles (1970, 90–135); and Allan (1989). For a detailed description of the sociology of friendship along age, class, gender, ethnicity, and geographic lines, see Allan (1996).

16. In keeping with Montaigne's views, these authors maintain that kinship and friendship embody various kinds of social communication. The authors are opposed to any fixed contrast between friendship and kinship, believing that many societies are structured after imbricate rather than rival kinds of relationship. Supporting this view, Guichard and his colleagues argue that friendship affinities should not be treated in isolation; instead they should be integrated into kinship discourses as forms of social assimilation (2003, 10). In spite of these efforts to view friendship and kinship as two spheres of divergent yet related areas of social synergies, Bell and Coleman strongly hold that friendship is subordinated under kinship. In fact, they contend that forces of all social relations are enunciated under the watchword of kinship. (1999, 6–7).

17. See, for example, Bloom (1993); and Rouner (1994). See also Bell and Coleman (1999, 6–7).

18. One could compare this with, for example, Allan Silver's observation of how new forms of friendship that emerged during the Enlightenment in the eighteenth century were instigated by the rationalizations of a pecuniary commercial society. He posits that earlier forms of friendship relied more on a rigid judgment of gratification rather than amicability (1990, 1474–1504). See also Spencer and Pahl (2006).

CHAPTER 5

1. Emerging concepts of cosmopolitan political tradition define the cosmopolitan individual not in terms of connections to one's nationality, family, or class but from a

broader context as worthy citizens of the world. For example, Martha Nussbaum (2019) confronts the pressures arising from flawed vision and failed ideologies within pluralistic societies through her concept of the cosmopolitan political person. See, among others, Luczak, Pochmara, and Dayal (2019); and Caraus and Paris (2019). For some historical contexts to cosmopolitanism, see Vertovec and Cohen (2002); Hannerz (1990); Hannerz (1996); Skrbis, Kendall, and Waldinger (2004); Szerszynski and Urry (2002); Robbins (1998a); Robbins (1998b); Archibugi and Held (1995); Held (2003); Cheah (1998); Cheah (2006); Hall (2002); Lamont and Aksartova (2002); Appadurai (2002); Roudometof (2005); Featherstone (2002); B. Turner (2002); and Appiah (1997).

2. See, for example, Nussbaum (2019); and Archibugi and Held (1998a).

3. See Mustafa (1998, 20). Long histories of trade and appropriation were already evident in Nigeria from the fifteenth century (being a period of slave trade) down to the independent years (see chapter 2). Michael Echeruo (1974) notes that by 1880, the cosmopolitanism of Lagos was already inevitable and that in the early nineteenth century the political organization of the entire British West Coast recognized only one single administrative unit, and Lagos was only a port and trading center. Since Nigeria was not in existence then, Lagos was not thought of as the capital of any homogenous and independent territorial entity. The "negro" community of Lagos saw itself as an extension of the larger "negro" world that, among other places, included Liberia and the United States. They came to see themselves as an embodiment of a cosmopolitan black ethos that is not overshadowed by any provincial character. See Echeruo (1974, 247).

4. Elisha P. Renne has tracked similar economies in her work "Contemporary Wedding Fashions in Lagos, Nigeria" (2010), where she remarks, "This proliferation of shops in Lagos specializing in bridal gowns, hats, and associated wedding items and services (*of which aso ebi is one of them*) began in the mid-1990s and was fostered by another development, namely fashion shows that specialized in bridal fashions" (italics added). Again, Kerstin Pinther has traced the connection between tailors and photographers in West Africa and how their interdependence provokes the emergence of a fashionable image. Leslie Rabine has also established a reciprocal transaction between fashion and photography in West Africa. New dresses did not only mark occasions for public spectacles before the camera, they also enacted a historically transformative change around questions of gender, aesthetic politics and public performance. Pinther & Julia (2007: 113–23); Rabine (2010: 305–30); See also Lamunière (2001).

5. For a scholarly insight into the dichotomies surrounding Western and local fashion, see Mustafa (1998, 20); Mustafa (2010, 127); Rabine (2002); Mustafa (2002, 28); and Hansen (2004b, 372).

6. This is suggestive of the fact that in Lagos, for example, the ability to transcend the city's continuous tendency to hide one's persona guarantees one's relevance in the scheme of things. *Owambe*, undoubtedly, removes the obscurity veil from the individual's social persona. See Raban (1998, 28). Elizabeth Wilson also remarked that "although anonymity was central to city life, dress subtly subverted it" (1995, 156).

7. For a spectacular fusion of the visual arts, aso ebi, Owambe and fashion see

(Sowole 2011; Orimolade 2014). In some sense these new ways of seeing might have given impetus to newer forms of dress styles in Nigeria toward the end of the twentieth century, as many Nigerians abandoned Western-style dresses in favor of the supposed "African styles." Elizabeth Hackspiel notes that "since the 1980s West African fashion has turned away from the readymade clothes in Western style" toward "African" fabrics (2008, 90). For the *Aso ebi Fashion Show*, which took place in February 2010 at the Civic Centre, Victoria Island, Lagos see "The *Aso ebi* Fashion Show 2010" Santiago, http://santiagopad.blogspot.com/2010/02/aso-ebi-fashion-show-2010.html. See also Berger (1972, 131); Sturken and Cartwright (2001, 196); Ash and Wright (1988); Peiss (1998); Breward (1995, 197); Thorp (1939, 113); Barber (2000, 244); and Meyer (2010, 8).

8. Compare Joanne Grabski's observation that "the city offers unparalleled creative and human resources," which have established fashion making as a quintessentially urban phenomenon (2003, 28–39).

9. In 1977 the government banned imported textiles such as lace, guinea brocade, and wax prints. However, despite this ban, many textiles were smuggled into the country.

10. Similar thoughts have been expressed in such texts as Tomlinson (1990, 34); Wilson (1995, 156); and Grabski (2009, 215).

11. See, for example, Gore (2001, 321–42). Flora Kaplan noted how in late nineteenth-century and early twentieth-century Benin, Nigeria, photographs became important not only for display in various contexts but also as a medium of exchange. See Kaplan (1991); Kaplan (1990); and Sprague (1978). For example, Erin Haney (2010) has shown how in nineteenth-century Ghana, portraits constituted part of the inaugural ceremonial spectacles in political supremacy rites and other larger public performances. Haney's study reveals how the photograph—in its earliest manifestation in Ghana—was inscribed into the everyday lives of Ghanaians as an accustomed object with complex meanings across a range of media. Also see Burt (1983, 62).

CHAPTER 6

1. As already shown in chapter 4, in some social events, *aso ebi* determined whether a celebrant received food or not.

2. Most studies on African photography have focused mainly on the role of the camera in colonial ethnographic surveys. See Vokes (2015: 95–112); Ranger (2001: 203–5); see also Apter (2002: 564–96); Hartmann and Hayes (1998); Faris (1992: 211–17); Morris-Reich (2016); Geary (1988); Banks and Vokes (2010: 337–49); Vokes (2012: 1–29, 4). Other recent studies have reinforced Africans' agency in colonial photographic discourses. See Richard Vokes & Darren Newbury (2018: 1-10); Jenifer Bajorek (2012: 140–65); Baloji and Jewsiewicki (2010); Erin Haney (2012: 127–39); Peffer and Cameron (2013); Sprague (1978: 9–28); Abiodun (1976); Abiodun (2013). Two of the most recent texts on African photography, Bajorek (2020) and Hayes and Minkley (2019) both have charted a more radical turn by highlighting previously undermined photographic

practices in Africa including the digital turn. Bajorek, for example, examined the role photography played in forging new decolonial identities and "reconfiguring new media networks" as Africa emerged from the twilight of colonial rule (2020: 14). She foregrounds the increased opportunities enabled by photography as Africans take control of their lives while Hayes and Minkley's text problematizes the "methodological implications of photographs and photography in their African setting;" one that they describe as 'ambivalent' (2019, 1–24). When the question of "the right to write about seeing" in Africa is posed, this book offers a totally radical methodological answer by exposing multiple modes of visibility in Africa to remove African photography from a linear, western technological determinism that privileges discourses of the camera as the only universally acceptable scopic regime.

3. For more on this, see, for example, Helms (1993); Miller and Hamell" (1986); Saunders (1999); and Thomas (1991).

4. Christopher Pinney explains "narrativized indexical depth" as the discourse of photography that borders on early European travel. He explains this as a photographic system that mapped the world as a picture. Using Samuel Bourne's 1866 "Narrative of a Photographic Trip to Kashmir," Pinney unveils this "paradigmatic text of the normative practice" whereby photography was understood as a view of the world in spatiotemporal certainty. This view of the world also involves forays in which lives became measured in terms of their "exploits" and the exploitation of the world as perspectivilized picturesque entity. According to Pinney, this system negates contemporary African and Indian postcolonial photography, which is concerned with a realm of the denarrativized, de-perspectivilized surface effects that operate in a zone of tactility quite different from the detached viewpoints advocated by early European practitioners such as Bourne. See Pinney (2003, 207–8).

5. Seydou Keita lived in Bamako, Mali, from 1921 to 2001. He was a self-taught portrait photographer. His portraits gained international acclaim through his studio, opened in Bamako in 1948. Malick Sidibé (1935–2016) gained a reputation for his black-and-white photographs of ordinary Malians in the 1960s. Sidibé and Keita were considered Mali's most important photographers of the mid- and late twentieth centuries. Sidibé's portraitures exemplify the dynamism and vigor of urban life in the Malian city of Bamako as African cities slowly emerged from the wrenches of colonial rule. The photographs reveal a deep search for urban fashionability and subjectivity amid the desperate pursuit for power and political future for post-independent African nations. Their style involved the use of brightly colored textile backdrops that often created a formal conflict with the striped textile dress of the subjects. Aihumekeokhai Ojeikere (J. D'Okhai Ojeikere, 1930–2014) was a Nigerian photographer who had his studio in Ketu, Lagos. Ojeikere's passion for photography became manifest in the 1950s when he purchased a modest Brownie D camera without flash and had a friend teach him the fundamentals of photography. Ojeikere's initial career was as a darkroom assistant in 1954 at the Ministry of Information in Ibadan. His interest in African women's fashion style

could be seen from the depiction of African hairstyles as a deft architecture of beauty and an apt display of Nigerians' decorative art of the body. See Ojeikere and Magnin (2000); Elam and Jackson (2005); and Lamuniere (2001).

6. For more on how the economic crisis engendered by the International Monetary Fund (IMF) Structural Adjustment Programme in Nigeria in 1986 impoverished the poor and demobilized the middle class and the rich, see chapter 5.

7. This type of photographic business is sometimes referred to as *kpaa kpaa kpaa* in Nigeria, and it involves street photographers who gate-crash into public events, take photos randomly, and make the printed copies available for the guests before the end of the event. Sometimes skirmishes erupt among the photographers in a bid to win prospective clients such that the first photographer to print the photos and rush back on the scene makes more money, and gets paid by the clients, to the detriment of the rest.

8. For more discussions on snapshot aesthetics, see Batchen (2008, 121); Marien (2002); and Frizot (1998).

9. "Place-loyalty" is Groening's metaphor for the new spatial categories promised by travel that connect one to the physical spaces of one's own surroundings as one travels through such modes as the bus. This, according to Groening, is destabilized by air travel, for example. I use this metaphor here to mean the physical spaces connecting one to one's memories. See Groening (2008, 24).

CONCLUSION

1. Henry John Drewal dwelled on this in his study "Pageantry and Power in Yoruba Costuming," where he specifically states that "substantial amount[s] of money are devoted to aso ebi," through a mobilization of uniformed membership used to indicate the stature of an individual or group in the society. See Drewal (1979, 189–229).

2. Eric Hobsbawn and Terence Ranger's (1983) position justifies the claim that both tradition and modernity are invented, but this time they could be represented through *aso ebi*, which, to some extent, has been modernized to suit changing realities of urban social life in Lagos. I argue that this entails a new tradition.

3. Lagos being originally a Yoruba settlement, a historical understanding of the meaning of clothes in certain Yoruba communities provides a footnote to similar contexts in colonial Lagos. Elisha Renne's study of the meaning of clothes in the social life of a Yoruba community called Bunu assists in contextualizing similar meanings in Lagos, especially during the era of rapid urbanization and in the preceding years of postcolonial rule. Renne notes that cloth was used to represent social unity and harmony and that it expressed ambiguous and contradictory messages in Bunu life whereby conflict coexists with general social ideals. In what George Simmel (1979, 91) calls an "awareness of dissonance" in social life, I liken Renne's study to the emerging conflicts that attend modifications in the modern use of *aso ebi*, of which a further explanation will help to provide an in-depth understanding of the research theme. See Renne (1995).

4. Anne Spencer echoed this idea when she noted that much can be learned about

West African history, values, and aspects of daily life through a study of photographs of people in different outfits. She made this statement in her study of the photographs of more than 175 Nigerian textile materials collected in the 1970s by Joanne Eicher, who lived in Eastern Nigeria then. I have extended this research by looking at the photographs of *aso ebi* textiles in this respect. See Spencer (2001, 43–64).

BIBLIOGRAPHY

"*Aso Ebi* Madness!—A Personal Encounter." March 9, 2009. http://www.bellanaija. com/2009/03/28/aso-ebi-madness-a-personal-encounter/

"*Aso ebi* Wahala." 2011. *234 Next*, January 8, 2011, 20.

Abimbola, Olumide. 2010. "Awakening the Giant." *TradeInvest Nigeria*. https://www. tandfonline.com/doi/full/10.1080/13688790.2011.542114?scroll=top&needAc cess=true, accessed December 15, 2020.

Abiodun Rowland. 1976. "A reconsideration of the function of Àkó, Second Burial Effigy in Owo" *Africa* 46, no, 1:4–20.

Abiodun Rowland. 2013. "Àkó-graphy: Òwò Portraits" In *Portraiture & Photography in Africa*. Edited by John Peffer and Elisabeth L. Cameron, 287–312. Bloomington: Indiana University Press.

Adams, John. Remarks on the Country Extending from Cape Palmas to the River Congo. London.

Adeboye, Olufunke. 2003. "Elite Lifestyle and Consumption in Colonial Ibadan." In *The Foundations of Nigeria: Essays in Honour of Toyin Falola*, edited by Adebayo Oye-bade, 281–303. Trenton, NJ: Africa World Press.

Adekoya, Shegun. 2010. Interview by Okechukwu Nwafor. Lagos. April 12.

Adeleke, Shola. 2010. Interview by Okechukwu Nwafor. Lagos. April 10.

Adepoyi. 2011. Interview by Okechukwu Nwafor. Lagos. February 15.

Aderemi, Ademola Pa. 2011. Interview by Okechukwu Nwafor. Yaba, Lagos. January 20.

Aderibigbe, A. B. 1975. "Early History of Lagos to about 1850." In *Lagos: The Development of an African City*, edited by A. B. Aderibigbe, 1–26. London: Longman Group.

Adesanmi, Pius. 2011. "*Aso ebi* on My Mind (Part One)." Keynote lecture delivered at the African Textiles Exhibition of Carleton University's Arts Gallery, February 16, 2011.

Adesokan, Akin. 1996. "Anticipating Nollywood: Lagos circa 1996." *Social Dynamics* 37, no. 1:96–110.

Adesola, Debo. 2011. Interview by Okechukwu Nwafor. Lagos. March 5.

Adjaye, Joseph K. 1997. "The Discourse of Kente Cloth: From Haute Couture to Mass Culture." In *Language, Rhythm, and Sound: Black Popular Cultures into the Twenty-*

First Century, edited by Joseph K. Adjaye and Adrianne Andrews, 23–39. Pittsburgh: University of Pittsburgh Press.

Agbadudu, A. B., and F. O. Ogunrin. 2006. "Aso-oke: A Nigerian Classic Style and Fashion." *Journal of Fashion Marketing and Management* 10, no. 1:97–113.

Ajayi, J. K. Ade. 1965. *Christian Missions in Nigeria, 1844–1891*. London: Longman.

Ajisafe, Ajayi Kolawole. 1931. *Abeokuta Centenary and Its Celebration*. Lagos: Ife-Olu Printing Works.

Akande, Shola. 2011. Interview by Okechukwu Nwafor. Lagos. January 22.

Akerele, Ronke. 2010. Interview by Okechukwu Nwafor. Lagos. December 22.

Akinrinade, Sola, and Olukoya Ogen. 2008. "Globalization and De-Industrialization: South-South Neo-Liberalism and the Collapse of the Nigerian Textile Industry." *The Global South* 2, no. 2:159–70.

Akinwumi, Tunde. 1981. "Persistence and Change in Yoruba Costume: A Case Study of Oyo." MA thesis. Ahmadu Bello University, Zaria, Nigeria.

Akinwumi, Tunde. 1990. "The Commemorative Phenomenon of Textile Use among the Yoruba: A Survey of Significance and Form." PhD diss. University of Ibadan, Ibadan. *Social Forces* 41, no. 1:6–12.

Akinwumi, Tunde M., and Elisha Renne. 2008. "Commemorative Textile and Anglican Church History in Ondo Nigeria." *Textile, Cloth, and Culture* 6, no. 2:126–45.

Aldous, Joan. 1962. "Urbanization, the Extended Family, and Kinship Ties in West Africa." *Social Forces* 41, no. 1:8–12.

Allan, Graham. 1989. *Friendship: Developing a Sociological Perspective*. Boulder, CO: Westview Press.

Allan, Graham. 1996. *Kinship and Friendship in Modern Britain*. Oxford: Oxford University Press.

Allman, Jean, ed. 2004. *Fashioning Africa: Power and the Politics of Dress*. Bloomington: Indiana University Press.

Alpers, Svetlana. 1983. *The Art of Describing: Dutch Art in the Seventeenth Century*. Chicago: University of Chicago Press.

Anheier, Helmut K., and Yudhishthir Raj Isar. 2012. *Cultures and Globalization: Cities, Cultural Policy, and Governance*. London: Sage Publications.

Anisulowo, Toyin. 2010. "Dale Alake for Senate." Dale Alake for Senate: An Action Congress Candidate. http://www.alakeforsenate.com/, accessed June 23, 2010.

Appadurai, Arjun. 1986. "Commodities and the Politics of Value." In *The Social Life of Things: Commodities in Cultural Perspectives*, 3–63. Cambridge, UK: Cambridge University Press, 1986.

Appadurai, Arjun. 1996. *Modernity at Large*. Minneapolis: University of Minnesota Press.

Appadurai, Arjun. 2002. "Spectral Housing and Urban Cleansing: Notes on Millennial Mumbai." In *Cosmopolitanism*, edited by C. A. Breckenridge, S. Pollock, H. K. Bhabha, and Dipesh Chakrabarty, 54–81. Durham, NC: Duke University Press.

Appiah, Kwame Anthony. 1997. "Cosmopolitan Patriots." *Critical Inquiry* 23, no. 3:617–19.

Apter, A. 2002. "On Imperial Spectacle: The Dialectics of Seeing in Colonial Nigeria." *Comparative Studies in Society and History* 44, no. 3: 564–596.

Archibugi, Daniele, and David Held. 1995. *Cosmopolitan Democracy: An Agenda for a New World Order*. Cambridge, MA: Polity Press.

Aremu, P.S.O. 1982. "Yoruba Traditional Weaving: Kijipa Motifs, Color, and Symbols." *Nigeria* 140: 3–10.

Arhin, Kwame. 1983. Rank and Class among the Asante and Fante in the Nineteenth Century." *Africa: Journal of the International African Institute*. 53, no. 1: 2–22.

Asakitikpi, A. 2007. "Function of Hand-Woven Textiles among Yoruba Women in South-Western Nigeria." *Nordic Journal of African Studies* 16, no. 1:101–115.

Ash, Juliet, and Lee Wright, eds. 1988. *Components of Dress: Design, Manufacturing, and Image-Making in the Fashion Industry*. London: Routledge.

Ashley, David, and David Michael Orenstein. 1990. *Sociological Theory: Classical Statements*. Boston: Allyn and Bacon.

"The *Aso ebi* Fashion Show 2010," Santiago. http://santiagopad.blogspot.com/2010/02/aso-ebi-fashion-show-2010.html.

Aṣọ *Ebi* Was Banned by the Ijebu (Women's Undesirable Practices) Order of 21 October 1946. National Archives, Ibadan [NAI] Ije Prof 3366/2.

Atanda, Salawu, and others. Petition of December 12, 1946, to Oba Alaiyeluwa, the Awujale of Ijebuland. National Archives, Ibadan [NAI] Ije Prof 3366/1 5–16.

Atanda, Taiwo. 1980. *An Introduction to Yoruba History*. Ibadan, Nigeria: Caxton Press.

Awolowo, Obafemi. 1947. *Path to Nigerian Freedom*. London: Faber and Faber.

Awusa, Femi, 2011. Interview by Okechukwu Nwafor. Ikorodu, Lagos. March 6.

Ayandele, Emmanuel A. 1981. *The Missionary Impact on Modern Nigeria, 1842–1914: A Political and Social Analysis*. London: Longmans.

Ayegboyin, Deji Isaac. 1991. "Women in Missions: A Case Study of the Baptist Women's Missionary Union in Nigeria." PhD diss. University of Ibadan.

Babalola, Ademola. 2010. "Pandemonium as Thugs Sack Ibadan Council over Jonathan's *Aso Ebi*." *Nigerian Compass*. Wednesday, October 20.

Bajorek, J. 2012. "Ca Bousculait!: Democratization and Photography in Senegal." In *Photography in Africa: Ethnographic Perspectives*, edited by Richard Vokes, 140–65. Oxford: James Currey.

Bajorek, Jenifer. 2020. *Unfixed, Photography and Decolonial Imagination in West Africa*. Durham: Duke University Press.

Baker, Pauline H. 1974. *Urbanization and Political Change: The Politics of Lagos, 1917–1967*. Berkeley: University of California.

Bakhtin, M. M. 1981. "Forms of Time and the Chronotope of the Novel." *The Dialogic Imagination*, translated by Caryl Emerson and Michael Holquist. Austin: University of Texas Press.

Baloji, S., and B. Jewsiewicki. 2010. *The Beautiful Time: Photography by Sammy Baloji*. New York: Museum for African Art.

Banks, M., and R. Vokes. 2010. "Introduction: Anthropology, Photography and the Archive." *History and Anthropology* 21, no,4: 337–49.

Barber, Karin. 1987. "Popular Arts in Africa." *African Studies Review* 30, no. 3:1–78.

Barber, Karin. 1991. *I Could Speak until Tomorrow: Oriki, Women, and the Past in a Yoruba Town*. London: International African Institute.

Barber, Karin. 1995. "Money, Self-Realization, and the Person in Yoruba Texts." In *Money Struggles and City Life: Devaluation in Ibadan and Other Urban Centres in Southern Nigeria, 1986–1996*, edited by Jane I. Guyer, LaRay Denzer, and Adigun Agbaje. 210–11. Portsmouth, NJ: Heinemann.

Barber, Karin. 2000. *A Generation of Plays: Yoruba Popular Life in Theatre*. Bloomington: Indiana University Press.

Barker, Chris, and Dariusz Galasinski. 2001. *Cultural Studies and Discourse Analysis: A Dialogue on Language and Identity*. London: Sage Publications.

Barnes, Ruth, and Joanne Eicher, eds. 1993. *Dress and Gender: Making and Meaning in Cultural Contexts*. Oxford: Berg Press.

Barnes, Sandra. T. 1986. *Patrons and Power: Creating a Political Community in Metropolitan Lagos*. London: Manchester University Press.

Bascom, William. 1951. "Social Status, Wealth and Individual Differences among the Yoruba." *American Anthropologist* 53, no. 2:490–505.

Bastian, Misty. 1996. "Female 'Alhajis' and Entrepreneurial Fashions: Flexible Identities in Southeastern Nigeria Clothing Practice." In *Clothing and Difference: Embodied Identities in Colonial and Post-Colonial Africa*, edited by Hildi Hendrickson, 97–132. Durham, NC: Duke University Press.

Batchen, Geoffrey. 2008. "Snapshots, Art History, and the Ethnographic Turn." *Photographies* 1, no. 2:133.

Bell, Sandra, and Simon Coleman, eds. 1999. *The Anthropology of Friendship*. Oxford: Berg.

Benjamin, Walter. 1968. "The Work of Art in the Age of Mechanical Reproduction." In *Illuminations*, edited by Hannah Arendt, translated by Harry Zohn, 217–51. New York: Schocken Books.

Berg, M. 2003. "Asian Luxuries and the Making of the European Consumer Revolution." In *Luxury in the Eighteenth Century: Debates, Desires, and Delectable Goods*, edited by M. Berg and E. Eger, 228–44. London: Palgrave Macmillan.

Berger, John. 1972. *Ways of Seeing*. London: British Broadcasting Cooperation.

Berreman, G. D. 1962. *Behind Many Masks: Ethnography and Impression Management in a Himalayan Village*. Ithaca, NY: Society for Applied Anthropology.

Berry, Sara. 1989. "Social Institutions and Access to Resources." *African Agriculture* 59, no. 1:41–55

Bhatia, N. 2003. "Fashioning Women in Colonial India." *Fashion Theory* 7:327–44.

BL, Sierra Leone. 1796. "Extract of a Diary kept by E. L. Parfitt on board the Sierra Leone Company's ship Calypso, William Cole Master from the River Sierra Leone to the River Gabon & back commencing 17th June & terminating the 29th December 1796 ff." 136r–156r.

Blau, Peter. 1964. *Exchange and Power in Social Life*. New York: Wiley.

Bledsoe, Caroline H. 1980. *Women and Marriage in Kpelle Society*. Stanford, CA: Stanford University Press.

Bloom, A. 1993. *Love and Friendship*. New York: Simon and Schuster.

Blumer, Herbert. 1953. "Collective Behaviour." In *Principles of Sociology*, edited by A. M. Lee. 219–88. New York: Barnes and Noble.

Bolland, Rita. 1991. *Tellem Textiles: Archeological Finds from Burial Caves in Mali's Bandiagara Cliff*. Amsterdam: Royal Tropical Institute.

Borgatti, Jean. 1983. *Cloth as Metaphor: Nigerian Textiles from the Museum of Cultural History*. Los Angeles: University of California, Los Angeles. Museum of Cultural History.

Bourdieu, Pierre. 1977. *Outline of a Theory of Practice*. Cambridge, UK: Cambridge University Press.

Bowdish, Thomas Edward. 1966. *Mission from Cape Coast to Ashantee with a Descriptive Account of That Kingdom*. London: Griffith & Farran.

Brenninkmeyer, I. 1973. "The Diffusion of Fashion." In Fashion Marketing, edited by G. Willis and D. Midgley, 259–302. London: Allen and Unwin.

Breward, Christopher. 1995. *The Culture of Fashion: A New History of Fashionable Dress*. Manchester, UK: Manchester University Press.

Bryson, Norman. 1983. *Vision and Painting: The Logic of the Gaze*. New Haven, CT: Yale University Press.

Buckley, C. H., and H. Fawcett. 2002. *Fashioning the Feminine: Representation and Women's Fashion from the Fin de Siècle to the Present*. London: I. B. Taurus.

Burnett, Ron. 2004. *How Images Think*. Cambridge: Massachusetts Institute of Technology Press.

Burns, Alan. 1978. *History of Nigeria*. London: George Allen and Unwin.

Burt, Eugene C. 1983. "Mural Painting in Western Kenya." *African Arts* 16, no. 3:60–63.

Burton, Richard Francis. 1863. *Abeokuta and the Cameroons Mountains: An Exploration*, vol. 1. London: Tinsley Brothers.

Byfield, Judith. 2002. *The Bluest Hands: A Social and Economic History of Women Dyers in Abeokuta (Nigeria), 1890–1940*. Portsmouth, NH: Heinemann.

Byfield, Judith. 2004. "Dress and Politics in Post–World II Abeokuta (Western Nigeria)." In Allman, *Fashioning Africa*, 36–43.

Callaway, Helen. 1992. "Dressing for Dinner in the Bush: Rituals of Self-Definition and British Imperial Authority." In Barnes and Eicher, *Dress and Gender*, 232–47.

Caraus, Tamara, and Elena Paris, eds. 2019. *Migration, Protest Movements, and the Politics of Resistance: A Radical Political Philosophy of Cosmopolitanism*. New York: Routledge.

Chaudhuri, Nirad C. 1976. *Culture in the Vanity Bag, Being an Essay on Clothing and Adornment in Passing and Abiding India*. Bombay: Jailo.

Cheah, Pheng. 1998. "Introduction, part II: The Cosmopolitical—Today." In *Cosmopolitics: Thinking and Feeling beyond the Nation*, edited by P. Cheah and B. Robbins, 91–114. Minneapolis: University of Minnesota Press.

Cheah, Pheng. 2006. "Cosmopolitanism." *Theory, Culture & Society* 23, nos. 2–3:486–96.

Cheal, D. 1988. *The Gift Economy*. London: Routledge.

Chinemelum, Mbadimma. 2013. Interview by Okechukwu Nwafor. Awka.

Chuks, Kinglsey. 2010. Email conversation with Okechukwu Nwafor. October 19.

Clark, Ebun. 1974. "Ogunde Theatre: The Rise of Contemporary Professional Theatre in Nigeria 1946–72 (First Part)." *Nigeria Magazine* 114:6–7.

Clarke, William H., ed. 1972. *Travels and Exploration in Yorubaland, 1854–1858*. London: Routledge and Kegan Paul, 1972.

CMS Archives CA 2/o43. Charles Gollmer. Journal Extracts for the Year 1845. 86.

Cohen, Yahudi. 1961. "Patterns of Friendship." In *Social Structure and Personality: A Casebook*, edited by Yahudi Cohen, 351–86. New York: Holt, Rinehart & Winston.

Cohn, B. S. 1996. *Colonialism and Its Forms of Knowledge: The British in India*. Princeton, NJ: Princeton University Press.

Cole, P. D. 1975. *Modern and Traditional Elites in the Politics of Lagos*. Cambridge, UK: Cambridge University Press.

Comaroff, Jean, and John Comaroff. 1997. *Of Revelation and Revolution: Dialectics of Modernity on a South African Frontier*. Chicago: University of Chicago Press.

Cordwell, Justine M. 1979. "Appendix: The Use of Printed Batiks by Africans." In Cordwell and Schwarz, *Fabrics of Culture*, 495–96.

Cordwell, Justine M. 1983. "The Art and Aesthetics of the Yoruba.," *African Arts* 16, no. 2:56–59

Cordwell, Justine, and Ronald A. Schwartz, eds. 1979. *The Fabrics of Culture: The Anthropology of Clothing and Adornment*. The Hague: Mouton.

Cornwall, Andrea. 2007. "Of Choice, Chance and Contingency: 'Career Strategies' and Tactics for Survival among Yoruba Women Traders." *Social Anthropology/Anthropologie Sociale* 15, no. 1:27–46.

Craik, Jennifer. 1994. *The Face of Fashion: Cultural Studies in Fashion*. London: Routledge.

Craik, Jennifer. 2005. *Uniforms Exposed: From Conformity to Transgression*. Oxford: Berg.

Crill, Rosemary, ed. 2006. *Textiles from India: The Global Trade*. Calcutta: Seagull Books.

Crowder, Michael. 1962. *The Story of Nigeria*. London: Faber.

Danjuma, Shuaibu. 2011. Interview by Okechukwu Nwafor. Lagos.March 4.

David, Nona. 2009. "Bend down, shake to the beat." *Top Traveller*. http://toptraveler.groups.vox.com/library/post/6a11017b8a484860e0110167cd374860d.html, accessed October 1, 2009.

Darling, Bunmi. "Owambe party, would you?" *Bunmi's Blog*. http://bunmidarling.com/bunmiblogs/?p=68, accessed September 9, 2011.

Dean, Jodi. 1996. *Solidarity of Strangers: Feminism after Identity Politics*. Berkeley: University of California Press.

DeNegri, Eve. 1962. "Yoruba Women's Costumes." *Nigerian Magazine* 72: 4–12

Denzer, LaRay. 1994. "Yoruba Women: A Historiographical Study." *International Journal of African Historical Studies* 27, no. 1:1–39.

Denzer, LaRay. 2002. "Fashion and Fluctuating Fortunes: The Nigerian Garment Indus-try under Structural Adjustment." In *Money Struggles and City Life: Devaluation in Ibadan and Other Urban Centers in Southern Nigeria, 1986–1996*, edited by Jane I. Guyer, LaRay Denzer, and Adigun Agbaje, 93–114. Portsmouth, NH: Heinemann.

Deutsch, Eliot. 1994. "On Creative Friendship." In *The Changing Face of Friendship*. Leroy S. Rouner, 15–27. Notre Dame, IN: University of Notre Dame Press.

Development of a Middle Class in Tropical and Sub-Tropical Countries. Record of the XXIXth Session held in London, September 1955. Brussels: International Institute of Differing Civilizations, 1956. Vi:467.

Dike, Theodora. 2010. Interview by Okechukwu Nwafor. Ojuelegba, Lagos. December 6.

Docker, John. 1994. *Postmodernism and Popular Culture: A Cultural History*. Cambridge, UK: Cambridge University Press.

Dosekun, Simidele. 2020. *Fashioning Postfeminism: Spectacular Femininity and Transna-tional Culture*. Urbana: University of Illinois Press.

Douglas, M. 1990. Foreword to *The Gift: The Form and Reason for Exchange in Archaic Societies*, edited by M. Mauss, ix–xxiii. London: Routledge.

Douglas, Mary. 1973. *Rules and Meanings: The Anthropology of Everyday Knowledge*. Harmondsworth, UK: Penguin.

Douglas, Mary, and Baron Isherwood. 1979. *The World of Goods: Toward an Anthropol-ogy of Consumption*. London: Allen Lane.

Drewal, Henry John. 1979. "Pageantry and Power in Yoruba Costuming." In Cordwell and Schwarz, *Fabrics of Culture*, 189–229.

Drewal, Henry John, and Margaret Thompson Drewal. 1984. *Gelede: Art and Female Power among the Yoruba*. Bloomington: Indiana University Press.

Dudley, B. J. 1964. "Marxism and Political Change in Nigeria." *Nigerian Journal of Eco-nomics and Social Studies* 6, no. 2:155–65.

Eades, J. S. 1993. *Strangers and Traders: Yoruba Migrants, Markets, and the State in North-ern Ghana*. Edinburgh: Edinburgh University Press.

Echeruo, Michael J. C. 1974. "Nnamdi Azikiwe and Nineteenth-Century Nigerian Thought." *Journal of Modern African Studies* 12, no. 2:245–63.

Echeruo, Michael J. C. 1977. *Victorian Lagos: Aspects of Nineteenth-Century Lagos Life*. London: Macmillan Educational Press.

Edwards, Elizabeth. 1997. "Beyond the Boundary: A Consideration of the Expressive in Photography and Anthropology." In *Rethinking Visual Anthropology*, edited by Marcus Banks and Howard Morphy, 53–80. New Haven, CT: Yale University Press.

Edwards, Michael. 1967. *The Growth of the British Cotton Trade, 1780–1815*. New York: Augustus M. Kelly.

Eicher, Joanne, ed. 1995. *Dress and Ethnicity: Change across Space and Time*. Oxford: Berg

Eicher, Joanne B. 2001. "Fashion of Dress." In *National Geographic Fashion*, edited by Cathy Newman. Washington, DC: National Geography Society.

Eicher, Joanne B., and Doran H. Ross, eds. 2010. *Encyclopedia of World Dress and Fash-ion: Africa*. Oxford: Oxford University Press.

Eicher, Joanne Bubolz. 1976. *Nigerian Handcrafted Textiles*. Ile-Ife, Nigeria: University of Ife Press.

Eicher, Joanne, and Tonye Erekosima. 1987. "Kalabari Funerals: Celebration and Display." *African Arts* 21:38–45.

Eicher, Joanne, and Tonye Erekosima. 1995. "Why Do They Call It Kalabari? Cultural Authentication and Demarcation of Ethnic Identity." In Eicher, *Dress and Ethnicity*.

Eicher, Joanne, Tonye Erekosima, Martha Anderson, and Philip Peek. 2002. "Fitting Farewells: The Fine Art of Kalabari Funerals." In *Ways of the Rivers: Arts & Environment of the Niger Delta*, edited by Martha Anderson and Philip Peek, 307–329. Los Angeles: UCLA Fowler Museum of Cultural History.

Ekwensi, Cyprian. 1963. *People of the City*. London: Heinemann.

Elam, Harry J., Jr., and Kennell Jackson Jr., eds. 2005. *Black Cultural Traffic: Crossroads in Global Performance and Popular Culture*. Ann Arbor: University of Michigan Press.

Elegante, Diva. 2007, August 13. "9jers & Owanbe!" *Verity* (blog). http://divaelegante. blogspot.com/2007/08/9jers-owanbe.html, accessed October 2, 2009.

Elkins, James, ed. 2007. *Photography Theory*. New York: Routledge.

Emerson, Ralph Waldo. 1902. "Gifts." In *The Works of R. W. Emerson: Essays*. London: Grant Richards.

Entwistle, J. 2000. *The Fashioned Body: Fashion, Dress, and Modern Social History*. Cambridge, UK: Polity Press.

Enwezor, Okwui, et al. 2002. *Under Siege, Four African Cities--Freetown, Johannesburg, Kinshasa, Lagos: Documenta II Platform 4*. Ostfildern-Ruit: Hatje Cantz Publishers.

Essah, Doris. 2008. "Fashioning the Nation: Hairdressing, Professionalism, and the Performance of Gender in Ghana, 1900–2006." PhD diss., Department of History, University of Michigan.

Euba, Titilola. 2002. "Dress and Status in 19th Century Lagos." In *History of the Peoples of Lagos State*, edited by Ade Adefuye, Babatunde Agiri, and Jide Osuntokun, 108–115. Lagos: Lantern Books.

Evenson, Sandra Lee. 1994. "A History of Indian Madras Manufacture and Trade" PhD diss., University of Minnesota.

Evenson, Sandra Lee. 2007. "Indian Madras Plaids as Real India." In *Dress Sense: Emotional and Sensory Experiences of the Body and Clothes*, edited by Donald Clay Johnson and Helen Bradley Foster, 96–108. Oxford: Berg.

Ezekiel, May Ellen, Sam Smith Bryson, Rolake Omonubi, and George Otiono. 1985. "The Swing of Fashion." *Newswatch*. December 30, 13.

Faiers, Jonathan, and Mary Westerman Bulgarella, ed. 2016. *Colors in Fashion*. London: Bloomsbury Academic, an imprint of Bloomsbury Publishing.

Falola, Toyin, and Matthew M. Heaton. 2008. *A History of Nigeria*. Cambridge, UK: Cambridge University Press.

Familusi, O. O. 2010. "The Yoruba Culture of Aso Ebi (Group Uniform) in Socio-ethical Context." *Lumina* 21, no. 2.

"Fashion in Motion." 2016. Victoria and Albert Museum. https://www.vam.ac.uk/search?q=fashion+in+motion&astyped=.

Featherstone, Mike. 2002. "Cosmopolis: An Introduction." *Theory, Culture & Society* 19, nos. 1/2:1–16.

Femenias, Blenda. 2005. *Gender and the Boundaries of Dress in Contemporary Peru*. Austin: University of Texas Press.

Ferme, Mariane. 2001. *The Underneath of Things: Violence, History, and the Everyday in Sierra Leone*. Berkeley: University of California Press.

Frizot, Michel, ed. 1998. *A New History of Photography*. Cologne: Konemann.

Gardi, Berhard, ed. 2009. *Woven Beauty: The Art of West African Textiles*. Basel: Museum der Kulturen.

Gardi, René. 1970. *African Crafts and Craftsmen*, translated by Sigrid MacRae. New York: Van Nostrand Reinhold.

Gardiner, Michael E. 2000. *Critiques of Everyday Life*. London: Routledge.

Gbelegbuwa II, Awujale of Ijebuland. Letter of October 16, 1946, to Resident, Ijebu Province. National Archives, Ibadan [NAI] Ije Prof 3366/1.

Geary, C. M. 1988. *Images from Bamum: German Colonial Photography at the Court of King Njoya, Cameroon, West Africa, 1902–15*. Washington, DC: Smithsonian Institution Press.

Gell, Alfred. 1998. *Art and Agency: An Anthropological Theory*. Oxford: Clarendon Press.

Godelier, Maurice. 1999. *The Enigma of the Gift*. Chicago: University of Chicago Press, 1999.

Goffman, Erving. 1963. *Stigma: Notes on the Management of Spoiled Identity*. Englewood Cliffs, NJ: Prentice-Hall.

Gondola, Ch. Didier. 1999. "Dream and Drama: The Search for Elegance among Congolese Youth." *African Studies Review* 42, no. 1:31.

Gore, Charles D. 2001. "Commemoration, Memory, and Ownership: Some Social Contexts of Contemporary Photography in Benin City, Nigeria." *Visual Anthropology* 14, no. 3:321–42.

Gott, Suzanne. 2010. "The Ghanaian Kaba: Fashion That Sustains Culture." In *Contemporary African Fashion*, edited by Suzanne Gott and Kristyne Loughran, 11–27. Bloomington: Indiana University Press.

Grabski, Joanne. 2003. "Dakar's Urban Landscapes: Locating Art and Artists in the City." *African Arts* 36, no. 4:28–39.

Grabski, Joanne. 2009. "Making Fashion in the City: A Case Study of Tailors and Designers in Dakar, Senegal." *Fashion Theory* 13, no. 2:215–42.

Grabski, Joanna. 2010. "The Visual City: Tailors, Creativity, and Urban Life in Dakar, Senegal." In *Contemporary African Fashion*, edited by Suzanne Gott and Kristyne Loughran, 29–38. Bloomington: Indiana University Press.

Groening, Stephen Francis. 2008. "Connected Isolation: Screens, Mobility, and Globalized Media Culture," PhD diss., University of Minnesota.

Groom, Nick. 2003. "Original Copies; Counterfeit Forgeries." *Critical Quarterly* 43, no. 2:6–18.

Guichard, M., P. Heady, and W. G. Tadesse. 2003. *Friendship, Kinship, and the Bases of Social Organization. Max Planck Institute for Social Anthropology Report, 2002–2003,* 7–17. Halle/Saale: Max Planck Institute for Social Anthropology. https://voidnetwork.gr/wp-content/uploads/2016/08/Friendship-kinship-and-the-bases-of-social-organisation.pdf.

Guyer, Jane. 1995. "Wealth in People, Wealth in Things." Introduction. *Journal of African History* 36:83–90.

Guyer, Jane I., and Samuel M. Eno Belinga. 1995. "Wealth in People as Wealth in Knowledge: Accumulation and Composition in Equatorial Africa." *Journal of African History* 36, no. 1:91–120.

Hackspiel, Elizabeth. 2008. "Modernity and Tradition in a Global World: Fashion in Africa." Exhibition review. *African Arts* 41, no. 2:90.

Hall, Stuart. 2002. "Political Belonging in a World of Multiple Identities." In Vertovec and Cohen, *Conceiving Cosmopolitanism,* 26–31.

Haney, Erin. 2010. "Film, Charcoal, Time: Contemporaneities in Gold Coast Photographs." *History of Photography* 34, no. 2:119–33.

Haney, E. 2012. "Emptying the Gallery: The Archives' Fuller Circle." In *Photography in Africa: Ethnographic Perspectives,* edited by Richard Vokes, 127–39. Oxford: James Currey.

Hannerz, Ulf. 1990. "Cosmopolitans and Locals in a World Culture." *Theory, Culture & Society* 7, no. 2:237–51.

Hannerz, Ulf. 1996. *Transnational Connections: Culture, People, Places.* London: Routledge.

Hansen, Karen Tranberg. 2000. *Salaula: The World of Secondhand Clothing and Zambia.* Chicago: University of Chicago Press.

Hansen, Karen Tranberg. 2003. "Fashioning Zambian Moments." *Journal of Material Culture* 8, no. 3:301–309.

Hansen, Karen Tranberg. 2004a. "Dressing Dangerously: Miniskirts, Gender Relations, and Sexuality in Zambia." In Allman, *Fashioning Africa,* 166–85.

Hansen, Karen Tranberg. 2004b. "The World in Dress: Anthropological Perspectives on Clothing, Fashion, and Culture." *Annual Review of Anthropology* 33:369–92.

Hansen, Karen Tranberg. n.d. "Colonialism and Imperialism." *LoveToKnow.* https://fashion-history.lovetoknow.com/fashion-history-eras/colonialism-imperialism, accessed February 12, 2017.

Hartmann, W., J. Silvester, and P. Hayes, eds. 1998. *The Colonising Camera: Photographs in the Making of Namibian History.* Cape Town: University of Cape Town Press.

Hay, Margaret Jean. 1996. "Hoes and Clothes in a Luo Household: Changing Consumption in a Colonial Economy, 1906–1936." In *African Material Culture,* edited by Mary Jo Arnoldi, Christraud M. Geary, and Kris L. Hardin, 243–61. Bloomington: Indiana University Press.

Hay, Margaret Jean. 2004. "Changes in Clothing and Struggles over Identity in Colonial Western Kenya." In Allman, *Fashioning Africa,* 96–111.

Hayes, Patricia, and Gary Minkley, eds. 2019. *Ambivalent: Photography and Visibility in African History*. Ohio: Ohio University Press.

Haynes, Jonathan, and Onokome Okome. 2000. "Evolving Popular Media: Nigerian Video Films." In *Nigerian Video Films*, edited by Jonathan Haynes, 209–241. Athens: Ohio University Center for International Studies.

Heathcote, David. 1972. "Hausa Embroidered Dress." *African Arts* 5, no. 2:12–19.

Held, David. 2003. "Cosmopolitanism: Globalisation Tamed?" *Review of International Studies* 29, no. 4:465–80.

Helms, Mary W. 1993. *Craft and the Kingly Ideal*. Austin: University of Texas Press.

Hendrickson, Hildi, ed. 1996. *Clothing and Difference: Embodied Identities in Colonial and Post-Colonial Africa*. Durham, NC: Duke University Press.

Hilling, David. 1969. "The Evolution of the Major Ports of West Africa." *Geographical Journal* 135, no. 3:365–78.

Hobsbawn, Eric, and Terence Ranger, eds. 1983. *The Invention of Tradition*. Cambridge, UK: Cambridge University Press.

Hodgkin, Thomas. 1961. *African Political Parties*. Harmondsworth, UK: Penguin.

Hopkins, Antony. G. 1973. *An Economic History of West Africa*. New York: Columbia University Press.

Horn, Marilyn, and Lois Gurel. 1968. *The Second Skin*. London: Houghton Mifflin.

Ibekwe, Ifeoma. 2010. Interview by Okechukwu Nwafor. Lagos. August 10.

Ibenegbu, Chidi. 2011. Interview by Okechukwu Nwafor. Lagos. February 25.

Idiens, Dale, and K. G. Ponting. 1980. *Textiles of Africa*. Leeds: Pasold Research Fund.

Idike, Uche. 2015. Interview by Okechukwu Nwafor. Lagos. August 27.

Idun-Arkhurst, Isaac, and James Laing, eds. 2007. *The Impact of Chinese Presence in Africa*. London: African Practice.

Imnakoya. 2005. "Nigerian Owanbe Party: Is It Custom, Craze, or Curse?" *Grandiose Parlor*. http://grandioseparlor.com/2005/11/nigerian-owanbe-party-is-it-custom-craze-or-curse/, accessed 1 October 1.

Irabor, Judith. 2010. Interview by Okechukwu Nwafor. Lagos. February 15.

Iriah, Peter. 2011. Interview by Okechukwu Nwafor. February 2011.

Janus. 1915. "Lagosians on Dits." *Lagos Standard*, February 24, 1915.

Jay, Martin. "Scopic Regimes of Modernity." In *Vision and Visuality*, edited by Hal Foster. Seattle: Bay Press. 17.

Jenkins, David. 2003. *The Cambridge History of Western Textiles*. Cambridge, UK: Cambridge University Press.

Jimoh, Azimazi Momoh. 2007. "Senate Seeks Measures to Revamp Textile Industry." *The Guardian*. Monday, October 29:1–3.

Johnson, Marion. 1974a. "Cloth on the Banks of the Niger." *Journal of the Historical Society of Nigeria* 6, no. 4:353–63.

Johnson, Marion. 1974b. "Cotton Imperialism in West Africa." *African Affairs* 73, no. 291:178–87.

Johnson, Samuel. 2001. *The History of the Yorubas*. Lagos: C.S.S. Limited.

Kaplan, Flora S. 1990. "Some Uses of Photographs in Recovering Cultural History at the Royal Court of Benin, Nigeria." *Visual Anthropology* 3:317–41.

Kaplan, Flora S. 1991. "Fragile Legacy: Photographs as Documents in Recovering Political and Cultural History at the Royal Court of Benin." *History in Africa* 18:205–237.

Kareem, Azeezat. 2017. "Saraki's daughter weds, aso ebi is N200,000." Encomium. http://encomium.ng/sarakis-daughter-weds-aso-ebi-is-n200000/, accessed March 13, 2019.

Kellner, Douglas. 1995. *Media Culture, Cultural Studies, Identity and Politics between the Modern and the Postmodern*. London: Routledge.

Kemi, Silva. 2015. Interview by Okechukwu Nwafor. Lagos. August 10.

Kennedy, Dane. 1990. "The Perils of the Midday Sun: Climatic Anxieties in the Colonial Tropics." In *Imperialism and the Natural World*, edited by John M. Mackenzie, 118–40. Manchester, UK: Manchester University Press.

Keyes, Carolyn Marion. 1993. "Adire: Cloth, Gender and Social Change in Southwestern Nigeria, 1841–1991." PhD diss., University of Wisconsin, Madison.

Kickasola, Joseph G. N.d. "Cinemediacy: Theorizing an Aesthetic Phenomenon." http://www.avila.edu/journal/kick.pdf, accessed July 28, 2010.

Kilson, Martin L., Jr. 1958. "Nationalism and Social Classes in British West Africa." *Journal of Politics* 20, no. 2:368–87.

Knappett, Carl. 2006. "Beyond Skin: Layering and Networking in Art and Archaeology." *Cambridge Archaeological Journal* 16:239–51.

Komter, Aafke. 2005. *Social Solidarity and the Gift*. Cambridge, UK: Cambridge University Press.

Koolhas, Rem. 2002. "Fragments of a Lecture on Lagos." In Enwezo, *Under Siege*, 20–33.

Kopytoff, Jean Herskovits. 1965. *A Preface to Modern Nigeria: The "Sierra Leonians" in Yoruba, 1830–1890*. Madison: University of Wisconsin Press.

Kraus, John. 2002. "Capital, Power, and Business Associations in the African Political Economy: A Tale of Two Countries, Ghana and Nigeria." *Journal of Modern African Studies* 40, no. 3:395–436.

Kraus, Rosalind. 1984. "A Note on Photography and the Simulacra." *October* 31 (Winter):49–68.

Kriger, Colleen. 2005. "Mapping the History of Cotton Textile Production in Pre-Colonial West Africa." *African Economic History* 33:87–116.

Kriger, Colleen. 2007. *Cloth in West African History*. Lanham, MD: AltaMira Press.

Ladoja, Rukky. 2010. "Spirit of Owambe." *Time Out/Nigeria, Celebrating Nigeria at 50*. Special collectors' edition. October.

Lagos State Ministry of Information Year Book. 1999. Lagos: Lagos State Government Press.

Lagos, Annual Reports of the Colony of Southern Nigeria for the Year 1889.

Lagos, Annual Reports of the Colony of Southern Nigeria for the Year 1909.

Lamb, Venice, and Judith Holmes. 1980. *Nigerian Weaving*. Lagos: Shell Petroleum Development Co. of Nigeria.

Lamont, Michele, and Sada Aksartova. 2002. "Ordinary Cosmopolitanisms: Strategies for Bridging Racial Boundaries among Working-Class Men." *Theory, Culture & Society* 19, no. 4:1–25.

Lamuniere, Michelle, ed. 2001. *You Look Beautiful Like That: The Portrait—Photographs of Seydou Keïta and Malick Sidibé*. New Haven, CT: Yale University Press.

Lander, Richard. 1967. *Records of Captain Clapperton's Last Expedition to Africa*. 1830; reprint, London: Frank Cass.

Lau, George F. 2010. "The Work of Surfaces: Object Worlds and Techniques of Enhancement in the Ancient Andes." *Journal of Material Culture* 15, no. 3:259–86.

Lawal, Babatunde. 1996. *The Gelede Spectacle: Art, Gender, and Social Harmony in an African Culture*. Seattle: University of Washington Press.

Lawuyi, Olatunde Bayo. 1991. "The Social Marketing of Elites: The Advertised Self in Obituaries and Congratulations in Some Nigerian Dailies." *Africa: Journal of the International African Institute* 61, no. 2:247–63.

Lefebvre, Henri. 1991. *Critique of Everyday Life*. Vol. 1, *Introduction*, translated by J. Moore. London: Verso.

Lester, Alan. 1998. *Colonial Discourse and the Colonization of Queen Adelaide Province, South Africa*. London: Historical Geography Research Series no. 34.

Lewis, Victor, 2009. Discussion on Fashion shows, Haute FashionAfrica.com. http://www.fashionafrica.com/features/ankara-the-rebirth/

Lipovetsky, Gilles. 1994. *The Empire of Fashion: Dressing Modem Democracy*. Princeton, NJ: Princeton University Press.

Lise, Skov. 2003. "Fashion-Nation: A Japanese Globalization Experience and a Hong Kong Dilemma." In *Re-Orienting Fashion: The Globalization of Asian Dress*, edited by Sandra Niessen, Ann Marie Leshkowich, and Carla Jones, 215–42. Oxford: Berg.

Lister, Martin, ed. 1995. *The Photographic Image in Digital Culture*. London: Routledge.

Little, Kenneth. 1962. "Some Traditionally Based Forms of Mutual Aid in West African Urbanization." *Ethnology* 1, no. 2:197–211.

Little, Kenneth. 1972. "Voluntary Associations and Social Mobility among West African Women." *Canadian Journal of African Studies / Revue Canadienne des Études Africaines* 6, no. 2:275–88. Special Issue: The Roles of African Women: Past, Present, and Future.

Lloyd, P. C., A. L. Mabogunje, and B. Awe, eds. 1967. *The City of Ibadan*. London: Cambridge University Press.

Lloyd, Peter. 1953. "The Integration of the New Economic Classes into Local Government in Western Nigeria." *African Affairs* 52:327–34.

Lock, Margaret. 1993. "Cultivating the Body: Anthropology and Epistemologies of Bodily Practice and Knowledge." *Annual Review of Anthropology* 22:133–55.

Luczak, Ewa Barbara, Anna Pochmara, and Samir Dayal, eds. 2019. *New Cosmopolitanisms, Race, and Ethnicity: Cultural Perspectives*. Warsaw; Berlin: De Gruyter Open Poland.

Lutz, Hazel A. 2003. "Design and Tradition in an India–West Africa Trade Textile: Zari-Embroidered Velvets." PhD diss., University of Minnesota.

Maiwada, S., and E. Renne. 2013. "The Kaduna Textile Industry and the Decline of Textile Manufacturing in Northern Nigeria, 1955–2010." *Textile History* 44, no. 2:171–96.

Maiwada, Salihu, and Elisha Renne. 2007. "New Technologies of Embroidered Robe Production and Changing Gender Roles in Zaria, Nigeria, 1950–2005." *Textile History* 38, no. 1:25–58.

Malinowski, Bronislaw. 1920. "Kula: The Circulating Exchange of Valuables in the Archipelagoes of Eastern New Guinea." *Man* 20 (July):97–105.

Malinowski, Bronislaw. 1978. *Argonauts of the Western Pacific: An Account of Native Enterprise and Adventure in the Archipelagos of Melanesian New Guinea*. London: Routledge.

Malinowski, Bronislaw. 1997. "The Principle of Give and Take." In *The Logic of the Gift: Towards an Ethics of Generosity*, edited by Alan D. Schrift, 15–17. New York: Routledge.

Malkan, Jeffrey. 2005. "What Is a Copy?" *Cardoza Arts and Entertainment Law Journal* 23:419–63.

Mann, Kristin. 1981. "Marriage Choices among the Educated African Elite in Lagos Colony, 1880–1915." *International Journal of African Historical Studies* 14, no. 2:201–228.

Mann, Kristin. 1985. *Marrying Well: Marriage, Status, and Social Change among the Educated Elite in Colonial Lagos*. Cambridge, UK: Cambridge University Press.

Mann, Kristin. 2007. *Slavery and the Birth of an African City: Lagos, 1760–1900*. Bloomington: Indiana University Press.

Manovich, Lev. 2001. *The Language of New Media*. Cambridge, MA: MIT Press.

Marien, Mary Warner. 2002. *Photography: A Cultural History*. New York: Harry N. Abrams.

Marris, Peter. 2004. *Family and Social Change in an African City: A Study of Rehousing in Lagos*. London: Routledge.

Martin, Phyllis. 1994. "Contesting Clothing in Colonial Brazzaville." *Journal of African History* 35, no. 3:401–426.

Martin, Phyllis. 1995. *Leisure and Society in Colonial Brazzaville*. Cambridge, UK: Cambridge University Press.

Martin, Phyllis M. 2004. "Afterword." In Allman, *Fashioning Africa*, 227–30.

Mauss, M. 1990. *The Gift: The Form and Reason for Exchange in Archaic Societies*. New York: W. W. Norton.

Mauss, Marcel. 1954. *The Gift: The Form and Reason for Exchange in Archaic Societies*. Transl. Ian Cunnison. London: Cohen & West.

McIntosh, Marjorie Keniston. 2009. *Yoruba Women, Work, and Social Change*. Bloomington: Indiana University Press.

McLuckie, Craig. 1993. Review of *Self-Assertion and Brokerage: Early Cultural Nationalism in West Africa*. In *African Literatures in the Eighties, Matatu*, No. 10, edited by Dieter Riemenschneider and Frank Schulze-Engler, 215–25. Amsterdam: Rodopi.

Meyer, Birgit. 1998. "Christian Mind and Worldly Matters: Religion and Materiality in Nineteenth-Century Gold Coast." *Journal of Material Culture* 2:311–37.

Meyer, Birgit. 2010. "Tradition and Colour at Its Best: 'Tradition' and 'Heritage' in Ghanaian Video-Movies." *Journal of African Cultural Studies* 22, no. 1:7–23.

Micheli, Angelo. 2008. "Doubles and Twins: New Approach to Contemporary Studio Photography in West Africa." *African Arts* 41, no. 1:70.

Miers, S., and I. Kopytoff, eds. 1977. *Slavery in Africa: Historical and Anthropological Perspectives*. Madison: University of Wisconsin Press.

Miller, Christopher L., and George R. Hamell. 1986. "A New Perspective on Indian–White Contact: Cultural Symbols and Colonial Trade." *Journal of American History* 73:311–28.

Miller, Joseph Calder. 1988. *Way of Death: Merchant Capitalism and the Angolan Slave Trade, 1730–1830*. Madison: University of Wisconsin Press.

Miller, Vincent. 2005. *Consuming Religion: Christian Faith and Practice in a Consumer Culture*. New York: Continuum International Publishing.

Mitchell, W.J.T. 2002. "Showing Seeing: A Critique of Visual Culture." In *The Visual Culture Reader*, edited by Nicholas Mirzoeff, 2nd ed., 86–101. New York: Routledge.

Mokake, Flavius Mayoa. 2010. "The Kabba Dress: Identity and Modernity in Contemporary Cameroon." In *Marginality and Crisis: Globalization and Identity in Contemporary Africa*, edited by Akanmu G. Adebayo, Olutayo C. Adesina, and Rasheed O. Olaniyi, 71–80. Lanham, MD: Lexington Books.

Moloye, O. 2004. "Traditional High Fashion in Transition." In *Understanding Yoruba Life and Culture*, edited by S. N. Lawal, M.N.O. Sadiku, and A. Dopamu, 377–88. Trenton, NJ: Africa World Press.

Montaigne, Michel de. 1972. *Essays of Michel de Montaigne*. Garden City, NY: Doubleday.

Moore, Shaun. 1993. *Interpreting Audiences: I Ethnography of Media Consumption*. London: Sage Publications.

Morris-Reich, A. 2016. *Race and Photography: Racial Photography as Scientific Evidence, 1876–1980*. Chicago: University of Chicago Press.

Motunrayo, Ayokanmi, Tolulope Oyedele, and Obisesan Babatunde. 2013. "The Resurgence of Ankara Materials in Nigeria," *Journal of Education and Practice* 4 no. 17: 167.

Murray, K. C., and A. Hunt-Cooke. 1936. *Extracts of Reports on "Native Minor Industries in Oyo and Abeokuta Provinces."* May.

Mustafa, Hudita Nura. 1998. "Satorial Ecumenes: African Styles in a Social and Economic Context." In *The Art of African Fashion*, edited by Els Van der Plas and Marlous Willemsen, 13–45. Trenton, NJ: Africa World Press.

Mustafa, Hudita Nura. 2001. "Ruins and Spectacles: Fashion and City Life in Contemporary Senegal." *Nka: Journal of Contemporary African Arts* 15:47–53.

Mustafa, Hudita Nura. 2006. "La Mode Dakaroise, Elegance, Transnationalism, and an Africa Fashion Capital." In *Fashion's World Cities*, edited by Christopher Breward and David Gilbert, 177–99. Oxford: Berg.

Mustafa, Hudita Nura. 2010. "Intersecting Creativities: Oumou Sy's Costumes in the Dakar Landscape." In *Contemporary African Fashion*, edited by Suzanne Gott and Kristyne Loughran, 122–37. Bloomington: Indiana University Press.

NAI Ije Prof 3366/2. 1946. "Women's Undesirable Practices." *Colonial Order*. October 21.

Nathan, Joseph. 1986. *Uniforms and Nonuniforms: Communication through Clothing*. New York: Greenwood.

Ndubuisi, Obiorah. 2007. "Who Is Afraid of China in Africa? Towards an African Civil Society Perspective on China-Africa Relations." In *African Perspectives of China in Africa*, edited by Firoze Manji and Stephen Marks, 35–36. Cape Town: Fahamu.

Nielsen, Ruth. 1979. "The History and Development of Wax-Printed Textiles Intended for West Africa and Zaire." In Cordwell and Schwarz, *Fabrics of Culture*, 467–98.

Niessen, Sandra, Ann Marie Leshkowich, and Carla Jones, eds. 2003. *Re-Orienting Fashion: The Globalization of Asian Dress*. Oxford: Berg.

Norris, Katherine Lucy. 2003. *The Life-Cycle of Clothing: Recycling and the Efficacy of Materiality in Contemporary Urban India*. PhD thesis, University College London.

Nunley, John W. 1987. *Moving with the Devil: Art and Politics in Urban West Africa*. Urbana: University of Illinois Press.

Nussbaum, Martha C. 2019. *The Cosmopolitan Tradition: A Noble but Flawed Ideal*. Cambridge, MA: Harvard University Press.

Nwafor, Maria Nneka. 2011. Interview by Okechukwu Nwafor. Texas. November 11.

Nwafor, Okechukwu. 2011. "The Spectacle of *Aso Ebi* in Lagos: 1990–2008." *Postcolonial Studies* 14, no. 1:45–62.

Nweke, Antonia. 2011. Interview by Okechukwu Nwafor. Apapa, Lagos. February 3.

Nwike, Nnenna. 2010. Interview by Okechukwu Nwafor. Lekki Peninsula, Lagos. April 5.

Nwokoye, Ifeoma. 2010. Interview by Okechukwu Nwafor. Lagos. April 3.

Nwosu, T. C. 1965. "Aso-ebi." *Nigeria* 86: 221.

Obese, Ayo. 2010. Interview by Okechukwu Nwafor. Surulere, Lagos. December 10.

Obiekwe, Ada. 2010. Interview by Okechukwu Nwafor. Lagos. April 1.

Odhiambo, Atioeno. 1992. "From Warriors to Jonanga: The Struggle of Nakedness by the Luo of Kenya." In *Sokomoko: Popular Culture in East Africa*, edited by Werner Graebner, 11–26. Amsterdam: Rodopi.

Ofeimun, Felix. 2010. Interview by Okechukwu Nwafor. Tejuosho, Lagos. April 6.

Ofeimun, Odia. 2005. "Imagination and the City." In *Lagos: A City at Work*. Lagos: Glendora Books.

Ogbonna, Chidimma. 2010. Interview by Okechukwu Nwafor. Lagos. November 30.

Oguchi, Ifeyinwa. 2010. Interview by Okechukwu Nwafor. November 30.

Oguibe, Olu. 2001. "The Photographic Experience: Towards an Understanding of Photography in Africa." In *Flash Afrique: Photography from West Africa*, edited by Kunsthalle Wein Steidt. London: Penguin.

Ogundana, Babafemi. 1972. "Oscillating Seaport Location in Nigeria." *Annals of the Association of American Geographers* 62, no. 1:110–21.

Ogunlana, Abiola. 2009. Interview by Okechukwu Nwafor. December 16.

Ogunlana, Vera. 2010. Interview by Okechukwu Nwafor. Lagos. February 15.

Ogunleye, Jide. 2010. "Adenuga's Daughter's Wedding: Aso Ebi Goes for N350,000." April 3. Jide Ogunleye's blog http://www.jideogunleye.com/blog/?p=690.

Ogunyemi, Chikwenye Okonjo. 1996. *Africa Wo/Man Palava: The Nigerian Novel by Women*. Chicago: University of Chicago Press.

Ojeikere, J. D., and Andre Magnin. 2000. *Okhai Ojeikere: Photographs*. Zürich: Scalo.

Ojeikere, Pa J. D. 2010. Interview by Okechukwu Nwafor. Ketu, Lagos. March 15.

Ojo, Aderonke. 2011. Interview by Okechukwu Nwafor. Surulere, Lagos. February 10.

Ojo, B. 2006. "An Appraisal of Weaving Cottage Industry in South-Western Nigeria." In *Potentials of Visual Arts and Creativity*. Lagos: CCAF Publication.

Okon, Edith. 2010. Interview by Okechukwu Nwafor. Lagos. April 10.

Okoro, Shedrack 2010. Interview by Okechukwu Nwafor. Lagos. April 5.

Okoye, Adaobi. 2009. Interview by Okechukwu Nwafor. Lagos. December 15.

Okoye, Chioma. 2010. Interview by Okechukwu Nwafor. Lagos. March 20.

Olajumoke, Busayo. 2010. Interview by Okechukwu Nwafor. Lagos. April 25.

Olaniyan, Tejumola. 2004. *Arrest the Music! Fela and His Rebel Art and Politics*. Bloomington: Indiana University Press.

Olatunji, Segun. 2007. "UNTL Shut Down, Sacks over 4000 Workers." *The Punch*. October 9.

Olukoju, Ayodeji. 2006a. "Maritime Trade in Lagos in the Aftermath of the First World War." *African Economic History* 20:119–35.

Olukoju, Ayodeji. 2006b. "Ports, Hinterlands, and Forelands." Inaugural lecture delivered at the University of Lagos on Wednesday, June 21, 2006.

Olukoya, Bisi. 2011. Interview by Okechukwu Nwafor. Lagos. March 26.

Olusanya, G. O. 1992. "Charlotte Olajumoke Obasa." In *Nigerian Women in Historical Perspective*, edited by Bolanle Awe, 105–120 Lagos: Sankore/Bookcraft.

Olusoga, Babalola. 2011. Interview by Okechukwu Nwafor. Lagos. March 10.

Olutayo, A. O., and O. Akanle. 2009. "Aso-Oke (Yoruba's Hand-Woven Textiles) Usage among the Youths in Lagos, Southwestern Nigeria." *International Journal of Sociology and Anthropology* 1, no. 3:62–69.

Omolara, Sade. 2010. Interview by Okechukwu Nwafor. Lagos. April 23.

Omoregbe, Johnson, Pa. 2010. Interview by Okechukwu Nwafor. Mushin, Lagos. December 20.

Omu, Fred I. A. 1978. *Press and Politics in Nigeria, 1880–1937*. Atlantic Highlands, NJ: Humanities Press.

Onimode, Bade. 2000. *Africa in the World of the 21st Century*. Ibadan, Nigeria: Ibadan University Press, 2000.

Onyegbula, Esther. "The *Ankara* Revolution and the Nigerian Aso-ebi Culture." *MyNAIJA News*. http://www.mynaijanews.com/content/view/1441/46, accessed May 10, 2009.

Onyewuenyi, Remy N. 1990. "The Evolution and Spatial Diffusion of Informal Sector Activity in Nigeria: A Case Study of Informal Tailoring Industry in the Oyo State Metropolitan Areas." PhD diss, University of Ottawa.

Orimolade, Adefolake Odunayo. 2014. "Aso ebi: Impact of the Social Uniform in Nigerian Caucuses, Yoruba Culture and Contemporary Trends. PhD Dissertation. University of South Africa.

Oyelami, Rose. 2010. Interview by Okechukwu Nwafor. Yaba, Lagos. March 30.

Oyelola, Pat. 1980. *Everyman's Guide to Nigerian Art.* Lagos: Nigeria Magazine.

Oyelola, Pat. 2007. "The Acculturation of Factory Print." *The Nigerian Field* 72, no. 3.

Pallinder, Agneta. 1990. "Adegboyega Edun: Black Englishman and Yoruba Cultural Patriot." In *Self-Assertion and Brokerage: Early Cultural Nationalism in West Africa,* edited by P. F. de Moraes Farias and Karin Barber, 11–34. Birmingham, Eng.: Centre of West African Studies, University of Birmingham.

Parsons, Timothy. 2006. "Consequences of Uniformity: The Struggle for the Boy Scout Uniform in Colonial Kenya." *Journal of Social History* 40, no. 2:361–83.

Peel, J.D.Y. 1968. *Aladura: A Religious Movement among the Yoruba.* London: Oxford University Press for International African Institute.

Peffer, John, and Elisabeth L. Cameron. 2013. *Portraiture and Photography in Africa.* Bloomington: Indiana University Press.

Peiss, Kathy. 1998. *Hope in a Jar: The Making of America's Beauty Culture.* New York: Henry Holt.

Perani, Judith, and Norma H. Wolff. 1999. *Cloth, Dress, and Art Patronage in Africa.* Oxford: Berg.

Picton, John, ed. 1988. *Tradition, Technology, and Lurex: Some Comments on Textile History and Design in West Africa.* Washington, DC: National Museum of African Art.

Picton, John. 1995. "Technology, Tradition and Lurex. The Art of Textiles in Africa." In *The Art of African Textiles Technology. Tradition and Lurex.* Edited by John Picton, 6–31. London. Barbican Art Gallery.

Pinney, Christopher. 2003. "Notes from the Surface of the Image: Photography, Postcolonialism and Vernacular Modernism." In *Photography's Other Histories*, edited by Christopher Pinney and Nicolas Peterson, 202–220. Durham, NC: Duke University Press.

Pinney, Christopher, and Nicolas Peterson, eds. 2003. *Photography's Other Histories.* Durham, NC: Duke University Press.

Pinther, Kerstin, and Julia Ng. 2007. "Textiles and Photography in West Africa." *Critical Interventions* 1, no. 1:113–23.

Plankensteiner, Barbara, and Nath Mayo Adediran, eds. 2010. *African Lace: A History of Trade, Creativity, and Fashion in Nigeria.* Ghent, Belgium: Snoeck.

Poole, Deborah. 2005. "An Excess of Description: Ethnography, Race, and Visual Technologies." *Annual Review of Anthropology* 34:159–79. Portsmouth: Heinemann.

Raban, Jonathan. 1998. *Soft City.* London: Harvill Press.

Rabine, Leslie W. 1997. "Not a Mere Ornament: Tradition, Modernity, and Colonialism in Kenyan and Western Clothing." *Fashion Theory* 1, no. 2:145–68.

Rabine, Leslie W. 2002. *The Global Circulation of African Fashion.* New York: Berg.

Rabine, Leslie W. 2010. "Fashionable Photography in Mid-Twentieth-Century Senegal." *Fashion Theory* 14, no. 3:305–30.

Raheja, Gloria Goodwin. 1988. *The Poison in the Gift: Ritual, Prestation, and the Dominant Caste in a North Indian Village.* Chicago: University of Chicago Press.

Ranger, T. 2001. "Review: Colonialism, Consciousness and the Camera." *Past and Present* 171: 203–15.

Reke, Jude. 1960. "*Aso Ebi*, Culture or Crisis." *Nigerian Outlook*. June 13.

Renne, Elisha. 1992. "The Decline of Women's Weaving among the North East Yoruba." *Textile History* 1, no. 5:87–96.

Renne, Elisha. 1995. *Cloth That Does Not Die: The Meaning of Cloth in Benin Social Life.* Seattle: University of Washington Press.

Renne, Elisha P. 2010. "Contemporary Wedding Fashions in Lagos, Nigeria." In Gott and Loughran, *Contemporary African Fashion*, 68–86.

Renne, Elisha. 2004. "From Khaki to Agbada: Dress and Political Transition in Nigeria." In Allman, *Fashioning Africa*, 125–43.

Renne, Elisha P. 2010. "Figured, Textured, and Empty Spaces: An Aesthetics of Textiles and Dress in Nigeria." In Plankensteiner and Adesiran, *African Lace*, 71–89.

Renne, Elisha P. 2015. "The Changing Contexts of Chinese-Nigerian Textile Production and Trade, 1900–2015." *TEXTILE* 13, no. 3:212–33.

Roach, Mary Ellen, and Joanne Bubolz Eicher. 1965. *Dress, Adornment, and the Social Order.* New York: John Wiley.

Robbins, Bruce. 1998a. "Comparative Cosmopolitanisms." In *Cosmopolitics: Thinking and Feeling beyond the Nation*, edited by P. Cheah and B. Robbins, 246–64. Minneapolis: University of Minnesota Press.

Robbins, Bruce. 1998b. "Introduction Part I: Actually Existing Cosmopolitanisms." In *Cosmopolitics: Thinking and Feeling beyond the Nation*, edited by P. Cheah and B. Robbins, 1–19. Minneapolis: University of Minnesota Press.

Roberts, R.E.L., L. N. Richards, and V. L. Bengtson. 1991. "Intergenerational Solidarity in Families: Untangling the Ties That Bind." *Marriage and Family Review* 16:11–46.

Roces, Mina. 2007. "Gender, Nation, and the Politics of Dress in Twentieth-Century Philippines." In *The Politics of Dress in Asia and the Americas*, edited by Louise Edwards and Mina Roces, 354–77. Portland, OR: Sussex Academic Press.

Ross, Doran. 1998. *Wrapped in Pride: Ghanaian Kente and African American Identity.* Los Angeles: UCLA Fowler Museum of Cultural History.

Ross, Robert. 2008. *Clothing: A Global History: or, The Imperialists' New Clothes.* Cambridge, UK: Polity.

Roudometof, Victor. 2005. "Transnationalism, Cosmopolitanism, and Glocalization." *Current Sociology* 53, no. 1:113–35.

Rouner, Leroy, ed. 1994. *The Changing Face of Friendship.* Notre Dame: University of Notre Dame Press.

Rovine, Victoria. 2001. *Bogolan: Shaping Culture through Cloth in Contemporary Mali.* Washington: Smithsonian Institution Press.

Rovine, Victoria L. 2004. "Working the Edge: XULY.Bët's Recycled Clothing." In *Old Clothes, New Looks: Second-Hand Fashion*, edited by Alexandra Palmer and Hazel Clark, 215–28. Oxford: Berg.

Rovine, Victoria. 2014. *African Fashion, Global Style: Histories, Innovations, and Ideas You Can Wear*. Bloomington: Indiana University Press.

Rubinstein, Daniel, and Katrina Sluis. 2009. "A Life More Photographic: Mapping the Networked Image." *Photographies* 1, no. 1:13.

Ruther, Kirsten. 2001. *The Power Beyond: Mission Strategies, African Conversion, and the Development of a Christian Culture in the Transvaal*. Munster: Lit Verlag.

Santos-Granero, Fernando. 2007. "Of Fear and Friendship: Amazonian Sociality beyond Kinship and Affinity." *Journal of the Royal Anthropological Institute* 13, no. 1:1–18.

Saunders, Nicholas J. 1999. "Biographies of Brilliance: Pearls, Transformations of Matter, and Being, c. AD 1492." *World Archaeology* 31: 243–57.

Scheld, Suzanne. 2007. "Youth Cosmopolitanism: Clothing, the City, and Globalization in Dakar, Senegal." In *City and Society* 19, no. 2:232–52.

Schwartz, Hillel. 1996. *The Culture of the Copy: Striking Likenesses, Unreasonable Facsimiles*. New York: Zone.

Sharpe, William, and Leonard Wallock. 1987. "From 'Great Town' to 'Nonplace Urban Realm': Reading the Modern City." In *Visions of the Modern City*, edited by William Sharpe and Leonard Wallock, 1–50. Baltimore: Johns Hopkins University Press.

Shonibare, Salau. 1946. Letter of November 18, 1946, to His Worship the Resident, Ijebu-Ode. National Archives, Ibadan [NAI] Ije Prof 3366/13–14.

Shubayo, Jumoke. 2010. Interview by Okechukwu Nwafor. Lagos. May 10.

Silver, Allan. 1990. "Friendship in Commercial Society: Eighteenth-Century Social Theory and Modern Sociology." *American Journal of Sociology* 95:1474–1504.

Silverman, Kaja. 1986. "Fragments of a Fashionable Discourse." In *Studies in Entertainment: Critical Approaches to Mass Culture*, edited by Tanio Modleski, 32–65. Bloomington: Indiana University Press.

Simmel, Georg. 1997. "The Philosophy of Fashion." In *Simmel on Culture*, edited by David Frisby and Mike Featherstone, 187–206. London: Sage Publications.

Simmel, George. 1979. *On Individuality and Social Forms*. Chicago: University of Chicago Press.

Sklar, Richard L. 1963. *Nigerian Political Parties*. Princeton, NJ: Princeton University Press.

Sklar, Richard L. 1979. "The Nature of Class Domination in Africa." *Journal of Modern African Studies* 17, no. 4:531–52.

Skrbis, Zlatko, Gavin Kendall, and Roger Waldinger. 2004. "Locating Cosmopolitanism." *Theory, Culture & Society* 21, no. 6:115–36.

Smith, Daniel Jordan. 2001. "Ritual Killing, 419, and Fast Wealth: Inequality and the Popular Imagination in Southeastern Nigeria." *American Ethnologist* 28, no. 4:803–826.

Smythe, Hugh H., and Mabel M. Smythe. 1960. *The New Nigerian Elite*. Stanford, CA: Stanford University Press.

Snow, David A., Sarah Anne Soule, and Hanspeter Kriesi. 2004. *The Blackwell Companion to Social Movements*. Oxford: Blackwell.

Sowole, T. 2011. Photographer, Jide Alakija in *Aso Ebi*: From the Diaspora, Politics of *Aso*

Ebi via Photography. http://africanartswithtaj.blogspot.com/2011/11/from-diaspo-ra-politics-of-aso-ebi-via.html, accessed June 2014.

Spencer, Anne. 1982. *In Praise of Heroes: Contemporary African Commemorative Cloth*. Newark, NJ: Newark Museum.

Spencer, Anne. 2001. "Of Polomints and Alphabets: The Eicher Collection of African Wax Printed Cloths." In *Cloth Is the Center of the World: Nigerian Textiles, Global Perspectives*, edited by Susan J. Torntore, 43–64. Minnesota: Goldstein Museum of Design, Department of Design, Housing and Apparel, University of Minnesota.

Spencer, Liz, and Raymond E. Pahl. 2006. *Rethinking Friendship: Hidden Solidarities Today*. Princeton, NJ: Princeton University Press.

Spitzer, Leo. 1974. *The Creoles of Sierra Leone: Responses to Colonialism, 1870–1945*. Madison: University of Wisconsin Press.

Sprague, Stephen. 1978. "How I See the Yoruba See Themselves." *Studies in the Anthropology of Visual Communication* 5, no. 1:9–28.

Steiner, Christopher. 1985. "Another Image of Africa: Towards an Ethnohistory of European Clothes Marketed in Africa, 1873–1960." *Ethnohistory* 32, no. 2:91–110.

Strathern, Marilyn. 1988. *The Gender of the Gift: Problems with Women and Problems with Society in Melanesia*. Berkeley: University of California Press.

Sturken, Marita, and Lisa Cartwright 2001. *Practices of Looking: An Introduction to Visual Culture*. Oxford: Oxford University Press.

Suttles, Gerald. 1970. "Friendship as a Social Institution." In *Social Relationships*, edited by George McCall, Michal McCall, Norman Denzin, Gerald Suttles, and Suzanne B. Kurth, 95–135. Chicago: Aldine.

Suttles, Gerald. 1989. "Friendship as a Social Institution." In *Friendship: Developing a Sociological Perspective*, edited by Graham Allan, 90–135. Boulder, CO: Westview Press.

Sylvanus, Nina. 2007. "The Fabric of Africanity: Tracing the Global Threads of Authenticity." *Anthropological Theory* 7:201–216.

Sylvanus, Nina. 2016. *Patterns in Circulation: Cloth, Gender, and Materiality in West Africa*. Chicago: Chicago University Press.

Szerszynski, Bronislaw, and John Urry. 2002. "Cultures of Cosmopolitanism." *Sociological Review* 50, no .4:461–81.

Talbot. P. A. 1926. *The Peoples of Southern Nigeria*. London: Oxford University Press.

Tarlo, Emma. 1996. *Clothing Matters: Dress and Identity in India*. Chicago: University of Chicago Press.

Taussig, M. T. 1980. *The Devil and Commodity Fetishism in South America*. Chapel Hill: University of North Carolina Press.

Tcherkezoff, Serge. 2003. "Of Cloth, Gifts, and Nudity: Regarding Some European Misunderstandings during Early Encounters in Polynesia." In *Clothing the Pacific*, edited by Chloé Colchester, 51–75. Oxford: Berg.

Thomas, Edith. 2010. Interview by Okechukwu Nwafor. Mushin, Lagos. December 2.

Thomas, Nicholas. 1991. *Entangled Objects*. Cambridge, MA: Harvard University Press.

Thompson, Krista. 2009. "The Sound of Light: Reflections on Art History in the Visual Culture of Hip-Hop." *Art Bulletin: A Quarterly Published by the College Art Association* 91, no. 4:481–505.

Thorp, Margaret Ferrand. 1939. *America at the Movies*. New Haven, CT: Yale University Press.

Tkbridals. 2019. Interview by Okechukwu Nwafor.

Tomlinson, Alan, ed. 1990. *Consumption, Identity, and Style*. London: Routledge.

Trager, Lillian. 2001. *Yoruba Hometowns: Community, Identity, and Development in Nigeria*. Boulder, CO: Lynne Reinner Publishers.

Trowell, Margaret. 1960. *African Design*. London: Faber.

Tulloch, Carol. 1998. "Out of Many, One People: The Relativity of Dress, Race, and Ethnicity to Jamaica, 1880–1907." *Fashion Theory* 2, no. 4:359–82.

Tulloch, Carol, ed. 2004. *Black Style*. London: V&A Publications.

Turner, Bryan. 2002. "Cosmopolitan Virtue, Globalization, and Patriotism." *Theory, Culture & Society* 19, nos. 1/2:45–63.

Turner, Terence. 1993. "The Social Skin." In *Reading the Social Body*, edited by Catherine B. Burroughs and Jeffrey David Ehrenreich, 15–39. Iowa City: University of Iowa Press.

Uchendu, Benson. 2009. Interview by Okechukwu Nwafor. Lagos. November 30.

Udenta, Nkemakonam. 2011. Interview by Okechukwu Nwafor. Lagos. March 7.

Udenwa, Chiamaka. 2010. Interview by Okechukwu Nwafor. Lagos. December 17.

Udobang, Kate 2011. Interview by Okechukwu Nwafor. Lagos. March 17.

Ugwu-Oju, D. 1997. "Aso ebi." In *Aso ebi: Cloth of the Family, Benin City, Nigeria, Christmas and New Year, 1991–1994*, edited by P. Galembo, *Benin City, Nigeria* page. Exhibition catalog.

Ujam, Joy. 2010. Interview by Okechukwu Nwafor. Lagos. December 15.

Umunna, Ifeyinwa. 2010. Interview by Okechukwu Nwafor. Lagos. December 12.

Uwem, Clement. 1975. "Is It Our Culture"? *New Nigeria*. December 28.

Uzoeche, Johnson. 2010. Interview by Okechukwu Nwafor. Lagos. April 6.

van der Laan, H. Laurens. 1983. "A Swiss Family Firm in West Africa: A. Brunnschweiler & Co., 1929–1959." *African Economic History*, no. 12, Business Empires in Equatorial Africa, 287–97.

Vansina, Jan. 1990. *Paths in the Rainforests: Toward a History of Political Tradition in Equatorial Africa*. Madison: University of Wisconsin Press.

Verhezen, P. 2005. "Gifts and Bribes: An Essay on the Limits of Reciprocity." PhD diss., Hoger Instituut Voor Wijsbegeerte, Catholic University of Leuven.

Vertovec, Steven, and Joshua Cohen, eds. 2002. "Introduction: Conceiving Cosmopolitanism." In *Conceiving Cosmopolitanism: Theory, Context, and Practice*, 1–22. New York: Oxford University Press.

Veblen, Thorstein. 1899. *The Theory of the Leisure Class: An Economic Study in the Evolution of Institutions*. New York: Macmillan.

Vokes, R. 2015. "The Chairman's Photographs: The Politics of an Archive in South-

Western Uganda." In *The African Photographic Archive: Research and Curatorial Strategies*, edited by C. Morton and D. Newbury, 95–112. London: Bloomsbury.

Vokes, Richard. 2012. "Introduction." In *Photography in Africa: Ethnographic Perspectives*, edited by R. Vokes, 1–29. Oxford: James Currey.

Vokes, Richard, and Darren Newbury. 2018. "Photography and African Futures." *Visual Studies* 33, no. 1:1–10.

Wallerstein, Immanuel. 1967. "Class, Tribe, and Party in West African Politics." In *Party Systems and Voter Alignments*, edited by Seymour M. Lipset and Stein Rokkan, 497–518. New York: Free Press.

Wass, Betty. 1979. "Yoruba Dress in Five Generations of a Lagos Family." In Cordwell and Schwarz, *Fabrics of Culture*, 551–48.

Watson, Ruth. 2003. *"Civil Disorder Is the Disease of Ibadan": Chieftaincy and Civic Culture in a Yoruba City*. Athens: Ohio University Press.

Weiner, Annette. 1992. *Inalienable Possessions*. Berkeley: University of California Press.

Wells, Karen. 2007. "The Material and Visual Cultures of Cities." *Space and Culture* 10, no. 2:136–44.

Welters, Linda, and Abby Lillethun. 2018. *Fashion History: A Global View*. New York: Bloomsbury Academic.

Wickramasinghe, Nira. 2003. *Dressing the Colonised Body: Politics, Clothing, and Identity in Sri Lanka*. Hyderabad: Orient Longman.

Williams, Akin. 2009. Interview by Okechukwu Nwafor. Ikeja, Lagos. December 22.

Williams, Gavin. 1970. "The Social Stratification of a Neo-Colonial Economy: Western Nigeria." In *African Perspectives*, edited by Christopher Allen and R. W. Johnson, 225–50. Cambridge, UK: Cambridge University Press.

Wilson, Elizabeth. 1995. *Adorned in Dreams: Fashion and Modernity*. London: Virago Press.

Wilson, Elizabeth, and Amy de la Haye, eds. 1999. *Defining Dress as Object, Meaning, and Identity*. Manchester, UK: Manchester University Press.

Wilson, Eric. 2009. "Bloggers Crash Fashion's Front Row." *New York Times*. December 24, 14.

Wolf, Eric. 1977. "Kinship, Friendship, and Patron-Client Relations in Complex Societies." In *Friends, Followers, and Factions: A Reader in Political Clientelism*, edited by Steffen Schmidt, James C. Scott, Carl Lande, and Laura Guasti, 167–77. Berkeley: University of California Press.

Wollen. P. 2003. "The Concept of Fashion in the Arcades Project." *Boundary* 2, 30, no. 1:131–42.

Young Men of Ijebu-Ode Comprising of Various Age-Groups Petition of October 7, 1946, to Oba Alaiyeluwa.

Zorn, Elayne. 2004. *Weaving a Future: Tourism, Cloth, and Culture on an Andean Island*. Iowa City: University of Iowa Press.

419, 124, 230

Abeokuta, 26, 61, 62, 116, 192n20, 193n25
Abeokuta Women's Union (AWU), 46–47, 50, 195n46
Abuja, 63, 115, 153
Adams, John, 28, 191n3
Adeboye, Folu, 202n3
Adenuga, Wale, 84, 86, 89, 90, 94, 95
Aderibigbe, A. B., 27
Adesanmi, Pius, 75, 201n9, 202
adire, 34; *alabere*, 61, 62; *eleko*, 61, 62, 63; *kampala*, 63, 64, 66, 67; *oniko*, 61; origins, 61–64; use for aso ebi, 54, 66, 68, 71
Ado-Ekiti, 88
agbada, 31, 32, 56, 66–67, 71, 198n17, 200n6
Agbebi, Majola, 33–34
Agudas, 25
Ajah, 127
Ajayi Crowther, Samuel, 35
Akinwumi, Tunde, 37–38, 42, 43, 50, 194n42
Akitoye, Oba, 28, 29, 191n1
Akosombo, 51
Aladura Church, 40
Allada, 8, 189n2
Allman, Jean, 20
The Ambassador, 160
Anambra State, 1
Animasaun Digital Studio, 159, 161, 162

ankara, 1, 2, 16, 22, 51–53, 54, 57, 58, 60, 66, 67, 68–69, 70–71, 72, 75, 76, 80, 108, 115, 116, 184, 189n1, 196n2, 196n3, 199n18
Appadurai, Arjun 72
art history, 10, 169
Ash, Juliet, 190n4
ashobi, 100, 193n28
aso ebi, 1–23, 25,26, 33–36; class, 91–95; copies and copying, 153–57; crowd and money, 86–91; friendship, 106–7; "logic of gift," 99, 107–14; meaning as traditional dress, 74–80; moral economy, 51–53, 54–60, 64; moral economy of intimacy, 96–99; mutuality and cosmopolitanism, 121–36, 139–42, 144, 146, 148, 149, 151, 153; oneness and solidarity, 16, 99–106; origins, 37–50; political solidarity, 114–19; public visibility, 81–82; purchasing, 82–86; Structural Adjustment Programme, 22, 66–72, 131, 132, 198n15, 208n6; surfacist aesthetics, 158–80
aṣọ òkè, 22, 33, 34, 54–57; reinvention, 57–60, 64, 65, 66, 67, 68, 71, 72, 76, 80, 92, 93, 105, 186, 196n3, 197n4, 197n6, 199n18, 200nn6–7
AsoEbiBella, 15, 79, 128
AsoEbiBella.com, 15, 128
authenticity, 52, 154, 182, 195
Awori, 24
AWU. See Abeokuta Women's Union
Ayegboyin, Deji, 40

Babangida, Ibrahim Badamosi, 124
Badagry, 29,193n25
Bakhtin, Mikhail, 176, 178
Balogun textile market, 20, 51–54; 69–71, 149, 152, 199
Barber, Karin , 85, 86, 94, 131, 192n20, 199n3
Bascom, William, 90, 186
Bastian, Misty, 198n13, 198n17
Batchen, Geoffrey, 167, 168
Belinga, Eno, 48–49
BellaNaija, 14, 15, 96, 127
Benin, 7, 8, 194n44, 206n11; Oba of Benin, 24, 27, 189, 200n7
Benjamin, Walter, 154
Berger, John, 159, 160
Blaize, Charlotte, 34
Blaize, Richard B., 34
Blumer, Herbert, 117, 118
Bouffarick, 39
Bourdieu , Pierre, 117–18
Brazil, 10, 24–25, 27, 28, 29, 30, 50
British, 10, 25, 26, 29, 31, 34, 35, 36, 44, 45, 62, 64, 65, 182, 191n1, 192n21, 194n44, 196n3, 197n8, 198n10, 205n3
brocade, 67, 206n9
buba, 31, 32, 34, 46, 56, 58, 200n6
Buhari, Muhammadu, 132
Burton, Richard, 26
Byfield, Judith, 46–47, 61, 195n46

camera, 37, 128, 129, 130, 134, 155, 169, 205n4, 206n2; analog, 163, 166, 167, 168, 177; Brownie D, 207n5; digital, 23, 158, 162, 164, 165, 166, 177, 179; phone, 158, 168
Chi Ming, Cha, 196n2
China, 20, 52, 72, 73, 76, 199n20; ankara, 51, 52, 57, 66, 68, 70, 71, 76, 189n1, 199n18; Chinatown 73; Nigerian textile market 72–74; 76, 87, 199nn19–20
Church Missionary Society (CMS), 35, 37, 100, 193n25
Clapperton, Hugh, 8
Clarke, William H., 26, 38–39

Clinton, Bill, 73
cloth/clothing/clothe, 2, 6, 9, 11, 14, 16, 18–22; 24, 26–35, 39, 42, 44, 63, 190n5, 191n16, 192n21, 193n26, 196nn2–3, 197nn9–10, 198n13, 198n15, 199n3, 205n7, 208n3; Allada cloth, 8; anti-colonial resistance, 46–48, 50–52; ashigbo, 42; ban on imported, 198n12; batik, 64, 189n1; broad cloth, 31; class, 91, 93, 94, 99, 100–101, 115, 120, 125, 127, 132, 146, 152, 159, 163, 172, 182, 184–87, 200n7; European, 31, 65, 192n21; family cloth, 5; handwoven, 34, 61, 62; history, 187; Hollandais, 70; Jebu cloth, 8; language, 72; "loin," 30; laundering, 65; missionary expansionism, 36–37, 39, 40, 42, 43, 194n43; official, 36; "poor people," 61; prestigious, 57, 200n6; tai-lored, 45, 100, 152; uniform, 33, 37, 40, 43, 99, 189n2, 202n2; up-country, 54; wax-print, 70; wealth, 52, 80, 82–91, 93
CMS. See Church Missionary Society
color, 5, 16, 17, 22, 26, 38, 44, 45, 46, 47, 51, 52, 55, 56, 58, 60, 61, 62, 63, 64, 65, 66, 67, 70, 78, 79–84, 91, 93, 95, 96, 102, 105, 116, 149, 151, 152, 153, 155, 156, 161, 189n1, 197n9, 199n2, 207n5
Comaroff, Jean, 192n21
Comaroff, John, 192n21
Compagnie du Senegal, 64
Congo, 61, 191n3
copy/copying, 16, 52, 73, 79, 81, 122, 148–49, 152, 153–56, 157, 185
CorelDRAW, 164
cosmopolitanism, 5, 11, 12, 14, 15, 20, 25, 58, 121, 122–29, 156–57, 181, 183, 204n1, 205n3

Daily Times of Nigeria, 130
Dei, Benedetto, 64
Denzer, LaRay, 40, 132, 152, 190n13, 198n15, 203n8
digital photography, 6, 23, 128, 158–80, 183, 187, 206n2; analog to digital, 162–64; Animasaun Digital Studio, 159, 161, 162

Dior, Christian, 67
Dosekun, Simidele, 20, 21
dress, 1, 2, 5, 6, 8–23; 25–35; histories
    and friendship networks, 39–48; rise
    of uniformed dress and missionary
    impact 36–39, 41, 43–47, 50, 56, 58, 60,
    67; traditional dress, 20–21, 27, 71, 72–
    76, 77, 79, 81, 82, 90–93, 96, 100–102,
    104–6, 114, 116, 120, 122, 123, 126–29,
    132–36, 146, 148, 149, 151, 152, 154–56,
    163, 167, 168, 179, 182, 184, 185, 186,
    190n15, 191n18, 192nn20–21, 193n24,
    193n26, 194n43, 195n49, 198n13, 198n17,
    199n2, 200n4, 200n7, 202n4, 205n4,
    205nn6–8, 207n5
Drewal, Henry John, 208n1
Durkheim. Emile, 119
Dutch, 8, 64, 160, 182, 196, 197n8, 198n16
Dutch East Indian Army, 64
Dutch West India Company, 64

Echeruo, Michael, 205n3
Edo, 24, 200
Egba, 24, 34, 61
ẹgbẹ́, 39–40, 41, 43, 44, 45, 47, 48, 50, 51,
    63, 90
Ekwensi, Cyprian, 122, 123
Elkins, James, 168–69
England, 29, 39, 43, 67, 72, 190n4, 192n20,
    195n47, 197n8, 197n10
Enwezor, Okwui, 9, 187
Euba, Titilola, 26, 27, 28, 30, 33, 34, 191.
Europe/Europeans, 44, 48, 64, 113; archi-
    tecture, 25; art, 159, 160; banned export
    goods, 61; capitalist mediation, 182;
    class, 92; cloth/clothing, 31, 34, 63–63,
    65, 72, 192n21, 197n9; culture, 35–36;
    dress, 10, 28, 30, 31, 32, 33–34, 36, 37, 46,
    50, 58, 75, 192n20; intellectuals, 201n9;
    manufacturers, 65–66, 71–72, 196n3;
    merchants, 36–39, 48, 53; missionaries,
    9, 36–39, 193n25; photography, 161;
    slave dealers, 8; textiles, 29, 61, 64,
    65–66, 67, 76, 195n50, 196n3; traders, 8;
    travel, 161, 207n4

fake, 22, 52, 73, 91, 97, 114, 117, 154
family cloth, 5
fashion magazine, 2, 6, 7, 12, 14, 16, 17, 22,
    23, 82, 109, 111, 121, 126, 129, 130–34, 135,
    138, 139, 140, 141–42, 148, 149, 151, 152,
    155–57, 183, 184–86
Ferme, Mariane, 100, 200n4
Fila, 56, 57, 85
Fiske, John, 74
Freetown, 193n28, 195n50
friendship, 10, 12, 13, 17, 27, 38, 39–48,
    50, 53, 91, 98, 99, 100, 102, 103, 104,
    105, 117, 118, 120, 183, 185–86, 203n11,
    204nn14–16, 204n18; interrogating,
    106–7; logic of gift, 107–14

Gabon, 8
Gelede, 38, 193n28
george, 2, 54, 67, 196n3, 198n13
Georges, Selve de, 160
Gibson, James J., 161
Gibson, Mrs., 34
gift, 5, 13, 23, 81, 82, 84, 86, 87, 88, 95, 97,
    98, 102, 103, 117–18, 120, 183, 185, 190n11,
    204nn12–13; "logic of gift," 99, 107–14;
    wedding, 17, 56, 80, 104, 105, 179
Gold Coast, 8, 31, 34
Gold Coast Colony Advertiser, 34
Grabski, Joanne, 190n13, 206n8
Groening, Stephen Francis, 173,
    208
Gucci, 67
Guinea, 64, 206n9
Guyer, Jane, 48–49, 83, 89

Hackspiel, Elizabeth, 205n7
Haney, Erin, 206n11
Hansen, Tranberg Karen, 74, 190n15,
    192n21, 197n7, 205n5
Haynes, Jonathan, 92
Heathcote, David, 190n15
Hendrickson, Hildi, 16, 192n7
Henry VIII, 160
Hobsbawn, Eric, 208n2
Holbein, Hans, 160

Ibadan, 61, 62, 207n5
iborun, 56, 106
identity, 10, 14, 20, 25, 30, 33, 146, 154, 158, 161, 199n2; collective, 119, 176; cultural, 126; ethnic, 74; national, 74; social, 74, 89, 195n48
Ijebu, 8, 10, 24, 34, 35, 101, 189n2
Ikorodu, 116, 196n2
Instagram, 23, 79, 81, 82
ipele, 56
Iro, 30, 46, 56, 58, 200n6

Janus, 203n9
Java, 64, 196n3, 197n8
Java Wax, 196n3
Jebu cloth, 8
Johnson, Samuel, 30
Johnson, Marion, 100–101, 191n16, 197n10

Kaduna Textile Ltd., 196n2
kampala, 63, 64, 67
Kampa Peace Conference, 63
Keita, Seydou, 163, 169, 207n5
Kellner, Douglas, 156
Ketu, 168, 207n5
Keyes, Carolyn Marion, 41, 50, 68, 190n7, 194n34, 194n43
Kickasola, Joseph G., 166–67
kijipa, 61, 62
Komter, Aafke, 190n11, 204n12
Kopytoff, Igor, 89, 200n5
Kopytoff, Jean Herskovits, 34
Kosoko, Oba, 25, 28, 191n11
K'OTo, Aiye, 42
Kraus, Rosalind, 154, 155
Kriger, Colleen, 189n3

lace, 1, 2, 5, 6, 52, 54, 57, 58, 60, 67, 68, 80, 93, 102, 105, 108, 196n3, 197n9, 206n9
Lagos, 1, 2, 4–50, 51, 53, 54, 56–60, 64, 67–74, 76–77, 78, 79, 81, 84–87, 90–97, 100–103, 106, 108–10, 116, 121–57, 158, 159, 16, 162, 163, 164, 165, 167, 168, 170–74, 176, 177, 179–80, 181–87, 190n4,

190n7, 191n1, 192n20, 193n24, 194n34, 195nn46–47, 195n50, 196nn2–3, 197n8, 197n10, 199n18, 199n20, 200nn5–6, 201n8, 205nn3–4, 205n6, 207n5, 208nn2–3
Lagos Critic, 33
Lagos Daily News, 42, 130
Lagos Daily Record, 11
Lagos Standard, 11, 33, 34, 39, 42, 106
Lagos Times, 34, 130
Lagos Weekly Record, 33, 41, 200n5
Lander, Richard, 8
Lau, George, 161, 176
Lawal, Babatunde, 27
Lawuyi, Olatunde Bayo, 93, 131
Lefebvre, Henri, 76, 120
Lekki, 79, 134, 164
Lewis, Victor, 181
Lipovetsky, Gilles, 18–19
Lister, Martin, 23
London, 69, 85, 126, 128, 196n3, 201n8

Macaulay, O. E., 33
Madras, 195n50, 196n3, 197
Magnin, Andres, 168, 208
Maiwada, Salihu, 190, 196, 199
Malinowski, Bronislaw, 112, 190
Manchester, 64, 197n10
Manovich, Lev, 177
Martin, Phyllis, 46, 120, 192n21
Mauss, Marcel, 99, 112–13, 117
McIntosh, Marjorie Keniston, 40, 44, 47–48, 49
McLuckie, Craig, 192n20
Mercer, Kobena, 169
Miers, Susan, 89, 200n5
Miller, Joseph Calder, 89
Miller, Vincent, 76
modernism, 134
Moloney, Alfred, 64–65, 197n10
moral economy, 12–13, 84, 97, 99, 119, 202n1
Mouttet, L., 65
Muslims, 30, 31–32, 44
Mustafa, Hudita Nura, 15, 17, 183

National Council of Nigeria, 195n47
Nigeria, 1, 5–7, 9, 12–15, 17, 19–23, 26, 31–
 36, 40–45, 48, 50–57, 61, 63, 64, 68–81,
 83–85, 87–89, 91–93, 95, 98, 100, 101,
 106, 110, 112, 114–16, 120, 122–26, 129–
 34, 144, 152, 157, 159, 163, 164, 168, 179,
 181–87, 189, 190, 192–203, 205–9
Nigerian Chronicle, 42
Nigerian Pioneer, 32, 41, 50
Nunley, John, 193n28
Nussbaum, Martha, 204n1

oba (king), 10, 24, 27–29, 48, 83, 191n1,
 200n7
Obama, Michelle, 63
Obasa, Charlotte, 195n46
Obasa, Sisi, 34
Obasanjo, Olusegun, 115, 198n12
Obiesie, Kelechi, 1, 3
Ode-lay Society, 193n28
Ofeimun, Odia, 152, 153
Ogbomoso, 40, 47
Ogunde, Herber, 202n2
Ojeikere, J. D'Okhai, 58, 59, 163, 168,
 196n3, 207n5
Ojeikere, Pa, 168
Ojo, Aderonke, 56
Okome, Onokoome, 92
Okundaye, Nike Davies, 63
Olaniyan, Tejumola, 125
Olukoju, Ayodeji, 41–42, 50
oneness, 16, 46, 120; interrogating, 99–
 106
Onitsha, 1, 5, 7, 87
originality, 16, 52, 154–55
oriki, 194n41, 199n3
Oshodi, 45, 54, 140, 199n20
Oshodi, Abiola, 45
Osogbo, 44
Otunba Gbenga Daniel, 115
Ovation, 146, 147, 148
Owambe, 12, 121, 122–26, 129, 156, 157, 184,
 205nn6-7
Oyelola, Pat, 189n1
Oyo, 8, 114–15, 189n2, 199n3, 200n6

Pallinder, Agneta, 192n20
Parsons, Timothy, 104–5
Payne, Otunba, 34
Perani, Judith, 16–17, 185, 197n10, 200n7
Peru, 161
phone, cell, 2, 17, 108, 122, 136, 139, 146,
 158, 168
photogenic, 167
photography, 5, 12, 17, 22, 37, 80, 123, 129,
 134, 142, 144, 146, 154, 184, 186, 205n4;
 digital, 6, 23, 128, 158–80, 183, 187,
 206n2; postcolonial, 161, 168, 169, 175,
 180, 187, 207n4
Photoshop, 23, 158, 159, 162, 163, 164, 168,
 171, 173, 174, 175, 177, 178, 179, 180
Picton, John, 54, 189n1, 197n8
Pinney, Christopher, 159, 161, 166, 173,
 207n4
Pinther, Kerstin, 205n4
Poole, Deborah, 174
Portuguese, 8, 24, 27
postcolonial, 5, 7, 9, 10, 14, 18–21, 24,
 39, 54, 75, 78, 91, 113, 114, 121, 125, 157,
 193n24, 208n3; agency, 182; anxiety,
 35; crises, 15, 134; photography, 161,
 168, 169, 175, 180, 187, 207n4; ruin, 183;
 urbanism, 122
postfeminist self, 21

Raban, Jonathan, 129
Rabine, Leslie, 71–72, 182, 193n21, 205n4
Ransome-Kuti, Funmilayo, 46, 195n47
Recuay, 161
Redeemed Christian Church of God,
 202n3
Renne, Elisha, 43, 50, 193n24; "Contem-
 porary Wedding Fashions in Lagos,
 Nigeria," 205n4; meaning of cloth in
 Bunu life 208n3; Nigerian politicians
 and *agbada*, 198n17
Royal African Company, 64

Salami, Bello Babatunde, 31–32
Salami, Alhaji Olasunkanmi, 114–15
Santos-Granero, Fernandos, 118

Saraki, Bukola, 85, 86, 89, 90, 93
Saraki, Tosin, 85
Saros, 24, 30, 35
sartorial, 11, 14, 16, 18, 19, 21, 25, 26, 29, 32, 33, 34, 35, 41, 45, 46, 48, 50, 52, 53, 56, 57, 58, 66, 71, 72, 75, 76, 83, 84, 93, 120, 121, 122, 128, 142, 144, 155, 156, 158, 159, 181, 183, 184, 185, 186, 190n12, 192n7, 196n3, 200n7
sartorial ecumene, 17
Schwartz, Hillel, 154, 192n20
Senegal, 17, 61, 64, 65, 182, 190n13
Senegambia, 8
Sequeira, Ruy de, 24
sewing machine, 25, 38–39, 50
Shagari, Shehu, 78
Sidibé, Malick, 163, 207n5
Sierra Leone, 10, 24, 25, 29, 30, 33, 35, 36, 37, 50, 89, 100, 193n28, 194
Simmel, Georg, 76, 208
Singer, 38–39
Sklar, Richard, 201n8
snapshot, 14, 134, 164, 167–79, 208n8
Snow, David, 118–19
Sodake, Reverend, 43
sokoto, 56, 200n6
solidarity, 1, 10, 11, 12, 15, 18, 19, 22, 35, 45, 83, 98, 99, 100, 102, 103, 106, 109, 112, 120, 146, 181, 182, 186; communal, 17, 105; fake, 114; family, 185; group, 16, 84; political, 114–19; social, 84; symbolic, 105; uniformed, 104, 114
Soyinka, Wole, 115, 116
Steiner, Christopher, 65, 66, 182
Structural Adjustment Programme, 22, 66–72, 131, 132, 198n15, 208n6
surface, 23, 62, 97, 142, 158–62, 164, 166, 183; achronotopic, 178; altered, 167–79; Baroque. 160; de-perspectivilized, 207n4; digital, 163; pictorial, 162, 174; shallow, 120; spatiotemporal, 178
Suttles, Gerald, 113, 203n11

tailors, 2, 5, 11, 14, 23, 37, 38, 39, 47, 68, 71, 74, 100, 121, 127, 132, 134, 151–52, 154, 156, 157, 184, 185, 205n4

Taiwo, David Conrad, 200n5
Tejuosho, 148, 149, 152, 153
Texas, 152
textile, 1, 2, 5, 6, 8, 9, 10, 11, 13, 15, 19–23, 27–29, 38, 43, 44, 46, 50–55, 58, 60–77, 80, 82, 87, 92, 93, 98, 100–122, 128, 133, 134, 149, 151–54, 158–60, 161, 163, 164, 171, 173, 174–76, 183, 186, 189n2, 194n34, 196n2, 197n6, 199n20, 200n7, 207n5; *ankara*, 22, 70; Balogun, 51, 52, 53, 54, 69, 70; British, 182; cheap, 52, 54, 184; Chinese, 22, 52, 199nn19–20; cotton, 189n3; Dutch, 182, 198n16; European, 29, 65, 66, 196n3; foreign, 54, 63, 64–66, 67, 68, 71, 195n49; Freetown, 193n28; French, 182; global, 19, 191n16; hand-dyed, 61; handwoven, 54; imported, 7, 58, 182, 197n9, 206n9; Indian, 29, 64, 195n50; indigenous, 197n9; Java, 197n8; Madras, 195n50; Manchester, 64; Nigerian, 22, 52, 54, 61, 66–72, 198n15, 199n19, 208n4; Oshodi, 199n20; patterned, 196n3; Senegalese, 182; wax-print, 198n16
Thompson, Krista, 159, 175
Times of Nigeria, 31, 32
Tinubu, Bola Ahmed, 125
Tkbridals, 2, 4, 5–6, 14, 17
Today's Fashion Magazine, 109, 111, 142, 143
traditional, 41, 58, 68, 173; *adire*, 63; attire, 25, 34, 71, 74, 134; ceremonies, 56, 57, 112, 126, 152; costume, 28, 130; dress, 20–21, 27, 31, 71, 72–76, 133, 148, 182; elements, 182; funeral rituals, 194n41; handspun yarn, 197n6; historian, 27; identity, 74; institution, 40; Kalabari society, 200n7; marriage, 153; outfits, 71; parameters, 177; photography, 166; rulers, 132; style, 28, 31; textile materials, 175; weddings, 56, 57, 80, 152, 199n3; Yoruba society, 93–94
Trager, Lillian, 48, 105, 195n48, 203n8

uniforms, 1, 2, 5, 6, 11, 14, 15–18, 19, 21, 25,

26, 33, 36–39, 40, 41, 42, 43, 44–46, 47, 49, 50, 52, 58, 60, 71, 74, 75, 80–82, 83, 88, 90, 93, 95, 97, 99–100, 103, 104–6, 107–8, 114, 115, 116, 117, 118–20, 122, 123, 130, 132, 133, 135, 141, 142, 146, 148, 153–56, 157, 164, 167, 168, 179, 180, 185, 189n2, 191n18, 193n24, 193n26, 193n28, 194n42, 200n4, 202n2, 202n3, 203n6, 208n1
United Nigerian Textiles Ltd., 196n2
United States, 2, 73, 152, 153, 199n1, 205n3
urban, 1–23, 37, 48, 53, 56, 58, 61, 64, 67, 71, 72, 74, 76, 78, 97, 98, 101, 121, 124, 126, 127, 129, 134, 155, 157, 159, 181, 185, 186, 187, 190n4, 190nn12–13, 193n28, 206n8, 207n5, 208n2
urbanization, 47, 53, 122, 208n3

Vansina, Jan, 89
Veblen, Thorstein, 21, 85–86
Versace, 67
visibility, 5, 6, 18, 78, 81–83, 84, 90, 91, 121, 122, 129, 132, 133, 174, 199n3, 206n2
visual culture, 1, 6, 7, 9–10, 12, 79, 96, 129, 156, 157, 161, 169, 182, 187, 190n13
Vlisco, 2, 72, 198n16
Vlisco Dutch Wax 2, 8

Wallerstei, Immanuel, 201n8
Wass, Betty, 182

wax print, 37–38, 64, 67, 68, 70, 72, 189n1, 196n3, 198n16, 206n9
wealth, 6, 9, 10, 11, 12, 22, 24, 25, 30, 34, 41, 42, 56, 78, 79, 80–95, 100, 102, 108, 124–25, 127, 133, 163, 183–85, 194n35, 198n16, 200n5, 200n7
wedding, 1–3, 5, 14, 15, 16, 17, 22, 23, 35, 42, 51, 52, 56, 66, 68, 69–71, 75, 78–87, 90, 93, 94, 95, 96, 97, 98, 102, 104–6, 109, 126, 127, 129, 131, 133, 134, 135, 139–40, 142, 152, 153, 155, 157, 158, 159, 162, 164, 168, 170, 173, 178, 179, 193n28, 199n3, 205n4
Weiner, Annette: *Inalienable Possessions*, 13
Wells, Karen, 97
Wesleyan, 193n25
WhatsApp, 2, 14, 23
Williams, Mabel Aduka, 44, 133, 146
Wilson, Eric, 128
Wilson, Elizabeth, 205n6
Wolff, Norma H., 16–17, 56, 185, 197n6, 198n10, 200n7
Wollen, Peter, 85–86
wrapper, 27, 28, 30, 34, 37, 44, 46, 56, 58, 61, 62, 67, 198n13, 200n6
Wright, Lee, 190n4

Yaba, 2, 148, 149, 152